Rhythm and the Blues

Rhythm
and
the Blues

A LIFE IN AMERICAN MUSIC

541

Jerry Wexler
and
David Ritz

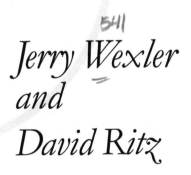

Alfred A. Knopf
New York
1993

Library of Congress Cataloging-in-
Publication Data
Wexler, Jerry.
Rhythm and the blues : a life in American
music / Jerry Wexler and David Ritz.
p.   cm.
Includes index.
ISBN 0-679-40102-4
1. Wexler, Jerry. 2. Sound recording exec-
utives and producers—United States—
Biography. I. Ritz, David. II. Title.
ML429.W4A3   1993
781.643'092—dc20
[B]   92-31704 CIP   MN

For Ahmet Ertegun

CONTENTS

ACKNOWLEDGMENTS

For love and support, we would like to thank our families—Lisa Wexler, Paul Wexler, Roberta Ritz, Alison Ritz, Jessica Ritz, and especially Jean Wexler, for her invaluable editorial input at a critical juncture.

We're especially grateful to our editor, Gary Fisketjon, who made this project possible, and to Pete Hamill and Stanley Booth, who (each separately) touted the idea of a Wexler story to Fisketjon. Thanks to Toby Byron for suggesting the formation of the Wexler/Ritz team, to the Aaron Priest Literary Agency, and to the many interviewees, including Ray Charles, David "Fathead" Newman, Hank Crawford, Renee Pappas, Cy Ampole, Berry Gordy, Jerry Leiber, Mike Stoller, David Geffen, Ahmet Ertegun, Arif Mardin, Dickie Kline, Etta James, Mark Myerson, Steve Paley, soul scholar Herb Boyd, Tom Dowd, Stanley Booth, Barry Beckett, Jimmy Johnson, Donnie Fritts, Rick Hall, Duck Dunn, David Hood, Roger Hawkins, Spooner Oldham, Jerry Greenberg, Milt Gabler, Connie Hillman, Alan Pariser, Earl McGrath, Shirley Aprea, Tommy Aprea, Lisa Wexler, Paul Wexler, Bonnie Bramlett, Mac Rebbenack, Lorraine Rebbenack, Barry Goldberg, John Bryant, Ray Baradat, Barry White, Isaac Hayes.

THE

MAN

*A*t *seventy-five,* Wexler is still a holy terror.

He runs around like an impatient kid, shopping for baby white eggplants at distant farm stands, booking acts for the local jazz association, talking on the phone to musician pals, celebrating the latest Hank Crawford or T-Bone Walker reissues, making Benny Goodman tapes for his butcher, dominating the dinner conversation with war stories of song pluggers and smash records. His eyes twinkle; his fingers nervously smooth over his white beard. The mind is racing. Compulsive, cunning, extravagantly verbal, he stays two beats ahead. His rapid-fire speech blends a promoter's hype with a scholar's precision, his lexicon a mixture of the mean streets and the graduate library. When you question a word he uses—say "ratiocination"—complaining that even an educated reader might balk at the meaning, he fires back in double-thick, unyielding New Yorkese, "Send the fuckers to the dictionary!"

Wexler loves language. What falls from his mouth aren't merely words but self-styled music, now harsh, now harmonious. His ego, fierce and battle-ready, has a soft underside. He's one of those tender tough guys. He relishes a good fight. His domain stretches from early swing to surrealism, from John O'Hara to Anita Brookner, and a litany of cultural stops in between.

Of his several obsessions, food is among the strongest. Ingredients must be fresh, wholesome, and handpicked; every meal must be perfect. As he once produced record sessions, he now produces lunches and dinners, supervising his Asian cook with the same firm finesse with which he supervised Dire Straits.

Over dessert, he's still going strong. He expounds on the greatness of clarinetist Pee Wee Russell; he analyzes the ironies of Magritte; he asserts his agnosticism, insisting on empirical rationalism. He wants you to listen. He wants you to fall in love with him. If his points of view are more papal edicts than opinions, his ability to laugh at himself saves the day. His energy is inexhaustible.

For years he's been waiting to tell these tales, to capture your attention and charm you into listening. His need to explain himself, to share his extraordinary adventures, is overwhelming. He demands attention. In his splendid digs in Sarasota, Florida, or East Hampton, New York— "I live like King Farouk!" he exclaims—his enthusiasm is contagious, his passion irresistible.

You give in. You sit and listen to the stories of New York in the thirties, the wonders of the Depression-era pool halls, the angst of Dad, the drive of Mom, the joys of stickball, the discovery of sex and jazz, the Army and the forties, the Brill Building Broadway buzz of the fifties, crude gangsters and crafty geniuses, his partnership with the Ertegun brothers, his soul-music talent hunts through the South, his forays into New Orleans and Nashville, Austin and Muscle Shoals, his pioneering work with Joe Turner and Ruth Brown and Ray Charles, his molding of Aretha Franklin, his nights with Willie Nelson and Bob Dylan, his method of buying in, making millions, cashing out, watching record labels evolve from seat-of-the-pants independents to massive conglomerates.

These stories are his life, a singular journey through the musical culture of our times.

—David Ritz

Rhythm and the Blues

TIME ON

IN

BULLSHIT

ALLEY

*W*ashington Heights was a lower-middle-class enclave of Jews, Italians, Irish—wage earners, civil servants, and small businessmen. We moved there when I was six. West of St. Nicholas Avenue was the Hudson River, buttressed by the imposing Palisades on the Jersey side. The streets in between had apartment houses ranging from simple five-story walk-ups to elegant buildings with doormen and elevator operators. East, towards the Harlem River, were Audubon and Amsterdam avenues, where many of the folks were on "home relief," the welfare of its day. There were very few cars, and north of 184th Street dirt roads ran into vast woods. From Riverside Drive down to the banks of the Hudson was a verdant jungle, a made-to-order wilderness for kids. Although strange objects came drifting by in the Hudson, the water was relatively clean, and its treacherous currents bred a bunch of damn good swimmers.

But it was an indoor sport that made Artie's poolroom the locus of my childhood. As in the recording studio—the most important arena of my adulthood—the poolroom was where lessons were learned, characters intermingled, battles won or lost. The poolroom was *it*.

Artie's had me enthralled. I couldn't stay out of the place, perched on the second floor of a double-story building—called "taxpayers" back then—on the corner of 181st Street and Bennett Avenue in Washington Heights. By my early teens, I was already something of a honcho. It was 1930, and the Depression was deep, hard, and dirty; anxiety lurked everywhere except in the imagination of a kid excited by the wonders and challenges of the streets. Robust and restless, I was considered gutsy by those I respected most, the guys in the poolroom.

Artie Goodman, the owner, was a tough guy himself. Bald as a cue ball, his face framed by glasses thick as the bottom of a Coke bottle, Artie brooked no nonsense. Given any shit, he might, for example, hook his middle finger in the corner of the miscreant's mouth and rip—either that or throw the troublemaker down two flights of ladder-steep stairs.

You had to be fifteen to get in, but I arrived early. I was big for my age, and Artie knew I could handle myself. That meant a lot to me, because Artie distributed heavy angst. The poolroom was filled with icons, figures larger than life, or at least larger than the life I was living within the narrow confines of my parents' apartment.

Physically and emotionally the poolroom was anything but narrow. It was there where I met No Hat Cohen, Shorty April, and the Three-Fingers Commissioner—"Three Fingers" because he lacked two on one hand, "Commissioner" because, while he never played, he arranged games. I hung out with Shortstop and Heavy, Slim O'Reilly and the Green Archer, dressed all in green after the cartoon character—green suede shoes, green tie—and a great pinball marksman who sometimes worked a hustle with the twins, Irving and Robbie, infamous for their lousy credit. Little Tommy Hopkins, at thirteen the best left-handed shooter in the joint, carried a note from his parish priest granting him permission to play; and Nero, a Sicilian shoeshiner whose accent prompted unmerciful teasing, actually lived in the hallway and slept on the tables.

It was mesmerizing. School wasn't doing it for me. I felt inadequate, unprepared, intimidated. No concentration. No respect for the teachers. I was a wise-ass kid who, ever since skipping his first day of kindergarten, sought ways to avoid the classroom. In contrast, the poolroom promised action.

Twenty green-felt tables stood under the yellow glare of hooded lights hanging from a high ceiling. The smell of chalk dust and furniture oil hung heavy in the air. The perfume of hot bagels, bialystokers, and freshly baked Danish emanated from the bakery below. Every so often the portly baker himself would run upstairs, incensed: whenever we banged our cues on the floor in celebration of a good shot, a snowstorm of white-flecked calcimine would fall from his ceiling and ruin his wares. Oscar the Ticker Man ran a ticker tape machine that spit out the baseball scores—an honor without recompense. Baseball betting was big, and Oscar, who chalked the scores on a giant blackboard, was disliked. A tightwad who always kept a container of cold water by his side, he realized the full extent of his unpopularity one day when, sipping his water, he tasted urine.

Seasons flew by. Big picture windows let in the heat of summer and the white of winter. On one snowy afternoon a guy came bursting in and screamed, "Who pissed on the steam?" Urinating on a radiator generates a most noxious effluvium, and we knew the perpetrators to be one of the two Zombies—either White Zombie, a giant albino, or Plain Zombie, a short tailor and Laurel and Hardy zealot with a hacking cough who always threw open a window, convinced freezing air would clear his phlegm.

Other patrons had more sense and style. Take Sidney "Benny the Gent" Greenberg—"Benny" because he came from Bensonhurst in Brooklyn, "the Gent" because, despite sparse resources, he dressed sharp. Most of us were homeboys, supported by our parents, but Benny was on his own. He was inventive, trimming his frayed cuffs with a scissors, pressing his pants under his mattress, ingeniously configuring his tie knot to cover the stains. Neither a swell nor a tough, Benny presented a picture of a gentleman. Benny had pride. Most importantly, his pool skills, unlike mine, were formidable; and whenever I could scrape together some change, I'd back him. Other hustlers would dump their friends and, without thinking twice, throw games by prearrangement. Not Benny. Benny was straight.

In the midst of the sharpshooting and sundry rites of machismo, all of which I found alluring, I also had a strange sense of being different from the others. Even at an early age, I was engaged by books and music, especially jazz and blues. Not that I looked down on my pals—far from it. They were my admired compeers. My artistic instincts, though, stood apart and, in fact, yielded no practical benefits for decades to come. My early life was a series of aimless meanderings. I couldn't focus, couldn't find my way out of the poolroom. But even there I demonstrated surprising signs of individualization.

Take charades, for example. I started a game in Artie's, and, as you can imagine, Artie wasn't thrilled. He charged twenty cents a half-hour for pool, a dime a man, and monitored the tables with a punch clock. As soon as time was up, he'd yell from his extra-high chair looking over the room, "Time off on table six!" We'd often ask him to swing it for us—let us run a tab—and Artie, good guy that he was, would usually comply. The second he saw us gathering around for a round of charades, though, he'd scream out, "Time on in bullshit alley!"

Our charades were notable for the adroitness of the players. The boys lacked stock knowledge in any particular area, but when it came to mimetics, they shone. They were brilliant at picking up syllabification. I remember how one of the players, a man-child who never graduated grammar school, was able to phonetically decipher "Dusolina Giannini sang the role of Cio-Cio-San in Puccini's *Madame Butterfly*"—no mean feat!

My pursuit of books, instead of causing resentment, added to my aura. In the world of adolescents, coolness is all. To be cool—to possess what the French call *adresse*—meant handling oneself with poise, being a good winner, a good loser, a good gambler, never overstating the obvious, and using one's fists with daring and effectiveness. If word leaked out that I was reading Hemingway, Dos Passos, and Fitzgerald and listening to remote dance band broadcasts, well, this only helped. I wanted to be the cool one and establish a high place in the poolroom pecking order.

No wonder I would arrive at ten in the morning, the minute the place opened, so I could help Artie's assistant Pop brush down the tables in return for a few tips on three-cushion billiards; no wonder that the most humiliating moment of my young life occurred when my mother, the beautiful and indomitable Elsa Wexler, appeared in the doorway and shouted for all the world that she would no longer tolerate my presence here and had come to take me home.

Artie hesitated. Stricken with shame, I cowered. Elsa, a fiery woman of singular determination, struck like lightning, picking up an empty Coca-Cola bottle and holding it menacingly over Artie's head.

"If you ever let my Gerald back in here," she warned him, "I'll brain you."

Artie coughed discreetly.

I slithered out with my mother, the sound of snickers following me down the steep staircase like the hissing of pit vipers.

WINDOW
WASHER'S
BLUES

Pa had them, and so did Ma. Later on, those same blues would come down on me. It was my father who washed the windows, but sometimes I think my mother suffered more for his fate than he did. The pail and ladder were symbols of his entrapment. Elsa fought her way out of the trap—sometimes escaping free, sometimes not—and was determined I join her in the flight. She was obsessed with me, no doubt. I was always her wunderkind, placed on a pedestal for the undefined gifts she just knew I possessed. My brother, Arthur, born eighteen months after me and one of the world's sweetest people, suffered from her flagrant favoritism.

An inordinate projection on Elsa's part trailed me throughout childhood. I was to be all she wasn't—a scholar, a writer, a contributor to culture—even as she herself underwent profound changes, leaving my father's domain of bare-bones subsistence in search of enlightenment and, I would later learn, romance.

Harry Wexler was a good man, filled with frustrations. I loved him and sorrowed for him, all at once. Arriving from Poland in 1912 at the age of nineteen, he discovered not streets of gold but a world of woe. In my heart, Pa became one of those Jewish heroes devoting body and soul to his family's survival. His Old World family—especially his zealously religious father—offered him no solace. His own childhood had been marked by abject poverty and the oppressiveness of ultraorthodoxy.

A year before he died, we sat down with a tape deck and recorded his recollections of the early days.

"Every day after studying the Talmud," he told me, "I'd go to my father's mill and watch a blindfolded horse going round and round in a circle, grinding buckwheat. In Europe, that was my life, watching that horse. And here in America . . ." His voice trailed off.

That he himself became a workhorse was a rancid irony. He died in harness like a beast of burden, well into his seventies, in 1968, still washing windows.

Six decades earlier, when the ship *New Amsterdam* landed in New York, Harry was with his cousin, a girl he'd promised to marry in exchange for the boat tickets she bought with her meager savings.

"At the dock I still wore my long black coat, my long black beard, and my *payess,*" Pa told me, describing the ritual locks of a Hasidic Jew. "I really wanted to shave them off, but I was afraid that if I happened to be turned back without them my father would disown me."

"There was no feeling of any kind between this cousin and me," said Harry, ever frustrated in an inchoate yearning for romantic love. "She died a couple of years after we came to America."

"My first job," he went on, "was washing windows. I hated it. I finally found a plumber who took me in. But he'd leave me to watch the shop. He never trained me. That was no good. I saw I had no choice. I went back to washing windows. I traveled all over the Bronx from my aunt's house in Harlem. I rode the trolley, working from six to six for four dollars a week. It was murder. When I met your mother, I was nineteen and she was sixteen. She was working in her father's bakery on Courtlandt Avenue near 161st Street. I was washing the windows and I looked in and saw this lovely girl. Elsa Spitz was a regular doll. She was also from a good home, and that appealed to me. Believe me, I was lucky to find her."

"Harry flirted with my mother," said Elsa. "At first she liked him, but not after we got engaged. We were German and he was Polish, and there were social distinctions. She didn't want a Galitzianer son-in-law. But to me it was a way of getting out of the bakery."

They were married in 1916, and I was born a year later. From the beginning of my memory, I viewed my father as a strong man, a powerful physical presence whose limp, the result of a fall from a ladder and an improperly set hip, symbolized his lousy luck. I was six when he broke his hip, and when Elsa and I visited him in Fordham Hospital in the north Bronx, I cried like a baby. Though my childish understanding couldn't encompass the situation, I'd made a vague but sad connection between my father and bad luck.

He washed windows—washed them in Harlem, washed them in

Portrait of the producer
as a young man

midtown, washed them on Wall Street skyscrapers during World War I, clearing the view for the captains of industry at Lehman Brothers, the Corn Exchange Bank, and the New York Trust Company. Once the war was over and the regular workers returned, Harry switched gears and bought a new route for between five and ten thousand dollars and brought home something under one hundred dollars a week. This was the early twenties, when we moved from Webster Avenue in the Bronx to Pinehurst Avenue in Washington Heights. Even though we survived the Depression—there were always windows to wash—his business never took off. As Elsa never failed to remind him, Harry chose bad partners, disloyal and dishonest.

Pa always talked about David Sarnoff's brother, an immigrant like himself, who had the window-washing concession at the RCA Building in Rockefeller Center. That was the pinnacle. Between my father and the mighty Sarnoffs, though, was a gradation of janitorial entrepreneurs, most of whom became wealthy. For all his goodwill, Harry never rose above the lowliest station. Aside from menial labor, his life consisted of the weekend poker game, reading newspaper editorials, railing against the fascists, venting a fearful temper, and enjoying an occasional glass of schnapps. I remember him sitting in front of the radio in the early thir-

Pop, Gerald, and Arthur, 1930

ties with his father-in-law, my maternal grandfather, Rudolph, inveighing against Father Coughlin's proto-fascist, anti-Semitic broadcasts.

Elsa pushed, prodded, and goaded Harry to higher things. Throughout my childhood, in fact throughout my life, they bickered horribly and blamed each other for their financial woes. Nevertheless, Elsa never tried to turn me away from Harry. Sparked by an inquisitive spirit and innate good taste, she spent all the money he made not simply on an immaculate apartment and gourmet meals—my mother was a gifted homemaker—but also on clothes for herself. This set the neighbors' tongues a-wagging. They saw her as self-indulgent, but Elsa couldn't have cared less. She went her own way, dead determined to drag me along.

I, too, was resolved to go my own way—I wasn't sure just where—but I grimly resisted Ma's insistence that I excel. She wangled a way for me to start school a year early—that's how anxious she was that I get ahead. But I bolted. I waltzed through public school, doing quite well on a bluff. I was cocky. I felt I could ad-lib answers to almost any question, and there was no studying in the true sense of the word; I got by with the help of opportunistic skimming and a good ear.

Junior high school, though, was a disaster, with countless days spent ·skipping, traversing back alleys, and racing over the rooftops of Washington Heights. The Heights was a marvel. We were lucky to wind up with an apartment on Bennett Avenue, one of the good streets west of Broadway. East of Broadway was the rough territory ruled by Irish and Italian toughs. I'd guess I was eleven or twelve, so the year was 1928 or '29. Sometimes word would go out—a gang was about to invade our territory carrying broken bats and rock-loaded socks. Like the vernal equinox, these eruptions would come a certain time of year, and I'd be ready. I'd be on the front line, and once I even whomped notorious bully Whitey Walsh into bad health. (This guy was so bad he wound up in the electric chair in Sing Sing.) I was impervious to pain. You could bust my nose and I'd still fight like mad. I was known for stalking the neighborhood with a pair of boxing gloves around my neck, the symbols of my readiness. It wouldn't take much, a wrong look or cross word, to provoke me into action—the same terrible temper that, later in my life, damaged my family. But it also served as an engine and a defense.

I was always happy playing—swimming, stickball, running the streets, which in my mind's eye still appear pristine and inviting. The Hudson was a stone's throw away, and in summer we'd swim off the point where the George Washington Bridge now stands or ferry across to Jersey, where we'd hike up the Palisades and picnic in a park, Manhattan's skyline shimmering before us.

On one blistering day I jumped in and, with my friend Abie the Window Cleaner, fought the powerful undertows all the way across to Jersey. We wound up a mile upriver without a nickel for the Dyckman Street ferry. Looking like two drowned rats, we begged on and, once on the other side, raced down Riverside Park as the sun melted in the river. It was dark by the time we arrived home, and Elsa was beside herself, screaming about how she'd told my father, my aunts, and half the neighborhood that I was drowning in the Hudson. A lifelong rationalist, I still can't explain my mother's hunch, premonition, or whatever it was.

Outside, away from the aggravation of my parents' marriage, there was a sense of lovely isolation in the summertime of my childhood. School was out and the rich kids, like Cy Ampole and Hoppy Adler, were off at camp. The deserted streets belonged to us. Sitting on the curb, entranced by points of mica sparkling in the cement, we'd wait for the ice truck and chip off chunks to quench our thirst or rub over our burning cheeks, me and my buddies, always restless, always ready for a stickball game on Bennett Avenue.

As a test of adolescent skill, stickball even rivaled pool. There was the ball itself, an object of considerable beauty, pink, lightly powdered, and empowered with a terrifically high bounce. This was the classic Spaulding, bought from the stationery store. Its rubber smell had a definite allure, and given the right whack, the thing flew from here to Canarsie.

Philly Girard, the neighborhood Ty Cobb, was king of the arcane stickball game. He was a good-looking kid who'd think nothing about taking us on a joyride in a stolen car. I admired him less for his loose scruples, though, than for his ability to knock the Spaulding into any open window of his choosing. Retrieving the ball, he'd scamper up the fire escape and, if the apartment was vacant, burglarize the joint in nothing flat.

Big leagues—the Polo Grounds and Yankee Stadium—were within walking distance. I paid half a buck to sit in the bleachers to watch Babe Ruth, Lou Gehrig, and the artistry of Mel Ott. I remember how at bat Mel stepped out with his right foot, the way he played right field like he owned it, throwing behind the runner and nailing him rounding first—McGraw baseball, we called it. In our neighborhood, we loved the Giants, Carl Hubbell and Prince Hal; loved it when the Cubbies came to town with their trio of tipsy pitchers—the historic drunks Charlie Root, Guy Bush, and Pat Malone—and heavy-bearded first baseman Charlie Grimm, toughest guy in the game.

Barney Ross, the great welterweight, was the tough guy we idolized most. Because he was Jewish, we couldn't help but identify. He had three epic fights with Jimmy McLarnin. They split the first two, and on the third Cy and I went to a strange poolroom on Audubon Avenue and put all our money on Barney, waging against some rough-and-ready Irish fans of McLarnin's. We were holding the bet and, convinced Ross was unbeatable, took the dough and wagered it with another group. If we had lost, we'd have been doubly dead; but Barney prevailed, thank God.

*L*ife in winter had its own special feeling; the Heights had its own beautiful hues. At the foot of Bennett Avenue were superb clay courts. In the winter they were flooded and turned into a glistening ice rink where I'd skate until my feet fell off. Back in our apartment—even now I can smell the aroma of Pa's heavy Turkish Murad or Helmar cigarettes and Ma's noodle pudding—I'd love to lie on the floor by the radiator near the window, looking at the windswept Hudson and listening to the radio. At six-thirty I'd get up and head out, because at six forty-five there was major conflict. Elsa and Harry had to hear "Easy Aces" with Jane and Goodman Ace, and I was hooked on Bing Crosby.

Cy and I would go to the Davega Sporting Goods store at 181st Street and St. Nicholas Avenue, stand in the open vestibule, and listen to Bing. He was my guru. Bing sent me into a state of voluptuous euphoria. He spoke to me. When he sang "Love in Bloom" or "We'll Make Hay While the Sun Shines," when he crooned "The Day You Came Along" ("My heart was fated the day you came along, two souls were mated the day you came along") or "Down the Old Ox Road," I levitated on his melodies. Bing started me, he stayed with me, he set me thinking about the mysteries of music and love. In 1977, I was in New Orleans working on the soundtrack of Louis Malle's *Pretty Baby* when the news of Bing's death came on the car radio, and I pulled over and wept.

I was also reading—not school lessons, mind you, but books of my choosing. I began with *Argosy* magazine and *Amazing Stories*. But soon I was reading Joseph Altsheler, a hipper version of James Fenimore Cooper who wrote about the French and Indian Wars. I loved Tom Sawyer and Huck Finn, dug the natural history books of Ernest Seton Thompson, and grew up on Haldeman-Julius's Little Blue Books, which were mail-ordered from a tiny town in Kansas, cost a nickel, and included the works of Shakespeare, Molière, Balzac, Freud, Havelock Ellis, William James, Plato, Plutarch, and Dante. Elsa made certain my brother and I had a complete set of *The Book of Knowledge*. Fixated on Theodore Dreiser's *American Tragedy*, Elsa was convinced her Gerald was going to write the Great American Novel.

Why did my brother receive less of my mother's attention? Maybe because I was firstborn. Maybe, too, because Arthur was born with a physical handicap, his right ear undeveloped. She did love him—compassionately, but with a deeply repressed guilt: she blamed herself for this congenital anomaly. Arthur grew up hard of hearing in an era when such handicaps were ignored; yet he excelled nonetheless, went to college, earned honors and graduate degrees, and wound up a brilliant chemist. Always, though, he bore the emotional scar of Elsa's obvious and tactless discrimination. As a kid, I felt my brother's pain; I became his defender. Anyone who teased Arthur knew they'd have to deal with me.

Harry was remote, Elsa was relentless; and still, in its own way, our family was close. Our extended family was spread over Manhattan, Brooklyn, and the Bronx. For the most part our relatives were poor but powerful in their influence on us. Aunt Ella, considered an angel, was much beloved. Above all, though, special mention must be made of the Mima.

When we started out in the East Bronx, we lived in the same building as my father's Aunt Goldberg, the Mima, the definite article a testament to her matriarchal status. The Mima was invincible. The Mima represented tradition, a clucking hen, a dominating housewife of archetypical proportions. She was Ma's mentor. And what an unlikely combination they made—the Mima, a tiny, feisty bundle of energy and shtetl smarts, and Elsa, the beautiful and ambitious girl with the high-toned German background. It was the Mima who taught my mother serviceable Yiddish, but it was my mother who plotted her own course away from the expected life of a Depression-era housewife.

As might have been expected, I endured the obligatory bar mitzvah. As usual, my mother was the mover, the architect of the event, my father the passive observer. Ma sent me to a Reform temple, where, in spite of my boredom, I actually took pleasure in writing about Moses and Joseph and the Old Testament prophets. This was the Temple of the Covenant. Rabbi Lux, a handsome American hunk, was head honcho. Inexplicably, he fell down the stairs of the poolroom on St. Nicholas Avenue one day and broke his leg—the same poolroom whose windows my father washed and where Rudy Wanderone, later known as Minnesota Fats, used to hustle. In those days he was probably shooting fourteen-ball rack straight pool from anywhere from five dollars to fifty dollars a game. The stakes for Chicago rotation pool might have been one dollar to ten dollars a point.

Back in temple, reformed Rabbi Lux was impressed by my ruminations on the biblical patriarchs, but the patriarchs from my father's family were not. They convinced Elsa to switch me from Lux's liberal domain to an Orthodox shul. Despondent and rebellious, I was brutalized by a long-bearded, garlic-reeking, sadistic *melamed* who used his ruler to deconstruct my antipathy for Hebrew. The ceremony came off nonetheless, though the take from my presents, given our pious but poor relatives, was pitiful. On the outside, I read my perfunctory bar mitzvah speech flawlessly; on the inside, I was laughing.

I can't remember a time when I wasn't a doubter. Never—not for a hot minute—have I believed in God. A half-century after my bar mitzvah, I was producing Bob Dylan's first gospel album. He had just been born again, and in an access of evangelism he pulled out the Bible and started to hit on me. When I told him to forget it, that he was dealing with a confirmed sixty-three-year-old Jewish atheist, he cracked up.

Granted, my atheism may belong in the same package as my other prejudices. But my convictions, or lack thereof, are lifetime friends. They nourish and sustain me. They satisfy me. If my colleagues disagree, I tolerate their aberrations. I glory in my disbelief. Disbelief, at least for me, is a source of strength.

Yet I see myself as deeply spiritual. My feelings for literature, art, movies, food, and wine are all invested with spirit. Above all, it's in my feeling for music. Music has brought me joy; it has given me a beat and a groove, sent me down the righteous roads.

ROADS

OF

RHYTHM

M*y mother* was proud of her legs and her looks, and she had every right to be. She had the classic visage of a dark-haired Viennese. She was gorgeous. She was a great reader, a diligent student of Freud, Marx, and Lenin. She was a freethinker, a liberal, a woman who instigated her own liberation sixty years before the movement began. She was one of those working-class, self-taught Jewish New Yorkers influenced by such icons as Eugene Debs, Samuel Gompers, and David Dubinsky. My mother and her wannabe-intellectual cronies would congregate in cafeterias like the Automat or Bickford's to drink endless cups of coffee and argue over Lenin and Trotsky. It's a pretty good bet she was a card-carrying member of the Party.

Pa didn't understand her and couldn't control her. As I moved through my teens, my parents' relationship worsened. As Harry busted his *cojones*, Elsa contrived to spend every penny he made. "Are you crazy, Elsa?" he'd scream. "Savings! Do you have no regard for savings?!" Elsa had none. In her mind, she'd already paid her dues.

She was ready to venture out into the world, comporting herself far above the level of a window washer's wife. She donated her time to the Travelers Aid Society and did volunteer work at the Presbyterian Hospital on 168th Street across from the Audubon Ballroom. She was an altruist, an idealist, a music lover whose piano playing never progressed above the mediocre. She'd sing light opera like *The Chocolate Soldier* in an out-of-tune coloratura that drove me to the street. She wanted me to become a concert pianist, but I had neither the chops nor the patience. I wore out six piano teachers before I was fifteen.

Elsa's interests expanded beyond politics and culture. She devel-

Young Gerald with, from left, Elsa, aunts Agnes and Gertrude

oped a passion for golf; and what a figure she cut, heading down 181st Street, clubs slung over her shoulder, neighbors agog at her snazzy outfit! I often caddied for her at the city-owned course at Van Cortlandt Park. But "Vanny" was no country club. To get there required three trolley transfers—total price, five cents—and to play eighteen holes, with a Parks Department season permit, cost a dime.

Elsa wasn't the only original in her family. She was the oldest of three sisters—Agnes next, Gertrude the youngest—and I adored my lovely, doting aunts. They brought me candies and pastries and often took me to museums, movies, picnics, ice skating—or to Brighton Beach in Brooklyn, where they taught me the crawl.

Like Elsa, Agnes was a beauty. She looked like a blond shiksa, an Episcopal flapper, a self-sufficient young woman who "went to business." A fabulous dresser, Agnes worked for the Hanes hosiery company and would rumble down Bennett Avenue in her own Model A Ford with me on the running board, the envy of my friends. As in the Johnny Mercer song "Weekend of a Private Secretary" (sung by Mildred Bailey), she went on a $49.50 cruise to Jamaica, where she promptly fell in love with an English Jamaican, heir to a huge sugar plantation. Just like that, they married. Alas, in the Depression sugar was worthless. Land poor, Agnes hung in with her cane baron and remained on the island for the rest of her life.

Agnes and my mother were at odds from then on. Maybe they were too much alike. Maybe Elsa was jealous that her sister had made the thrilling romantic leap she herself could never quite manage. I remember my mother, always the doctrinaire liberal, returning from Jamaica, relating with considerable ridicule that her sister was afraid of being slain by her own "ganja-crazed" black servants.

Gertrude was different. Softer, more girlish and vulnerable than her older siblings, she reminded me of a sweet Victorian heroine out of a storybook. She, too, was drawn to romance, though hers took an especially painful turn for my mother. Gertrude fell in love with and married a Greek immigrant, then working as a dishwasher, who decades later became chairman of the sociology department at Dartmouth. Early on, fearing her religion might hinder her husband's academic career, Gertrude renounced her Jewishness and cut off all contact with her family.

Agnes wasn't the problem—she was far away in Jamaica and, besides, married to a blue-eyed Anglo-Saxon. (In fact, some twenty years later, during a High Holy Day service in a Jamaican shul, a religious fever fell over Agnes, who arose, arms extended, and announced her recommitment to the Torah.) But in Gertrude's eyes, Elsa was the sister married to a Polish window washer, the one who'd squandered her intellectual potential and fallen to a social level far beneath her.

The separation of the sisters was a ghastly family tragedy. When I was a boy, it tore me up. I saw how it haunted my mother every day of her life. It plagued me so that after the deaths of Agnes and Elsa, I was compelled to reach out to Gertrude, to speak to her, then in her nineties, before she died. I sent word through her son, my cousin Mike, who gave me her number.

A frail voice, a voice I hadn't heard in six decades, said hello; and, holding back tears, I explained how good it was to hear her after so many years. "Gerald, I'm sorry," she replied. "I can't handle this." And with that she hung up. A few weeks later she was gone.

Cut off from her sisters, Elsa seemed to direct even more of her tireless attention on me. Through the sheer force of her will she maneuvered me into advance-placement programs, and at age twelve I entered Townsend Harris as a sophomore. It was the toughest preparatory high school in New York. A friend once described the precocious, astigmatic, mainly Jewish student body as looking like "Alexander Woollcott cut off at the knees." Graduating meant automatic admission to City College, which had impossibly high entrance requirements. But I never made it out of Townsend Harris. My first year there was my only year. I'd faked my way through elementary and junior high. Didn't know the first thing about studying. Never went to the library except to check out novels. Couldn't abide authoritative old-maid teachers, couldn't sit still. Fell behind, and exams were coming up, scaring me to death.

Feeling trapped, caught, I decided to run away. I rang Cy Ampole's bell and invited him to join me. Cy looked at me like I was nuts. He came from a well-to-do family with a fancy apartment in an elevator building across from our walk-up. Cy had a new bike and fine clothes. He had no interest whatsoever in flying the coop.

I took the streetcar to the Dyckman Street ferry and crossed the Hudson to Jersey, then walked up the Palisades. I was on my way to California. Or Canada. Or China. I didn't know where I was going, except that it would be far away from the pressures of school, from Elsa and Harry's miserable marriage, from my inability to stay out of trouble. Manhattan still in sight, I stuck out my thumb, determined to leave my old life behind.

A driver picked me up and wanted to know my destination. When I informed him I was "heading for the coast," he conveyed me to the nearest police station. My benefactor turned out to be a detective who promptly called Harry. Poor Harry, hard at work, had to put down his pail and ladder and shlep to Teaneck, New Jersey, to pick up the runaway schmuck. Back home, it all came spilling out—how I'd been fucking off, playing hookey, tottering on the brink of failure. Irate, Harry took a few good whacks at me. But vengeful little bastard that I was, I merely sneered back and invited him to take his best shot. There was no repentance. My only tears would be tears of rage.

But Elsa kept her cool. With a little psychological counseling, she figured, I'd be fine. A female shrink, a friend of hers, recommended I switch schools. Fine with me. They sent me to George Washington High at the northern end of Manhattan. Through the grace of God and Elsa's inexorable nagging, I managed to graduate. My mind, though, remained unfocused. Restlessness still ruled. I moved to the tempo of the streets, the rhythms of jazz.

There seems to be a certain kind of music addict who can trace his initiation to a specific singer or record—Laura Nyro, Joan Baez, Peter and Gordon, Chad and Jeremy, "The House of the Rising Sun," "Louie Louie." With me it didn't work that way. My imprint was cumulative. I was simmered in a slow-cooking gumbo of New Orleans jazz, small Harlem combos, big bands, Western swing, country, jukebox race music, pop schmaltz. The talismanic names would include Louis Armstrong, Red Allen, Duke Ellington, Bob Wills, Riley Puckett, the Harlem Hamfats, Gene Austin. "Hot rhythm stimulates me, deep rhythm captivates me," sang the sublime Billie Holiday with the Basie band in a song called "Swing, Brother, Swing."

I'm a product not solely of the Swing Era but of all those ingredients that melded into swing. I came of age during a springtime of syncopation which widened my tastes and excited my sense of surprise. Just as we loved the baseball Giants in our neighborhood, we loved the giants of swing—Fletcher Henderson and Jimmy Lunceford's marvelous big bands, the ethereal solos of Bix Beiderbecke, the hungry buzz and natural rasp of Roy Eldridge's fiery in-your-face horn, and, always, the ineffable trumpet playing of Red Allen.

I was blessed with friends who led me to the magic—blessed to know Al Bibbo, an Italian kid from Audubon Avenue on the wrong side of Broadway. Al was a great stickball player and superlative lindy hopper. You've seen those all black-and-white movies where the cooks and waitresses throw each other about with abandon. Al Bibbo could step out on the floor of the Savoy Ballroom with the best Negro steppers and immediately generate a ring of admiring dark-skinned beauties. His virtuosity was an uptown legend. He had fabulous ears; he could whistle every note of every solo played by any prominent swing musician. We thought Al was on the way to be a great trumpet player. Somehow, though, he couldn't hack it. He had desire, but no chops. He could never master that goddamn horn, and wound up, touchingly enough, being Roy Eldridge's best little ofay buddy, hanging out with Roy for years.

I remember an afternoon when we ran into Al at the 181st Street subway stop. He was just coming from the downtown electronics district with a discount brand-new Victor 78 single of Benny Goodman's "King Porter Stomp" and "Sometimes I'm Happy." The shellac glinted in the summer sun. The anticipation was unbearable, so we ran over to Al's place, where he made us iced coffee, pulled down the shade against the heat, and played that record all afternoon long. The Fletcher Henderson arrangements swung like crazy; Bunny Berigan's "King Porter" solo sent us soaring. And the unearthly saxophone choir on "Sometimes I'm Happy"—I know it by heart and still play the record. In my mind, the passage remains unsurpassed to this day.

A few months back I happened to hear on the radio Frankie New-

ton's driving trumpet on "Rocking the Blues," another Bibbo favorite
and a signature song of my early life. Newton's chorus put me into a
trance. I remembered every note of his solo, though I hadn't heard this
record for fifty years. Time stood still.

Back then, time was on my hands—time to get deeper into music,
to learn the ropes of record collecting. All that meant going to Harlem.
I loved the Harlem of the thirties, loved its look and feel, its dance halls
and nightclubs and especially its sounds. There were the after-hour cellar joints where the great dance-band and club musicians came to jam.
There were the piano flats—good-time flats, we called them—where an
impecunious tenant would throw himself a rent party, charging fifty
cents for admission. Once inside, you could get a dish of chicken backs,
a reefer, or a glass of gin for a dime per. As for female companionship, it
was "every tub on its own bottom." Comic Eddie Green had three rib
joints where for thirty-five cents you got ribs and a choice of two out of
three: coleslaw, potato salad, or the very un-Italian Franco-American
canned spaghetti, later referred to in my set as "rhythm-and-blues" spaghetti. You could also skip the side dishes and order "ribs all the way,"
which meant a washboard of the best barbecue ribs you ever tasted.

How did this white boy fare in darkest Harlem? As Leadbelly says
in "Midnight Special," "When you go to Houston, you better walk right."
In this one compressed line of blues poetry there are instructive layers
of meaning. A lot of Caucasians made it north of 110th Street in search
of poon. The demeanor, the look, the gait of these guys were excruciat-
ingly square. They didn't even know how to proposition. Heavy dues
were paid in the form of beatings and robbery by pimps, fancy men, and
street lookouts. I knew enough not to patronize or try to be overcool. I
knew not to pretend to be something I wasn't. I modeled myself after
older friends, white guys who were relaxed and comfortable uptown.
Besides, the racial climate was infinitely more mellow than it is today.
Not once was I ever accosted, threatened, or menaced.

And it wasn't just the Harlem of the night that mesmerized me; it
was the Harlem of a spring afternoon, when I'd get off the bus at Lenox
Avenue—a boulevard as fetching as its counterparts in Paris—and the
world seemed so soft and easy, a sweet breeze blowing across the brown-
stones, a gorgeous blue-eyed black woman allowing me to search
through the stock of her record store, where (glory, hallelujah!) I'd un-
earth an original Okeh of Louis Armstrong's "West End Blues" or the

pseudonymous Broadway Bellhops playing "There Ain't No Land Like Dixieland," the corniest song in creation except for a Bix solo that made it a collector's wet dream come true.

We'd go to Salvation Army depots and junk shops, where sometimes, in the back of beat-up old-fashioned Victrola cases, you'd luck up on priceless booty: sides by Muggsy Spanier, Pee Wee Russell (for me the greatest clarinetist in the history of that supple instrument), Red Allen, Ellington, Basie, Lucky Millinder, Coleman Hawkins, Bobby Hackett, Ben Webster, Lester Young, Edmond Hall, Charlie Christian, Fats Waller, Red Nichols, Don Redman, Zutty Singleton, Joe Venuti, Earl Hines, Chick Webb, Horace Henderson, Sid Catlett, Oran "Hot Lips" Page, Bud Freeman, Teddy Wilson, Artie Shaw, Mary Lou Williams, Harry Carney, Johnny Hodges, Cootie Williams, Jack Teagarden—all legends in the land of youth.

We were a new cult of record collectors, relentless in pursuit of our Grail, prospecting beyond Harlem, over to the Bronx, east to Queens, south to Brooklyn, deep into Bedford-Stuyvesant. We were especially tenacious under the els, on those shadowy streets beneath the elevated subways, under the incessant overhead roar of the trains. Els were the breeding grounds of used furniture stores, and where there was used furniture there were used phonographs and used records. We marched fearlessly into yards bristling with BAD DOG signs, following our muse down dark alleys into dusty rummage shops, sneaking past wary janitors to see if, by chance, someone had discarded a box of records in some vacant basement.

At the end of day, having scored or struck out, we'd be back in Harlem, our fixation switched from recorded sound to live music. The mecca was the Savoy Ballroom. With its big, beautiful stage and lines of tables and chairs where you'd sit and drink and watch the smoothest, most spectacular dancers pulsate to the smoking beat, the Savoy was fabulous. It cost a half a buck to get in, and I'd invariably go with a buddy. I was only seventeen, but my size fooled the ticket taker. I was also a good dancer—no Al Bibbo, mind you, but decent enough to get out on the floor and take a spin. That took guts. Most of the patrons, perhaps 80 percent, were black, meaning that the quality of dance was exceedingly high. The rhythm, though, overcame my inhibitions. The crazy rhythm got all over me.

The sight of the undulating, lindy-hopping dancers was one thing;

the beauty of the music, another. Fletcher Henderson's band exemplified the sounds of the Savoy. To hear the felicitous rhythm patterns played by the saxes on "Christopher Columbus," to follow the intricate and wildly swinging improvisations of Chu Berry or Roy Eldridge or Herschel Evans—shit, that was heaven on earth. When the Savoy Sultans, the superb house band, interpreted "Swanee River," the groove was so achingly slow you could have a baby during the bridge. On "Second Balcony Jump," altoist Rudy Williams tore it up, playing changes, a decade before Bird, that more than anticipated bop. Musically—even metaphysically—I was learning lessons about timing and patience. The marvel and mystery of great jazz was becoming clear—the point where relaxation and stimulation, cool and hot, meld together.

On other nights, in other ballrooms, the battles of the bands were waged to our eternal delight. I remember Red Norvo versus Chick Webb, Benny Goodman versus Jimmy Lunceford. In one dramatic confrontation at the Fordham Club in the Bronx, we heard Bunny Berigan take on Count Basie. Clustered around the bandstand, we stretched our necks to view our heroes as if at a prizefight. Bunny had Joe Bushkin and Georgie Auld. Count had Buck Clayton and Lester Young. In the final analysis, though, it came down to the drummers—Davie Tough for Berigan, Jo Jones for Basie. Davie was a bitch, but Jo cleaned him out. Basie's band blew Bunny out of the goddamn ballroom. It was a memorable night, not only for the decisiveness of Count's victory but for the presence of the man who brought Basie out of Kansas City into national prominence, John Hammond.

Hammond was one of my earliest idols. He was a demigod. He had started producing for Polyphone in 1930; his Fletcher Henderson sides were acknowledged masterpieces. John was a model of erudition, the first producer to earn a status as high as that of the musicians he recorded. Throughout the years, his look never changed. With his brush haircut, Brooks Brothers tweed, button-down Oxford shirt, and intellectual-radical periodicals—*New Masses, Masses and Mainstream, The Worker*—tucked under his arm, he stood there smiling at the music, his tall, spare frame unmistakable even in a crowd. John was a patrician, and meeting him that first time was an unbelievable gas: I was shaking hands with the man who had found Billie Holiday and Charlie Christian. Years later we became good friends, bonded in our preoccupation with jazz and blues.

My family's financial failures were brought home by one of the grisliest events of my early life, my grandfather's suicide. Having lost his bakery during the Depression, Elsa's father had worked at odd jobs until he became too old. He and my grandmother had a small house in Bensonhurst, but no savings. An insurance policy on his life was his only asset, and the act itself the only way he saw to ensure his wife's well-being. I remember Elsa's face at the funeral—humiliated, utterly despairing—and you'd think that would've been motivation enough for me to accomplish the one thing she'd dreamed of: academic success.

It wasn't. I was still in an egregious, seemingly endless period of fucking up. I'd graduated high school in 1932 at the tender age of fifteen and somehow got into City College for two semesters before dropping out. It was the depths of the Depression, and job prospects were dismal even for older, experienced applicants. For the likes of me there was nothing. I knew I needed a degree to have any chance at all, but I could deal with the classroom only if I turned it into my own personal theater, ridiculing the teacher and displaying what I considered my biting wit. No matter how much Ma nudged, I couldn't buckle down and wouldn't be told what to do.

In the parlance of modern psychology, though, Elsa was an enabler of epic proportions. She would not, she insisted, give up on my education. No matter that I'd busted out of City College; Ma was convinced that at New York University I'd find myself. So she found fifty dollars of *kishka gelt* to pay for five summer-school credits—but instead of taking the IRT downtown to University Place, I promptly headed for Artie's. It took me four and a half agonizing hours to blow it all on a game of straight pool.

There was no thought of admitting to Ma that I'd gambled my college funds away, so I had to think of some money-raising scheme in a flaming hurry. I turned to my buddy Cy. More loyal to me than to his own family, Cy helped me gather up his mother's silverware and carry the stuff off in a pillowcase; but the suspicious pawnbroker, rather than fork over cash, threatened to call the law. Not to be denied, we hurried back to Cy's, where we took his sister's textbooks—she was studying at Columbia—and sold them at Barnes & Noble. And if that weren't bad enough, we took that money and immediately ran to Artie's, where—

you guessed it—we blew it on still another game of three-cushion billiards.

And yet Elsa persisted in cleaning up after me, and structured yet
another plan to stick my obstinate ass in some ivory tower somewhere.
Indefatigable, she went to the almanacs and, with the help of my pal Joe
Orns, pored through the reference books. Together they came up with
a lulu:

Kansas.

A
MOTHER'S
KISSES

When I read Bruce Jay Friedman's brilliant seriocomic novel *A Mother's Kisses* in 1964, I was convinced he had invaded my psyche and stolen the story from me. So taken was I with the book that I knocked on Friedman's door—he happened to live nearby in Great Neck—and introduced myself. I congratulated him on his work and remarked on the uncanny similarity between his invention and my reality. He was interested to hear that my mother, like the larger-than-life Jewish matriarch in his novel, was proud of her shapely legs and, more to the point, bent on shaping her son's destiny. In Friedman's fiction, the mother buses to the midwestern college where she places herself in the center of her offspring's psychic, academic, and romantic life.

In getting me to Kansas, Elsa worked in conjunction with my great buddy Joe Orns, who was a couple of years older than me. We were bonded by a love for jazz, sports, foreign movies, slapstick comedy, and John O'Hara. Joe had a hypertrophied sense of the absurd, and we shared a terminal irreverence, running under the aegis of satire and irony, aways on the qui vive for pomposity, self-aggrandizement, and downright stupidity in friends, pols, teachers, and journalists.

Generally speaking, Joe was madder than me. Later on he would bust out of medical school in Edinburgh, acting out a story by Jerome Weidman about intransigent Jewish guys from Brooklyn who, victims of anti-Semiotic quota restrictions at American universities, went to study in Scotland. Instead of taking care of business, though, they dove into *la vie bohème*, cut classes, and went nutso. They were bounced out and returned home. Joe wound up in the rag trade, in which he had a long and productive career.

Elsa, 1930

Despite his patent dementia, Joe would talk to me like a concerned Big Brother, or the Dean of Men admonishing a wayward freshman. Around Elsa he assumed a seriously tutelary attitude toward me, wearing a mien of extreme *gravitas*. Elsa really bought it, calling on Joe for counsel on the subject of my frequent infractions. Together Elsa and Joe got me to college.

This new chapter in my life began in 1936 when Elsa accompanied me to Manhattan, Kansas, home of Kansas State College of Agriculture and Applied Science—today it's called Kansas State University—where Ma had discovered out-of-state tuition was one hundred dollars a term. She not only took me there but also, before heading back to New York City, made certain that we met Charles E. Rogers, chairman of the journalism department.

Her son, she announced to this elegant Presbyterian, old-line American, was going to be a great writer.

We were impressed by his cordiality and, even more, by his Jewish wife. His was the exact opposite of Aunt Gertrude's attitude, and it immediately endeared us to the man. Culturally we were proud, up-front Jews, even if we ignored the rituals; we were, after all, also atheists. Elsa went so far as to tell him about her sister, then ask whether he'd ever been worried that discrimination might hurt his career. A half-century later, I can still see him rising from the table, reaching for his goblet of wine, and announcing, "Here's the bottle, and here's the glass—if they don't like it they can kiss my ass."

Charles E. Rogers took me under his wing, and presently wrote to my mother: "Gerald is a most interesting young man. He surely has great talent. I am certain he will do great things in newspaper work and make us all proud."

At least for a while, I was going great guns. The change did me good. What a contrast between Manhattan, New York, and Manhattan, Kansas! For the first time, I broke free of the province of Washington Heights to experience a strange and wondrous world. There were golden wheat fields, clear blue skies, and people who spoke with a twang decidedly different from what I'd heard on the boardwalk at Coney Island. For a while I fulfilled my mother's dream and began writing little pieces for the school paper. My academic affairs were going well.

It didn't take long, though, for a far more compelling affair to take over my imagination. I met a local girl who turned my fancy, a scintillating young woman, the first true love of my life and one of the reasons Elsa grew alarmed. Pauline was not Jewish. Her aunt was a celebrated food writer for the *New York Herald Tribune,* and Pauline—called Patty—was spirited, smart, sexy, and willing to go my way. My way often led 114 miles east to Kansas City. That's where the rhythm was.

Patty and I played out our passionate affair over the mid-thirties music of Boss Pendergast's 12th Street gangster-era rag. Talk about good-time urban corruption! The atmosphere was as thrilling as a James M. Cain novel. And if there was a feeling of safety in all this, it's because the music, while fresh and new, soared with the same energy I'd learned to love back in Harlem. Swing was everywhere. And we made the scene, Patty and I, from the Reno Club, where John Hammond had scooped up Count Basie, to Dante's Inferno, where bottomless topless waitresses held my full attention. Here in the Wild West, the juke joints and blues clubs were in full cry. At the Elks I heard Joe Turner, that magnificent shouter, then a singing bartender, whom twenty-five years later I wound up producing. The big bands were roaring: Bennie Moten's, led by his accordion-playing brother Bus; Andy Kirk and his Clouds of Joy; Harlan

Leonard and the Rockets. In our room at the Puritan Hotel—no lie—Patty and I left the window open so the late-night sounds from the street, the blistering jazz of wide-open Kansas City, would fuel the fire of our lovemaking.

Back in Manhattan, Kansas, my out-of-the-classroom musical education was in full force. The jukeboxes in town, for example, had the most marvelous mixture of genres. Jazz like Louis Armstrong's "Ding Dong Daddy from Dumas" would be next to so-called race records like "Take It Easy, Greasy, You've Got a Long Way to Slide." Bing Crosby on button A-1; Adolph Hofner on A-2. The juxtaposition fascinated me. It was my first taste of country music, and I loved what I heard. I didn't know it then, but I was experiencing the Periclean Age of Western Swing, personified by the colloquial creativity of Bob Wills and the Texas Playboys.

My most important teacher was a fraternity boy, Dale Shrof, who later became a big-band trumpeter and called himself Dale Brody. As an undergraduate, he possessed a wide knowledge of jazz and the willingness to share good news. We'd climb up to the attic of the frat house, where, with only a flickering green light from the Victrola half-illuminating the tiny space, he filled in gaps in my education, introducing me to the glories of an older pre-swing music that was love on first hearing. I'm speaking of Jelly Roll Morton, King Oliver, Ma Rainey, Mamie Smith, Clara Smith, Jabbo Smith, Bessie Smith, Ida Cox, and especially Louis Armstrong, the main master, whose music's sweet afterglow lasted for days, for weeks—in truth, a lifetime. New Orleans, like Kansas City, seemed to call. The pioneers, early jazzmen and blues primitives excited me as much as the slick swing musicians at the Savoy. In fact, I heard it as one harmonious continuum.

But even more urgently, I heard from my mother. By now I was into my second year at Kansas, and, true to my pattern, my grades had turned to shit. Elsa was alarmed not only by my poor performance but also because she'd sensed between the lines of my letters an amorous state of mind. She wrote Professor Rogers for an evaluation, and I still have his response. (Like a magpie, I kept everything from those days—letters, tear sheets, newspaper clippings, photos, even some of my term papers—a sign, I guess, of my ingrained egocentrism.)

"I promised to send you some impressions of Gerald," Professor Rogers wrote Elsa, "that might be of use to a mental hygienist in advising you in solving the riddle of his personality. In short, Gerald is a young man of marked ability who is manifestly unable to integrate his own personality in his world. He is teacher's pet, yet teachers loathe him for his intolerable habit of trying—and too often succeeding—to steal their show. He simply cannot go on here. Something in him rebels. He is a man who *might* have succeeded, a person with a great potential blighted by a personality defect which he, you, or I cannot fathom."

That same spring my mother called to say she was coming to Kansas. My heart sank. "Gerald is talking crazy," I heard her tell Harry. "I'm bringing him home." Which is what she did.

Part of me didn't want to leave Patty, but a stronger part wanted to escape still another academic catastrophe. Elsa's rescue came just before exams which I would have surely flunked. She was brokenhearted that I had disappointed her once again, but told me before we left that we weren't going straight home. We were going via Niagara Falls. I asked why, not a little surprised by the odd turn my most recent failure had taken. "I've never had a honeymoon," she explained. "This might be my only chance."

Decades later, when someone joked with her about the oedipal implications of our relationship, Elsa smiled and said, "Freud, shmeud. I loved Gerald, but I never wanted to fuck him."

PICKING
UP
THE
PAIL

My brother, Arthur, had a brilliant political mind. I did not. He was an ecstatic Marxist, swept up in the emotion of the Revolution. He followed Trotsky and could analyze the complexities of Trotsky's splinter groups—the Cannonites versus the Shachtmanites—with absolute precision. Though my own leanings were left of center—in our household, how could they be otherwise?—not until I went to Kansas did I become emotional about politics. There I saw the New Deal in action. In the mid-thirties folks in the Midwest were dealing with the Dust Bowl and the Tennessee Valley Authority was under way, a massive operation that seemed to me ingenious. Saving the soil, erecting monumental dams down the Missouri and Mississippi, bringing electricity to rural America—being at a land-grant college brought all this home. I was awestruck.

Yet once I was back in New York City, the rest of America and its mighty resources receded like a half-remembered dream. I was back where I started, living at home in my parents' small apartment. Still doting, Elsa wouldn't give up on me. Now she had concluded that I didn't need to work, that since I'd written articles for the college paper I could become the next Dreiser. She bought me a Royal typewriter, placed a pile of yellow typing paper next to it on the desk, and, before leaving to do her marketing in the morning, would kiss me on the cheek.

"Write," she'd say.

But when she returned an hour later, I'd be asleep on the couch, not having written a comma. Inertia consumed me. Boredom knocked me out. Among other things, I lacked what the ancients called *furor scribendi*—the rage to write.

For years Harry had complained that she was spoiling me to death, and finally Elsa had to agree. It hurt her to admit it—perhaps more than it hurt me—but we both knew the game was up. We had no choice. The one thing Ma and I dreaded most was coming true. But what else to do? I'd managed to blow all my odd jobs—delivery boy, assistant clerk at Morris Rosenbaum's liquor store at 4247 Broadway, packer in the garment district, waiter in the Catskills during the summer (where I was fired for staying in bed too late). The truth is that I wasn't much of a worker or much of a writer. I was a cosmic fuck-up.

There was only one employer who wouldn't turn me down: my father. Only one sure thing remained: windows. I started washing windows with Harry, and I loathed every living minute of it. Today it puts me in mind of the old gospel tune "Carrying the Cross for My Boss." The stipend was eighteen dollars a week.

Winters were the worst. Pop would drag me out of bed at three-thirty a.m. I was numb with fatigue and horror. We'd traipse to Bickford's cafeteria, empty and bleak in the iron-cold morning, to wolf down the nineteen-cent bacon special: one egg, two strips of bacon, hash browns, buttered English muffin, and coffee. We'd get our pails, ladders, and buckets from a friendly storekeeper's backroom and hit the windows. Often we had to put alcohol in the water to keep it from freezing. Slick sidewalks and iron cellar doors posed a constant danger; our ladders could easily slide from under us, and often did. Unlike my father, I never broke anything. He knew how repugnant this life was for me, but there were two opposing dynamics at work: on the one hand was the inexorable economic necessity (he needed my help), and on the other was filial compassion (he pitied my misery). To cover the route we'd have to work till four or five in the afternoon, but many times he'd send me home early.

I remember being up in Riverdale, standing on the ladder and running the squeegee over a pane of beveled glass, looking into a home of such splendor that I couldn't help but stop to daydream. Inside were polished hardwood floors, a gleaming marble fireplace, a Bechstein grand piano. I yearned for such opulence, but in my heart I knew it was unlikely. I was qualified for nothing but the job before my nose. "Wash the window," Pa would call out. "Just wash the goddamn window."

The dreariness of my working life, though, only added to the zest with which I led my personal life. Kansas had stimulated my passion for jazz, and now record collecting exploded into a full-blown obsession. It was a mania both fraternal and competitive. There were the real pros— John Hammond, George Avakian—and there were the up-and-coming shleppers like me and Russ Sanjek, who, with our dog-eared copy of Charles Delaunay's sacred *Hot Discography,* made up in energy what we lacked in knowledge.

Russ came from Wadsworth Terrace north of 191st Street, a different world. His father was a Slovak minister, and although Russ never graduated high school, he was a world-class autodidact. Eventually he would come to write the classic, four-volume history *American Popular Music and Its Business,* a treasure of arcane information and colossal research. With his passion for Art—great books, foreign films, impressionist paintings, esoteric jazz—he both taught and inspired me; his sardonic manner and ironic quips seemed the quintessence of sophistication. Later he'd be the key to unlocking the doors to the music business for me. When we were young men, though, business was the last thing on our minds. We were record hunters, fierce and indefatigable. To discover, in the back of some basement in Far Rockaway, a carton of unopened, still-in-original-wrapper sets of Black Swans—a label owned by W. C. Handy and responsible for Ethel Waters's first recordings—was an experience second only to orgasm.

That, too, was a topic much on my nineteen-year-old mind. Fresh from my breakup with Pauline, I was especially motivated to find a replacement. My track record as a ladies' man was spotty, my desire always exceeding my success. I had been in love with sultry Kitty Campanioni. Because of my brawny build, she figured I was her age, but she dropped me when she learned I was three years her junior. Before Kitty I'd been crazy for Joan Edwards, later to become a singing star on radio's "Your Hit Parade," but Joan gave me the back of her hand. Pera, bless her heart, gave me a handful, but nothing more. Dottie was a terrific tease, and I took whatever I could get, which wasn't much.

My peers were waiting just where I'd left them—at Artie's poolroom. Much to Ma's chagrin, we'd meet there every Saturday and discuss options: do we make the scene in the Village, or Harlem, or 52nd Street, where the clubs—Jimmy Ryan's, the Onyx, Kelly's Stables— were going strong? Hiding under the bandstand at Nick's in the Village, we'd listen to Pee Wee Russell and Max Kaminsky for hours, or until we were discovered and booted out. No matter, at evening's end we'd regroup back in the Heights at the Willow Cafeteria, where, over toasted pound cake and steaming hot coffee, we'd lie about our sexual conquests.

There were, however, loftier interests. The Museum of Modern Art became a rich resource. On Sundays we'd sit in the sculpture garden, bask in the sun, and sip Rhine-wine spritzers while eying Giacomettis and Henry Moores. I developed an affinity for the surrealists, particularly Magritte. Along more traditional lines, I loved Edward Hopper and his straight-ahead style of storytelling.

The museum also showed a series of fabulous foreign movies. Jean Renoir's *Grand Illusion* touched my soul, and I can still quote lines spoken by Jean Gabin. Renoir's atmospheric adaptation of Gorky's *The Lower Depths*—a startling piece of modernity—also starred Gabin, whose work in Marcel Carné's *Port of Shadows* defined the model antihero, an outsider with whom I readily identified. We'd also run over to the Thalia on Broadway to catch *The Informer*—I saw it a dozen times—or one of Robert Flaherty's telling documentaries, *Nanook of the North* or *Man of Aran*. Other milestones were *Un Chien andalou*, Salvador Dalí's collaboration with Luis Buñuel, and *Spanish Earth*, Joris Ivens's account, narrated by Ernest Hemingway, of the plight of villagers during the Spanish Civil War; and above all, Jean Cocteau's haunting *The Blood of a Poet*.

On the lighter side, I was nuts for slapstick. The Marx Brothers, the Ritz Brothers, Laurel and Hardy, W. C. Fields, the deadpan Buster Keaton, Larry Semon, the sublime Charlie Chaplin—you couldn't keep me out of the movie houses. Earlier, I'd been knocked out by vaudeville. For a short while I'd ushered at the RKO Coliseum, a deluxe theater on 181st and Broadway. All the great acts came through—Bennie Rubin; Block and Sully; Sammy Timberg, Willie West, and McGinty, who came on as paperhangers and wound up plastering each other; Frank and Milt Britton's band, who threw lifelike dummies into the audience and beat one another over the head with trombones—and Phil Fabello led the full-sized house orchestra.

Absurdity in art, whether mainstream comedy or avant-garde painting, hit me between the eyes. I liked it subtle and I liked it wild. I also liked experimentation. And if music continued to be my central passion, the pleasure of listening was soon enhanced by something altogether new—my first hit of grass, thirties-style.

We were stone-age stoners, first-generation heads. Appropriately enough, my initial high came on 52nd Street, where my dear friend Dan Qualey had taken me on a Sunday afternoon in spring to a jam session produced by Milt Gabler, renowned jazz impresario. Dan was a Brooklyn bartender reputed to be the illegitimate son of John Barrymore. He was a Dodger rooter and Pete Reiser fan of undying devotion, a jazz scholar with an Irish dock worker's accent who, when drunk, wept for the brave Spanish rebels while swearing vengeance on the head of Franco. Later he started Solo Art Records—he was the guy responsible for bringing boogie-woogie piano to mainstream America—and became a major-league player in the music game.

Qualey was a role model, and when he offered me a joint, I didn't say no. It was no ordinary stick, but one rolled by Mezz Mezzrow, notorious as both a clarinetist and Louis Armstrong's pot supplier. Mezz's joints, as Dan showed me, were rolled with a perfect six-corner tuck. Just as Picasso signed his name on the lower right side of his canvases, the hexagonal fold was Mezz's signature, known wherever jazz was played.

Dan passed the reefer, showing me how to keep my mouth shut and hold in the precious smoke. It worked. It got me to that other place where I was supposed to go. I took the quantum leap, from the sunshine of an April afternoon to the darkness of Jimmy Ryan's smoke-filled club, where Roy Eldridge, one of my idols, was blowing "Heckler's Hop," every fiber of his music, every quavering note, piercing my bloodstream and flooding my brain with joy.

Window washing aside, my life was mostly music and hanging out. Back in the Heights, we hung at the Wall at Fort Washington Avenue and 175th Street. Constructed of fieldstone, the Wall was the neighborhood meeting spot for teens and young adults, a point of social reference and information exchange. On the Wall, my hipper friends would tap out Jo Jones's drum solos, using a matchbook to simulate his high hat and brushes. The Wall had a relaxed, slow-moving rhythm all its own. Low enough to sit upon, it overlooked a softball field where I chased many a long fly ball. You could see the Hudson from the Wall. Fort Tryon Park and the Cloisters, Rockefeller's museum of medieval art, were close by. On clear nights the lights of the Palisades flickered like fireflies.

I found love on the Wall. It was 1936, and the agony of working for my father was heavy on my heart. I was searching for romance, and when I saw this alluring womanchild—she was sixteen, three years younger than me—with green liquid eyes, a dark and delicate Modigliani face, lovely legs, a quick wit and supple mind, I was smitten. Her name was Shirley Kampf. She'd grown up only a block away from me. In fact her mother, Blanche, knew Elsa. Shirley was just graduating high school and about to enter a secretarial trade school. But, struck by the quality of her mind, I talked her out of it, insisting that someone like her belonged in college, and echoing Elsa's remarks about me.

Unlike me, though, Shirley was able to win a scholarship to New York University. Eventually she earned a graduate degree. She was a voracious reader, a lover of novels and poems, an appreciator of jazz; she was everything I could have hoped for.

I remember the summer afternoon when Shirley rang my doorbell. She stood in the doorway of my parents' apartment wearing a simple white-flowered summer dress—her waist so slim, the fabric so clinging. I was mad for her. On our first formal date, as an indication of her importance, I took her to the Apollo to hear Ella Fitzgerald and Chick Webb, themselves young lovebirds. I romanced her in record booths all over the city. "It was in a booth in my store," Milt Gabler remembers, "that Jerry Wexler courted his Shirley."

Gabler's Commodore Record Store on 52nd Street was a key setting in our affair. Shirley became a comrade, a regular participant in my search for rare records. Early in our romance, we were walking down Eighth Avenue when I spotted a rummage shop across the street from Madison Square Garden. Way in the back, underneath piles of dusty old curtains, I happened on a cache of unused records that took my breath away. The more I scrutinized the find, the harder my heart started hammering. Original King Olivers on Vocalion. New Orleans Rhythm Kings on Gennett. The Chocolate Dandies on Okeh. Bennie Moten on Victor. Don Redman on Brunswick. The Rhythmakers on Melotone. Pay dirt!

I was overwhelmed. To me, a rare record was a precious jewel, and I'd just found hundreds. The only problem, of course, was money. I had none. But I had Shirley wait. She became a live deposit while I ran over to Milt Gabler's to make a deal.

In my book, Milt Gabler is a prince. He put his money where his heart was—in music. Not only did he run the most exciting jam sessions and the best-stocked record store in the city, he also privately produced Billie Holiday's ethereal late-thirties music on his Commodore label. When his shop closed at night, he'd invite in a few fans for after-hours listening. Along with Dan Qualey, Russ Sanjek, Ted May, Abe Oriel, and Moe Danziger, I was happy to be an insider.

Jazz buddies in the forties: (clockwise from lower left) Ted May, Dan Qualey, Moe Danziger, Abe Oriel, Wex

"Milt!" I cried, bursting into the store. When I described the find, he reached for the cash—just like that. We went in as partners. It was my first minor-major record deal. I forget all the details, but we both wound up with a lot of inventory—his going into the store, mine going to Shirley's parents' apartment, the new warehouse for my burgeoning collection. Elsa wouldn't put up with the clutter. Besides, she'd want to know where I got the money.

How I managed my money still isn't clear to me. In the five years, 1936 to 1941, after my return from Kansas, I still hadn't accomplished a thing. Yet Shirley believed in me with unwavering conviction. Together we were discovering—through books, movies, music, and art—a life of the mind.

"I thought Jerry was extremely attractive, physically and mentally," Shirley remembers. "The first time I saw him I whispered to my girlfriend Bunny Keshin, 'Now there's a handsome beast.' But I also had never met a man with such an uncontrollable and violent temper. Jerry's father was sweet, but he also had a short fuse. Harry was a yeller. There was always a lot of yelling in Jerry's household. And tremendous preoccupation—on both Jerry's and Harry's part—with Elsa.

"I grew up in a household with two women, my mother and my aunt Ida, who knew Elsa well. They played bridge with her but were privately censorious, holding her in low esteem. She indulged herself with clothes and was not discreet about her outside men. In the beginning, I was taken by Elsa. She impressed and dazzled me. My own mother was someone remote, and Elsa seemed warm and caring. Only later, though, did I learn she cared for me only as a way to stay close to her Gerald. Her Gerald was her world. Jerry was charming and charismatic, but he was also a mess when we first met. He was surreptitiously following Elsa around the streets, trying to decipher whom she was having affairs with. At a certain point, there were two men, both well-established professionals. Elsa always went for the best. One was with the NBC orchestra, the other a respected physician."

When it comes to shadowing my mother, I confess to a memory lapse, but there can be no doubt that I was deeply concerned that her relationship with Harry was on the verge of collapse. Nineteen thirty-nine was an especially difficult year. Pa fell from a ladder and broke his back, so I had to cover his route as well as my own. If I remember, we had to deal with forty or fifty stores.

Later that same year my parents' relationship finally ruptured.

"Jerry and I were on our way to the World's Fair in Flushing when Harry called with a bulletin," Shirley recalls. "When we got to the apartment, he was threatening to jump out the window."

The news made us all crazy. I had never seen my father so distraught. Tears were streaming from his eyes as, barely able to speak, he told me that Elsa was gone, and so was our money. She'd cleaned out our bank account—the whole ten thousand dollars—and run off to Miami.

Money was always the main matter between Elsa and Harry. Elsa was a strange mix of thrift and profligacy. For example, she never shopped for food more than once a week. Even though we had three great meals a day, Arthur and I had ravenous appetites. To stretch the larder, Mom would padlock the fridge before leaving the house. To this day I'm stricken with embarrassment at this memory. Maybe there's an echo here; maybe this is where my lifelong preoccupation with food and wine started.

My brother and I, evicted from our bedroom by a roomer, had been sleeping in the living room even before our mother left. Even though Harry by now was making two hundred dollars a week or better washing windows—decent money during the Depression—Elsa insisted that we take in the roomer, Mr. Maxson, who walked in one afternoon when Shirley and I were smooching on the sofa. Too ashamed to explain who he was, I neglected to introduce him accidentally on purpose and later claimed he was a visiting relative.

"Elsa wanted the money," Shirley says about my parents' separation. In fact, she took the money and went to Miami for a divorce. I almost went nuts, shocked out of my mind. "Elsa got the divorce," according to Shirley, "so her children wouldn't see her as a tramp." I never agreed with this. To my mind, Mom divorced Harry out of sheer inanition.

She came back from Florida and moved in with a man on Third Avenue and 34th Street under the el. I couldn't stand the guy. I refused to accept my parents' separation, refused to see my mother. It was Shirley who convinced me that I was acting like a child. She admitted that she'd been visiting Elsa after her classes at NYU and urged me to come along.

I would have to go behind Harry's back—but I finally decided Shirley was right. I needed to see my mother. I thought of all the times Elsa had confidentially expressed her frustrations to me: Harry was not a good provider; Harry didn't know the meaning of romance; Harry was inadequate. Their marriage was one of convenience and habituation. So as Shirley and I walked up the narrow staircase to my mother's new domicile, I suppose I was expecting to see her shacked up with someone who looked like William Powell.

Instead, in this dingy apartment with cracked linoleum and peeling paint—certainly a scale down from our place on Bennett Avenue—I was introduced to an undersized Armenian, an importer, physically unprepossessing, rotund, and years younger than Elsa. This seemed miserable, but at least my relationship with Elsa was reestablished. In fact, several months later it was my mother who, with the war and Army service looming, convinced me to propose. I'll let Shirley explain:

"I still have nightmares about that. Jerry and I were on the subway and he stated it plainly. He was honest, I'll grant him that. He said, 'My mother's sure I won't get drafted right away if we get married. My mother thinks we should get married.' I was dumbfounded, but I was also terribly in love with Jerry. He was the most exciting thing that had ever happened to me and, Elsa or not, I wasn't about to lose him."

Shirley's parents had difficulties of their own. Her father, Morris, was one of those mute Jewish heroes with an apron and fallen arches who, for forty years, worked behind the counter of his little delicatessen slicing pastrami. When he came home, his wife, Blanche, would badger him.

Both Shirley and I were escaping households sodden with misery; we were looking for a better life. At the same time, the prospects were nil. Thus we were forced to make love (and eventually live) in those very apartments—the childhood homes we had outgrown and wanted to flee. The tension in our parents' marriages never subsided, and in looking to escape, Shirley and I went exactly nowhere. These were the inauspicious beginnings of my marriage to a woman I admired and adored.

STRANGE
CUSTOMS

In 1941, I married Shirley twice. The first time we eloped to Stamford, where Russ Sanjek and his wife, Betty, drove us from Washington Heights and served as witnesses. A second ceremony, conducted by a rabbi, was designed to please Shirley's parents. To give you an idea of our extended families' combined worth, total gifts amounted to around fifty dollars.

Tougher still was the fact we were living with my father at 1 Bennett Avenue. Arthur was away at graduate school in Nebraska, and Harry had hired a woman to keep house.

"Harry had been paying a woman thirty dollars a week to cook and clean," Shirley remembers. "When I came on the scene, he fired her and paid me twenty-five dollars to do the same work. Out of that twenty-five dollars, though, I also had to buy food. It was an interesting way to start a marriage. In many ways it was fun." Poor Shirley: not only were we newlyweds sleeping on a lumpy pullout couch, but she was suddenly keeping house and cooking for a pair of behemoths, me and Pa.

"When it came to our own food," Shirley recalls, "I would sneak over to Elsa, who was still living with Eddie the Armenian, and have her give me the recipes for dishes Harry and Jerry liked best. I suppose Harry presumed that all women cooked the same, because he never mentioned that I was preparing his wife's menu for him. I loved my father-in-law, but he could be picky and cruel, and you can imagine how relieved I was when Elsa came back."

This was 1942. I'm not sure whether Mama's boyfriend had begun playing around or whether they'd run through the ten-thousand-dollar dowry. Either way, Ma was ready to come home. The delicate negotiations were handled by Goldie, my father's niece, whom my parents had helped bring over from Poland. Harry and I were overjoyed. Elsa's days of restlessness were finally over.

"It was the wintertime," Shirley adds. "And the price of reconciliation included a new fur coat for Elsa."

I had washed my last window earlier in the year and was now a customs guard, patrolling the freezing docks of Manhattan, Staten Island, and Brooklyn from midnight till morning. The work was better than window washing, but only because of fewer physical demands: it was boring as all hell. Many a Saturday night I'd crawl into a berth on an empty ship and sleep until Sunday afternoon, when I'd head over to 53 West 52nd Street to join my pals at Jimmy Ryan's for one of Milt Gabler's fabulous jam sessions.

I arrived on Swing Street one day, still in uniform, my head still cobwebbed from sleep, when the drummer Kansas Fields asked me, "You packing your rod, man?"

"More than that, Kansas, I got the formula for making the best hash you ever dreamed of."

He followed me down to the basement of Ryan's, where Max Kaminsky and the boys—including my friends Dan Qualey and Ted May—were smoking a little tea. The place reeked. After I took a toke myself, I began to read passages from a government-written manual, meant for customs officers, describing in exacting terms the way marijuana was made: the flailing of cannabis, the treating of the residue, the caking of the plant. My buddies were enraptured, and some were even taking notes.

Upstairs the jazz roared inside my head until I thought I'd pass out from too much excitement, too much love, too much irresistible swing.

"There was a moment there," Max Kaminsky later wrote in his autobiography, "in 1941–42, at the Ryan sessions, when hot jazz seemed at its purest. At Ryan's the music was the thing, and when a musician was building a solo, you never heard a sound from the audience. You could *feel* them listening."

The place was always packed, and for sixty-five cents you'd hear Bobby Hackett, Brad Gowans, Zutty Singleton, Eddie Condon, Jack Teagarden, Dave Bowman, Sidney Bechet, Marty Marsala, Joe Sullivan, Teddy Bunn and the Spirits of Rhythm. You might see a young Shelly Manne on the drums—I remember him in short pants—or, if you were lucky, hear the ethereal Billie Holiday singing "Fine and Mellow," weaving a spell over the smoky Sunday afternoon.

Back on the Heights, Shirley and I had kept my parents' apartment, while Elsa and Harry had moved into another one-bedroom flat on the same floor. Occasionally Shirley and I would spend an afternoon on 14th Street, where I'd comb the used-record bins for hidden gems. The notes of Red Allen's "Meet Me in the Moonlight," for example, remain written across my heart. It was an accidental purchase; I didn't know what I was in for, didn't know that for the next fifty years Red would remain my favorite instrumentalist, a much-neglected virtuoso who was unfairly compared to his fellow Louisianian Louis Armstrong, in spite of the fact that Allen's unexpected tonal leaps and sophisticated sense of harmonics were futuristic, far closer to the beboppers of the forties than to the preswingers of the twenties.

On that particular day I bought two other 78s which I'll never forget—Rex Stewart leading a small Ellington ensemble called the 52nd Street Stompers playing "Tea and Trumpets" and "Rexatious," and Mildred Bailey singing "I Let a Song Go Out of My Heart."

In a trance confected of romance and music, Shirley and I, hand in hand, would stroll to midtown, where we'd meet Russ and Betty Sanjek at a small bistro. Those were the days when you could buy a memorable meal at a restaurant like Du Midi for fifty cents—vichyssoise, scallops St. Jacques, braised squab, medallions of veal, *pommes frites*, a fabulous Grand Marnier soufflé, and for another forty cents, a decent bottle of Bordeaux, *troisième cru*.

No matter how great the diversions, though, I knew I was just marking time. I'd received a draft notice in 1941, and my marriage put off induction for only a year.

One of the reasons Elsa came back was because, worried about my going into the Army, she wanted to see whether there was anything she could do to prevent it. There wasn't.

REVEILLE

Looking back, I see certain pivotal points in my life, events which turned me this way or that. The Army had a prodigious impact on me. If I was a fuck-up before I went in, by the time I left I was almost a mensch. The Army set me straight and made something of my capricious Jewish ass.

The minute I hit boot camp, I felt relief. Perhaps it was the absence of Elsa, or the presence of a reassuring structure. I no longer had to worry about what was to become of my life. The Army took care of that. The Army took care of everything. No more idle hours in the library stacks, no more idle jobs, no more leniency. I might get away with being a wisecracking smartass to my teachers or employers, but not in the Army. Oddly enough, I liked the discipline, liked being forced to behave.

I excelled. No one's shoes shone with greater luster, no one's belt buckle gleamed like mine, no one's trousers had sharper creases. At the weekly inspections called "guard mount," the best-groomed soldier, the one to win a weekend pass, was often me. "My main memory of visiting Jerry in Trenton," says Shirley, "was his obsession with shining his shoes. Over and again he kept asking, 'Where's my Kiwi? Who took my Kiwi?'"

Well, I found my Kiwi and I found my pride. I wanted to show my Christian colleagues—some of them country boys, some of them rednecks—that this New York City Jew could hang tough with the toughest. Most defensively, I felt they perceived me and my tribe as wimps, round-shouldered and humpbacked from leaning over prayer books, and pussy to the core. I was actively engaged in showing them otherwise.

In Trenton, I also was able to pursue my predilection for jazz music. I happened to have friends there—Bob Arthur, later to become a suc-

cessful playwright and scriptwriter, and his wife, Bea, later to become a famous actress—who took me to the local club to hear the great trumpeter Oran "Hot Lips" Page. Lips and I knew each other from the city, and it was a special treat to feel his fire on those cold Saturday nights in the industrial boondocks of Jersey. He was a gregarious, warm, and intelligent man, a magnificent player with an idiosyncratic down-home feel, ethnic in the primal sense of Delta bluesmen—more so, I felt, than other trumpet icons like Sidney de Paris, Bill Coleman, Frankie Newton, or Roy Eldridge. With the exception of Louis Armstrong, no one could touch Lips singing blues. He elevated "Gee Baby Ain't I Good to You" (not structurally a twelve-bar blues, but blues-feeling nonetheless) to anthem status. I'll never forget his castigation of a misbehaving female in "Fattening Frogs for Snakes" for "getting all glamorous and simple."

My first post-basic-training assignment was simple and unglamorous: the military police. My experience as a customs guard qualified me, I suppose, and they sent me to Oswego, New York, for training. I wasn't thrilled to become another sort of cop, but at the same time I wasn't being sent overseas. In order to maintain stateside status, I took every test that came along. Soon I was studying psychology at the University of Pennsylvania, a six-month course on administering and evaluating behavioral tests for military personnel. Suddenly I was surrounded

At the Copacabana: Shirley, Wex, Archie de Satuik, and Cy Ampole

by professional psychologists—clinicians, statisticians—many of whom had master's degrees and doctorates. In some sense, we were in competition. Doing well in the course meant an extra pass home, so I drove myself hard.

I made the Army work for me. I found a home. Were it not for the Army, my ongoing stupefaction—my unending pattern of sloth and self-indulgence—would have surely done me in. In testing situations, right answers were critical. I learned what answers they were looking for and was quickly rewarded: rather than being shipped to the landing beaches of France, I wound up on the beaches of Florida.

Shirley joined me, and we lived in Miami Beach for nearly a year. That's when I first fell in love with Florida. If it wasn't paradise, it was close, with all the clichés of the subtropical Eden—balmy breezes, swaying palm trees, glorious sunshine. We had an apartment in a tropical deco building across the street from the ocean. I was actually stationed at a seaside hotel called the White House. (It's still there, one of the ornaments of Miami's South Beach deco revival.) My job was to process test scores of Air Corps personnel. The tests purported to determine their best potential—as pilots, bombardiers, gunners, or navigators. Shirley found a great job teaching children at a private institution, the Mannheim School. On the weekends we played volleyball and listened to jazz.

I was transferred to Wichita Falls, Texas, to do the same job, and fortunately Shirley was able to come. By then she too was working for

*War duty at the White
House, Miami Beach*

the Army. They'd trained her in management, and she was soon design-
ing manuals for every department on the post. We lived in a converted
chicken coop, developed a nice nucleus of friends, and began a foreign
film club, renting movies from the Museum of Modern Art in New York.

This was a period of concentrated reading, a period where I also
concentrated on the ambition my mother had long harbored for me—to
become a writer. I was obsessed with the writers who spoke most
directly to me, including Hemingway, Faulkner, Lardner, Fitzgerald,
Tolstoy, Turgenev, Thomas Mann, James M. Cain, and John O'Hara.
Despite the fact that the literary establishment shut out O'Hara—only
his short stories were begrudgingly considered worthwhile—I found
him inspiring. Thanksgiving was my favorite holiday, not for turkey and
stuffing but because it meant the publication of a new O'Hara. I re-
sponded to his characters, I suppose, because they acted according to
inexorably logical mandates. I found that satisfying. Beyond that, I've
always listened for the music in writers, and O'Hara's prose moved to
the cadence of jazz. He swung. Reading *Appointment in Samarra* or

Butterfield 8, I heard Joe Venuti and Bix Beiderbecke. A jazz baby himself, O'Hara would actually name musicians known only to the initiate:
Ross Gorman, saxist for Paul Whiteman; Mike Pingatore, hunchback
guitarist; the Scranton Sirens, the Dorsey brothers' early orchestra.
O'Hara was accused of anti-Semitism and, maybe because I loved his
writing so immoderately, I argued that he wasn't, even if his characters
were. I needed to forgive him his bias.

I had my own prejudices. Contrary to the opinion of my contempo-
raries, I abominated Damon Runyon and such Runyonisms as "Me and
Harry the Horse was tearing a herring at Schmindy's." Jumping Jesus
Christ! My man was Ring Lardner. Lardner's dialogue rang true; his
people were real where Runyon's deli heroes were cartoonish and over-
drawn. When it came to hard-boiled, I was drawn to James M. Cain, not
Dashiell Hammett. Cain was more concerned with unreleased passion
than with some inane mystery. As well as anyone who came before or
after, he wrote about fucking—uninhibited, balls-out fucking.

Killing time was never a problem during my Army days, despite the
fact that my hours were light. My new mind-set—achieve, achieve,
achieve—led me to correspondence courses through Kansas University,
and I made up credits writing essays on Sherwood Anderson's small-
town America and studying European history. By the time I was dis-
charged in Midland, Texas, I was a corporal, and a motivated man. I
decided to go back to Kansas State to get my degree. Shirley was happy
to come along, and the school was happy to take me back.

In 1946, Manhattan, Kansas, and the middle of the country seemed
even more inviting. I'd always thought that the meat in the sandwich of
America is between the two coasts. Much later, while the music business
competed mostly in Hollywood and New York, I worked and thrived
in Alabama, Tennessee, Florida, Georgia, Texas, and Louisiana. Root
Americana always touched my heart—and I trace that connection to
Kansas.

I was also writing in Kansas. The school paper gave me my own
column, and my muse led me to write from the point of view of a rat
living in the laboratory of a psychologist. I even named my rodent Watson, after the behaviorist. Using the animal's voice, I expounded on
everything from modern literature to world affairs. (It was my jejune
cribbing of the immortal Don Marquis's mehitabel.) My literary ambi-
tions—or Elsa's—had resurfaced. One story was picked up by *Story,*
Whit Burnett's publication, which launched the careers of Irwin Shaw

and William Saroyan. The opening of "Lost Summer," written in this period, is a good example of my frame of mind.

> That was the summer when I wanted to be a writer, the summer of Elaine and me and George the elevator boy of the building across the street. It was when I had somehow stumbled onto Hemingway and Fitzgerald and Sherwood Anderson one right after the other, and all the beauty of George and Elaine and me in the lateness of the warm summer nights was in the wonderful books and I became Amory Blaine and George Willard and Nick Adams and didn't know what to do about it.

Despite my rhapsodic romance with literature, I was not above hustling. One article, for instance, about a man who built scale-model houses, was published in *Profitable Hobbies Magazine*. Whether highbrow, lowbrow, or no-brow, this stuff didn't prove exactly profitable in Kansas. As soon as I got my journalism degree, I was headed back to New York, where my hopes were high that someone would pay me decent money for words.

THE POSTWAR CAN'T-FIND- A-SLOT ABOUT-TO- DROP BEBOP HAPPY-TIME NEW YORK CITY BLUES

Wasn't self-pity. Wasn't self-degradation. Hell, it wasn't even depression. Just plain frustration, deep and long-lasting. Me and Shirley, back up in Washington Heights, living, of all places, with her parents. There were five of us in that small apartment on 177th Street between Broadway and Fort Washington Avenue—Blanche, Morris, Aunt Ida, Shirley, and me. We were paying her mom twenty dollars a week. The experience wasn't exalting.

While Shirley supported us by working for a furniture manufacturer, I hit the streets. With my degree in one hand and my hat in the other, I made the rounds for months on end, looking for work at magazines or newspapers. A couple of midwestern papers offered me cub reporter jobs, but no thanks. I was fixated on a big-city job, though in the big city they wouldn't even hire me as a copy boy. There were some nibbles here and there—the United Jewish Appeal needed someone to run their house organ—but salaries were so pathetic and the work so mindless I held out, for what I'm not sure. It was that strange mixture of cockiness and fear that motivated me to keep searching; soon, I was convinced, my change was going to come.

When it did, was it ever exiguous. The pay was thirty-five dollars a week, and the job could only loosely be described as writing. Significantly, though, it was my first foray into the music business. And once in, I'd never leave.

It was 1947, and my friend Russ Sanjek was working for Broadcast Music, Inc. (BMI), the renegade publishers' collection agency which rivaled the American Society of Composers, Authors, and Publishers (ASCAP). Their function was to collect fees and royalties from users of music such as radio, television, record companies, theaters, concert halls, nightclubs, and all other venues operating for profit.

Until 1940, ASCAP was monopolistic and, with few exceptions, lily white. ASCAP represented almost every major songwriter and music publisher in Tin Pan Alley, Broadway, and Hollywood. "Hundreds of regional composers and publishers who couldn't pass its picky admission tests," the *Wall Street Journal* would later report, "were on their own, powerless to collect performance royalties and dependent only on the sheet music they would sell."

Radio stations paid ASCAP to broadcast ASCAP music, and in 1940, when ASCAP raised its rates, the radio stations raised hell. That's when the big broadcasters started BMI. By year's end, BMI had fifty-two publishers, including three majors. But ASCAP, unimpressed by BMI's raggedy list of songs and songwriters, remained aloof. ASCAP controlled the music of the masters—Kern, Gershwin, Rodgers, Hammerstein, Berlin—and wasn't about to budge. Radio, they thought, couldn't get along without their precious catalogue of standards. ASCAP was wrong. In the last half of the decade, just when I stepped into the scene, the tables finally began to turn. Music heretofore ignored—a new kind of rhythmic blues emerging from the black urban centers, and hillbilly music coming out of the white South—was making commercial noise.

This became BMI's domain—the sort of sounds I'd always loved most. And it didn't hurt that my running buddy Russ was one of BMI's most energetic warriors. The work I did was hardly heroic, but it was a job. I wrote continuity copy for radio stations—in effect, pithy plugs for BMI songs. It was boring and uncreative, and didn't even require that I go to their office. It did mean, though, that in a rudimentary fashion I was in the music business. I could start moving around in that intriguing self-contained world of songwriters, song pluggers, producers, canaries, con men, and assorted nut cases. The problem, though, was that it didn't last long. I came down with viral pneumonia and was laid up in bed for six weeks.

Back in my infancy, during the influenza epidemic of 1918, I'd contracted pneumonia. When my fever hit 107, Elsa thought I was gone. A half-hour later the fever broke, but my lungs were left weak. For the rest of my life I'd suffer from upper-respiratory problems. It didn't help that I was a compulsive smoker from ages fourteen through fifty-eight.

By the time I recovered from this second bout of pneumonia in 1947, the freelance job at BMI was gone, and I was back on the streets, a fresh copy of my resumé in my hand and the stale taste of rejection in my mouth.

I searched for months, and for months saw the same doors slamming in my face—newspapers, publishers, record companies, no openings anywhere. The same anxieties that had washed over me when I'd come home from the Army—fear of being broke, of never finding my way—returned and redoubled. I was thirty years old with nothing to show. My in-laws and parents weren't very proud. And just when it looked like I might be washing dirty windows again, a man named Meyer Shapiro came through.

Shap was one of those wonderfully mellow, hip Broadway press agents, an old-time publicist who was working for BMI. He sent me to Joe Carlton, the music editor of *Billboard*. Thanks, Shap. Next thing I know, I'm in Carlton's office and the guy is grilling me. I've got on a white shirt, a Brooks Brothers paisley tie, and my best and only suit. I've presented myself as a music maven, but deep down I'm nervous as a motherfucker.

Carlton lays into me with a pop quiz. He wants to know the name of Nat Cole's label. I space. My memory bank has collapsed, and all I can do is gulp. "Capitol," he says. "You don't know Nat's on Capitol?" I figure that's it, but the conversation goes on. I regain some composure, and by the time we're through, Carlton sees I'm not a total disaster. When he calls the next day to say he's offering me a cub reporter's beat at seventy-five dollars a week, you'd think I just hit the daily double. I have my first real job, and the next thing Shirley and I do is move into a place of our own.

Lazy Sunday morning, springtime in the city. Shirley and I are just getting up, still settling into our new apartment in an old brownstone on West 89th Street off Central Park. Sunlight streaks through the blinds; from outside our bedroom door, the acrid aroma of marijuana; from the phonograph in the living room, the sounds of a jazz music I've never heard before. I throw on a robe and follow my nose.

Slouched over the couch where he's spent the night is my good pal Dan Qualey, a fat joint in hand.

"This is it," he says.

"What's 'it'?" I ask.

"Dizzy, Bird, 'Emanon.' Dig it."

He has a pile of 78s—Bird with Miles, Bird with Bud Powell, Bird with John Lewis and Max Roach and Curley Russell and Tiny Grimes, Monk and Tommy Potter, Duke Jordan and Kenny Dorham and Slim Gaillard, Kenny Drew, Jack McVea and Dodo Mamarosa, "Donna Lee" and "Little Willie Leaps," "Tiny's Tempo," "Half Nelson" and "Merry Go Round," "Poppity Pop," "Chasing the Bird," "Bird Gets the Worm," and "Ornithology." Feathers are flying all over the living room. I've never heard such speed, such syncopated frenzy—the frantic riffing and fire in the horns, the complexity in the chords, a relentless look-here-there-everywhere vision that shakes up my morning. I'm seeing the dawning of a new day in jazz; the light is brilliant. It takes me about a week of careful listening, but then I get it. And it's Dan, a connoisseur of swing and the jazz of early New Orleans, who leads me to the future.

New York of *fin de guerre:* America's got money. America's hopped up and hungry for happy-time music. The Swing Era is fading out while the beboppers are bopping in, and 52nd Street is caught in a creative schizophrenia. Cultures clash, merge. The Onyx, the Three Deuces, the Downbeat, the Famous Door, Minton's. The mainstream greats—Coleman Hawkins, Roy Eldridge, Erroll Garner—transcend category and can play with anybody. (Astonishingly, so can Pee Wee Russell.) The moderns—Bird and Bud, Miles and Max and Diz—are brimming with artistic integrity, experimentation, rebellious conviction. Some of the critics are outraged. Even my future mentor and role model, the erudite John Hammond, calls bebop "a manufactured craze that died a-borning." This is also a time when I fall in love with the greatest of all scat singers, Leo Watson, and the ineffable Spirits of Rhythm, a loose confederation of string specialists, masters of the guitar, mandolin, banjo, ukulele, and tipple. New jazz clubs are born—Bop City, Birdland—to showcase the new sounds, and I'm there, I'm digging, I'm ready.

I'm also further down Broadway, getting a whole different perspective on the music business. After the blackout of World War II, the lights are back on the Great White Way, good news circling round the Motogram on Times Square, the Camel man puffing perfect smoke rings, couples dancing on the roof club of the Astor Hotel, me snaking my way down the aisles of Lindy's.

Of all the great Broadway delis, none was greater than Lindy's in its prime. The perfume of kosher dills and corned beef greeted you at the door. The place—the second Lindy's, the one at 51st Street—was rigidly codified. The left-hand side was for tourists, the right-hand for regulars. The first table was for the comics—Milton Berle, Red Buttons, Buddy Hackett, George Jessel, Henny Youngman. Their cutting contests were lethal, and no one could top Jack E. Leonard. "If Moses saw you," Jack E. liked to tell his Borscht Belt competitors, "he would have invented another commandment."

The second prominent table was for the song pluggers, a group of guys right out of John O'Hara's *Pal Joey*. They had style, color, lingo, the look of the forties: smooth felt hats with tapered crowns, double-breasted gabardine suits, wide white-on-white collars and big-knotted hand-painted ties, shiny black wing tips, and ultrasheer rayon socks, always a smile, always a story to tell and a song to sell.

Primarily they were selling their personalities. Their job was to convince Guy Lombardo or Sammy Kaye to put a new number in the book, to make up an arrangement of a new song. In those days, record sales were insignificant; sheet music and live performances accounted for the real revenue. ASCAP had given up the fight for radio play to BMI, but music-only radio (radio as a mass-marketing tool for selling music wouldn't emerge until the fifties). Although in decline, some big bands like Les Brown's, Harry James's, and Jimmy Dorsey's under Lee Castle still ruled.

No one had greater rapport with big-band leaders than Juggy Gayles. Juggy was the Eddie Stanky, the Charlie Hustle of the song pluggers. He was close to Sinatra, Nat Cole, and Woody Herman, whose thundering Herds were breeding talents that informed the sounds of modern jazz—Stan Getz, Al Cohn, Zoot Sims, Jimmy Giuffre, Ralph

Burns, Nat Pierce. Everyone loved Juggy; his best friends were songwriter Jimmy Van Heusen and columnist Earl Wilson. Broadway personified, he lived at Lindy's and the track; his bibles were *Billboard* and the *Racing Form*. Four years older than me, Juggy was a street guide and Tin Pan Alley guru. He didn't read books, but if they gave out degrees in song plugging, he'd have a doctorate.

Juggy introduced me to some of my first music-industry parties. There'd be fabulous weekends, for example, at Fred Waring's Shawnee Inn resort on the Delaware, with golf, swimming, softball, boating, barbecue, an appearance by Perry Como, and round-the-clock big-pot poker games. The flashy pluggers who pulled down five hundred dollars a week plus expenses would murder each other with one-liners and lies about how tight they were with Benny Goodman or Artie Shaw.

Things were quickly changing for me. I'd gone from being an outsider—an impassioned record collector and obsessive fan—to someone suddenly confronted by hard-nosed reality, profit and loss, sheet music and salesmen, the world of fast money. Though college was behind me, my actual education was only beginning. For the next four years, as a reporter for *Billboard*, my vantage point of that crazy three-ring circus known as the music business would be unique. I'd get to see all the clowns close up.

DISKERS,

PUBBERS,

AND

CLEFFERS

*H*arry *Truman's* in the White House. The news around Times Square says Tokyo Rose is guilty. The late edition of the *Journal-American* has the Brooklyn Dodgers beating the Boston Braves in a double-header. Jackie Robinson's hitting .340.

Up Broadway at the corner of 49th Street is the Palace Theater Building, the Valhalla of vaudeville. Inside, past an ornate lobby gilded with fake gold, is a small elevator. Ride up to the sixth floor and you'll find a typical forties newspaper office—ticker machines and clanking typewriters, ringing phones and screaming editors. Welcome to *Billboard*.

My welcome was less than cordial. I was greeted by a crusty old hard-drinking Irish copy chief who got one whiff of my propensity for fancy English and read me the riot act. He stayed on my ass until he got what he wanted. "Make it clean," he'd command. "Make it clear. Make it concise." I already knew how to form a grammatical sentence, but *Billboard* taught me to write a lead and punctuate with precision; soon I was using semicolons.

Back in the nineteenth century, *Billboard* had begun by covering outdoor shows. Traveling carnivals used the magazine as a mail drop. Vaudeville came in, and so did nightclubs. By the forties, radio had become a major beat and, in its infantile form, television began attracting coverage. Outdoor entertainment—state fairs, carnivals—was handled out of Cincinnati. But in New York the concern was music.

When Joe Carlton left to become head of artists and repertoire for RCA Victor, Paul Ackerman took over as music editor. Few people have affected me as profoundly as Paul. He was a saint, and I said so at his

With Paul Ackerman

funeral in 1978. In Jewish lore, in every generation the hope of the world rests on ten pure souls—*tzaddikim*—without whom the universe would fragment. Paul was one such soul, an incarnation of decency, someone blessed with an excess of love, an extra chromosome of affection.

Paul was bald as an egg, a tall man with smoldering brown eyes who spoke ever so thoughtfully and slowly. He was the inheritor of a genteel German-Jewish culture, his physician father having raised him on Goethe, Heine, Schiller, Mendelssohn, and Strauss. Paul held a master's degree in English—his specialty was the Romantic poets—and displayed great reverence for the mother tongue. He had a balanced sense of news and knew how to apportion space—what rated a five-column head and what was better consigned to the permanent limbo of overset.

Ackerman's bias was *Billboard.* He had friends on the other trades, but looked on these papers with a studied astigmatism. Nothing would offend Paul more than to be asked to print verbatim the handouts of the record companies. He drew a hard line between puffery and news. Not that he was averse to helping a friend with a harmless plug, but his kindness was leavened with righteous intolerance. Ackerman believed in true editorial content; a trade paper was not just an appendage to a sales chart. Paul couldn't abide the self-promoting moguls who whipped their minions in an endless push for personal aggrandizement. Nor would he yield to the big bullying labels in their ongoing drive to control his news. He stood his ground, drawing more than one advertising boycott in his long career.

The man's musical iconography was fascinating and deep. His heroes were Ralph Peer and Frank Walker, explorers who went with portable equipment to the Smokies, the Delta, the Savannah, the Piedmont, and the cotton bottoms to find Ma Rainey and Bessie Smith, Jimmie Rodgers and Robert Johnson and Hank Williams. That's the stuff Paul loved best—the beginnings, the earliest strain. He would champion the next wave of country music—Fred Rose and Roy Acuff, Steve Sholes and Don Law. He'd also develop an extraordinarily close relationship with Sam Phillips, the Southerner behind Sun Records, Elvis, Johnny Cash, Jerry Lee Lewis, and Charlie Rich. Paul sensed stylistic evolutions and often championed those changes against stubborn traditionalists. His writing would wind up in the Country Music Hall of Fame.

For Paul, though, it always came back to Jimmie Rodgers and Hank Williams, the sounds of the crucible, the Great Depression, the deprived, the knights of the road, the circuit riders and easy riders but never the night riders. Like Studs Terkel, Ackerman had a great grasp of the America of the twenties and thirties. He also identified with the pioneers who started the independent blues and country labels. He introduced me to many of these men, later to become my competitors— Herman Lubinsky, Syd Nathan, Leonard Chess, Saul Bihari. He dug them because they broke the stranglehold of the pop record labels; he admired Russ Sanjek and BMI for similar reasons.

Despite an Army accident which cost him the power of his left arm, Ackerman had fabulous physical strength. He built his own greenhouse, maintained a crazy menagerie of cats and pigeons, and pursued an undying passion for camellias. Every springtime he'd vacation to camellia country in the Carolinas to hunt for new hybrids.

In the grungy, often greedy music business, Paul was my guru. There wasn't a penny's worth of malfeasance in the *Billboard* music department. Not that I was a prude. I'd load up on free meals and golf games. Christmas was always bountiful, with booze, candies, and coffee cakes. I loved the perks. At the same time, though, I was merely taking, not giving. If anything, I was giving the diskers, pubbers, and cleffers—

trade lingo for record companies, publishers, and songwriters—a hard time.

I'd start at the Brill Building, just down the street at 1619 Broadway, home of a thousand tunesmiths and assorted hustlers. From the top floor, I'd work my way down, poking my head into every office, nosing around for news. I'd jump over to Eleventh Avenue, down around 34th Street, where the record jobbers, distributors, and jukebox roughnecks operated. A lot of these guys were ex–cigarette machine bosses, a few were mobbed up, and they all had stories to tell. You'd hear everything—polka, salsa, Rumanian language records. It was a music bazaar, an exotic market of sounds.

The battle between ASCAP and BMI raged on, and I covered many of those major stories, infuriating both sides. I earned a reputation for finding and printing actual sales figures and concert grosses. Eventually, I was covering the whole smorgasbord, reviewing Lee J. Cobb in Somerset Maugham's TV adaptation of *The Moon and Sixpence* one day and the "Rootie Kazootie" kid show the next. "There's heavy sugar in gospel singing," I wrote about Sister Rosetta Tharpe's profitable one-nighter tour of the South. "For a solo performer whose only luggage is a guitar, Sister Tharpe is folding lettuce at a remarkable rate."

Erroll Garner and Lester Young at Birdland, Billy Eckstine and Charlie Ventura at the Royal Roost, Machito at the Palladium—I was making all the scenes. I also like to think I was making something of a contribution to the vernacular. Beginning in 1942, the *Billboard* chart for black records was termed the "Harlem Hit Parade," changing in 1945 to the euphemistic "Race Records." Granted, America's rubrics of race have always been peculiar. "Race" was a common term then, a self-referral used by blacks. "He's a race man to the bricks" was a compliment; it meant a musician's ethnicity was out-front and formidable. On the other hand, "Race Records" didn't sit well. Maybe "race" was too close to "racist." In 1949, my suggestion for change was adopted by *Billboard;* I came up with a handle I thought suited the music well— "rhythm and blues."

"Rhythm and blues," I wrote in a turn-of-the-decade essay for the *Saturday Review of Literature,* "is a label more appropriate to more enlightened times." I liked the sound of "rhythm and blues"—it sung and swung like the music itself—and I was happy when it stuck; it defined a new genre of music. The handle worked its way into our language and has managed to survive four decades. After having dropped it for any number of new designations—"Soul," "black," "urban"—*Billboard* has recently gone back to R&B.

In the same *Saturday Review* piece I made a distinction in 1950 black music between the hoke and the hot. "The most interesting labels," I wrote, "include Atlantic, Savoy, Regal, Apollo, National, King, Aladdin, Miracle, Modern, Imperial, and Sittin' In. These small, independent companies, more sensitive to changes in the world of rhythm and blues than less flexible major disceries, have virtually captured the field."

There were exceptions, of course. Louis Jordan, on Decca, was produced by Milt Gabler, who a few years later would infuse Jordan's spirit into the work of Bill Haley and the Comets, one of the first seeds of black rhythm and blues to bloom into white rock 'n' roll. If Gabler's one of my role models, it's because over the decades he truly understood the natural art of bending and blending genres.

Louis Jordan is a shining example. "For almost a decade after 1942," wrote scholar Arnold Shaw, "Jordan records were seldom off the 'Harlem Hit Parade.'" I was there when Jordan stepped out of Chick Webb's saxophone section in 1938. That was the same year Webb died and Louis formed his Tympany Five (though the group was usually seven strong). Like Cab Calloway before him, Jordan was an infectiously good-hearted, hard-swinging entertainer. But more than Cab, Louis was a true musician. His shuffle syncopations—those dotted eighth and sixteenth notes—became a foundation of commercial dance music, from jitterbug to boogaloo and back. His super-tight sextet would be the model of mean-and-lean rhythm-and-blues bands for decades to come—Ray Charles, James Brown, the Muscle Shoals configurations, Tower of Power, and, in the eighties and nineties, the Time.

Not to overlook Lionel Hampton. Hamp's brilliant forties aggregation, the one of "Flying Home" fame, built the bridge from big bands to small combos. Hamp had tenor men like Illinois Jacquet honking and blues divas like Dinah Washington shouting. Hamp was prerock, preroll, one of the sure-enough daddies of the Big Beat. Hamp was hip. But it was Louis Jordan who honed and refined the small-group concept, marrying the harmonic sophistication of jazz with the folk wit of the blues. Other bands—Tiny Bradshaw's, for instance—were nearly as good, but Jordan threw extra condiments into the stew. His humor and celebrations of a black lifestyle—"Saturday Night Fish Fry," "Beans and Cornbread," "Ain't Nobody Here but Us Chickens"—were picture-painting poetry. "The Mills Brothers like the Ink Spots were really black men singing white songs," my pal Ralph Gleason, a sharp jazz critic, once wrote. "But Louis Jordan sang black and sang proud."

Unlike the teenage market which would explode in the fifties, the rhythm and blues of the late forties was adult in flavor and often spiked with booze. Amos Milburn's "Bad, Bad Whiskey," Joe Liggins's "Pink Champagne," Bullmoose Jackson's "Who Threw the Whiskey in the Well?," "Drinkin' Wine Spo-Dee-O-Dee" by Stick McGhee (Atlantic Records' first hit, in 1949)—the list could fill a still.

In the mid-forties, Private Cecil Gant put his upright piano on a flatbed truck and toured the boondocks, singing "I Wonder," a song that would have as great an impact on the industry as Mamie Smith's "Crazy Blues" in 1920. It sold hundreds of thousands of copies each week, reminding white executives that a record by and for blacks only could still make a mint. A classic blues ballad, it foreshadowed a mellow style to come; it was a song I myself was to produce for artists as diverse as Chris Connor, LaVern Baker, Ray Charles, and Aretha Franklin.

Black people were moving, taking the shortest paths out of the South—from the Carolinas to New York, from the Delta to Chicago, from Texas and Louisiana to California. Southern California was especially fertile territory, if only for the presence of three innovators— Charles Brown from Houston, T-Bone Walker from Dallas, and Percy Mayfield from Minden, Louisiana. In the L.A. scene of the mid-forties, a huge clientele of blacks were working in war plants. There was money left over after grits and gravy. Nightclubs with singers backed by small combos were the places to go—to drink, dine, and dance.

You couldn't get the good-timing people's attention by singing over their chatter. You got it by mellowing down lightly and politely. You seduced them softly. Charles, Percy, and T-Bone each shared a blues sensibility that was smooth and salty at once, sweet but anguished, simple yet profound. The postwar Southern California blues had a mystique all its own, refined and relaxed. It was an original creation: Club Blues, the third in the trinity that included Dancehall Blues and Bar Blues.

Like Nat Cole, Charles Brown was a virtuoso pianist and principal of the Club Blues school. Also like Nat, his voice was velvet, his delivery an effortless exercise in emotional communication. As Malcolm Rebennack (a.k.a. Dr. John) put it years later, "Charles is like Ben Webster on tenor—they both got air to spare." Brown's "Drifting Blues" remains a benchmark of the art, his dynamics ranging from soft and quiet to zephyrs and whispers. Mother Charles—how I dearly love him!—is a master.

What Charlie Christian gave jazz guitar, T-Bone Walker gave blues guitar; he was one of the first to electrify, yet always with taste, restraint, and pure heart. His original licks live today in the repertoire of a thousand blues artists. I still see him in splendid attire, a diamond in his front tooth, jewels on his Gibson.

Mayfield, like T-Bone, was a beautiful, honey-toned singer, and a poet to boot, always on the verge of some fantastic disclosure which, like the name of the Hebrew god, could never be uttered. "Please Send Me Someone to Love," "River's Invitation," and "Hit the Road, Jack" (made famous in the sixties by Ray Charles) are but three of his best-known songs from a body of work distinguished by linguistic flair and wisdom. "Only you can tell," wrote Percy, "how deep is the well, 'cause the well is the soul of a man."

During this pivotal period I was also pointed in the direction of soulful singing by Moe Danziger. Like Dan Qualey, Moe was a Dixieland freak, one of our running buddies who took in the foreign films at the Museum of Modern Art and jam sessions at Ryan's. And just as Dan introduced me to bop, Moe tipped me off to quartet singing with a simple four-word admonishment: "Listen to the Ravens."

At first I was too quick to judge, too quick to associate them with the more middle-of-the-road pop of the Ink Spots and the Mills Brothers. I didn't get it. I was dead wrong. It turned out that the Ravens of the forties were the archetype for the great doo-wop, rhythm and blues, and gospel quartets of the fifties. Their rendition of "Ol' Man River," for example, with its sly, loping beat, was a model for the Drifters. The bass lines of the two groups—the harmony structures and rhythm patterns—are more than just genre resemblances; they're first cousins. With Jimmy Ricks's arresting bass and Howard Biggs's arrangements and songs ("Write Me a Letter," "Got You on My Mind"), the Ravens blazed a path that I myself was destined to pursue, once I wised up.

*A*t *Billboard,* the notion of pursuing destiny was far from my consciousness. I was just getting my pop music chops. There were times, though, when my instincts weren't half bad. A case in point is "Tennessee Waltz," one of the biggest hits of all time. Material was always crossing my desk—dozens of song demos, for example, looking for a label or singer. I also reviewed records. One day Coral sent over a copy of Ace Harris—the pianist who followed Avery Parrish (of "After Hours" fame) in Erskine Hawkins's band—doing "Tennessee Waltz." I'd never heard the original country version (by Pee Wee King), but Ace's reading stuck with me. A few days later I was working the Brill Building, looking for story leads, when I bumped into Jack Rael, who managed Patti Page. She was about to cover "Boogie Woogie Santa Claus," he explained, and needed a B side. Did I have any ideas? I gave him "Tennessee Waltz," which became Patti Page's career song. It was one of my first credits as a tune tout.

At the same time, my devotion to trade journalism wasn't undying. After four years of hacking out copy, I was losing enthusiasm. One of the first fissures came when an editor asked me to get a dossier on a folk group called the Weavers. The dark days of Joe McCarthy and blacklisting were upon us, and I wasn't about to do that kind of dirty work. I refused. I didn't quit—not right then and there—but the request left such a bad taste in my mouth that a few months later I found myself resigning. Besides, when I'd first arrived at *Billboard*, Bill Smith, the old-timer running the nightclub department, had told me, "Kid, if you're here more than three years, you're a goner." By 1951, I was already a year over the limit.

*T*he Big Three—Robbins, Feist, and Miller—was the music publishing arm of MGM. I was recommended by their promotion director, my good pal Howie Richmond, who'd quit to start a firm of his own (soon to score rich with Teresa Brewer's "Music, Music, Music"). I took Howie's place, and my job was to get exposure for Big Three songs. My boss was a mahoff named Abe Olman, an old-time songwriter who'd written "Down Among the Sheltering Palms" and "Oh, Johnny!" and who now sent me scurrying down to sell producers and disc jockeys on recording and playing Big Three tunes. My deal was $150 a week, plus $50 for expenses.

I hustled hard and did well, but I wasn't happy. There was a gap between the music I loved—hanging out at the bar at Birdland (the seated section was the bullpen, strictly for tourists and civilians), the Chicken Shack, the Embers, the Royal Roost, listening to Elliot Lawrence's big band with Gerry Mulligan in the saxophone section at Bop City—and the music I was pushing.

At the same time, I was pushing open doors to recording studios, seeing and learning things that, although far from the jazz, blues, and rhythm and blues I loved best, impressed me mightily. Enter Mitch Miller. We'd met when I was at *Billboard* and he was A&R man for Mercury. When he switched to Columbia in 1951, I brought him two songs that shot to #1—"Cry," a huge hit for Johnny Ray, and "Cold, Cold Heart" by Hank Williams, a million-selling smash Mitch produced for Tony Bennett (though I had Sammy Kaye in mind). It was "Cold, Cold Heart" that led Mitch to Hank Williams's great catalogue of songs and added momentum to mainstreaming country music.

I'm afraid the public's image of Mitch is just a guy with a goatee waving a baton over a smiling flock of sing-a-long freaks. At the dawning of the age of rock 'n' roll, Mitch might have also come out with some feckless pronouncements. An omnivorous reader, he once compared Jerry Lee Lewis's vocal antics to the farting friar in Chaucer's *Canterbury Tales.* I took issue with him on that score, but in other areas we couldn't have been more compatible. Mitch Miller became a lifelong friend, a man of courageous liberal politics, great intelligence, and rare erudition. Beyond that, he was also the first modern A&R director in the history of American music.

Mitch had graduated from the Eastman School of Music and was a virtuoso oboist. He played with the CBS Symphony and the Budapest String Quartet. One night you'd catch him at Town Hall interpreting a modernistic classical composition by Alec Wilder; the next night he'd be at Birdland blowing "April in Paris" with the Charlie Parker with Strings ensemble.

When Mitch came to Columbia, his rabbi was John Hammond. John realized a record company required diversity, and he knew Mitch could provide just that. Before Mitch's time, much of pop music was little more than steady thirty-two-bar boring songs sung to Victor Herbert behind-the-potted-palms, put-you-to-sleep charts. Producers could sleepwalk through their work; mainly they found material and made sure everyone turned up on time. Mitch turned all that upside down. With Frankie Laine—on "Mule Train" and "Cry of the Wild Goose"— he came on with cracking whips and exotic birds, and for Rosemary Clooney he supplied unusual material and unorthodox instrumentation:

Beard bonding with Mitch Miller

"Come On-a My House," "Mambo Italiano," the haunting "Hey There."
Back in 1948, he'd overdubbed Patti Page singing her own harmony on
"Money, Marbles and Chalk"—a first. He was years ahead in his use of
harpsichords, steel guitars, and percussion; he was a bold innovator, a
model of the producer as artist rather than traffic cop.

I also loved him for his patience. In 1952, for example, my second
year at Robbins, I managed to get him to a screening of the movie *High
Noon* in the middle of the day, no easy feat. Robbins owned the copyright of the theme song, "Do Not Forsake Me," which I wanted recorded. Mitch showed up, but the film didn't. I was mortified: I had the
biggest A&R man in town and nothing to show him. No problem, he
said; he'd come the next day. When he saw the film, he loved the song
and gave it to Frankie Laine.

A few years later, when I was with Atlantic, CBS hired one of our
discoveries, the arranger Ray Ellis, on an exclusive basis. (Ellis would
later be known for his lush charts on Billie Holiday's 1958 *Lady in Satin*
album.) In an unprecedented move for the cutthroat music business,
Mitch augmented the terms, allowing Ellis to continue to write for us.
He also made me some much-needed bucks in my *Billboard* days when
he put a tune I wrote with Bob Wells on the back of Frankie Laine's
"Jezebel." We called the song "Flamenco"—in truth, filched from the
melody of "Malagueña."

In 1952, I continued to dislike my job. To some degree I'd been

*At the beach with
Ahmet and his first
wife, Jan, 1951 (before
I joined Atlantic)*

deluded. When Abe had given me songs to take to the big A&R men of
the day—Harry Myerson at RCA (who'd done Sinatra's first session with
Tommy Dorsey) or Joe Carlton (who'd moved from *Billboard* to Mercury), Morty Palitz at Decca, or Bob Thiele at Coral—I'd run. I'd set up
the meetings, play the material and look terrifically successful. I was
getting songs recorded left and right. What I didn't realize, though, was
that Abe had often taken care of business in advance. He'd made the
covert arrangements with these guys to place the tunes. Without knowing it, I was just a messenger—a schmuck.

Even so, I had enough of a reputation to get a couple of job offers.
The first was to run Frank Loesser's music firm as a professional manager. Owning a piece of a publishing company would have been nice;
owning valuable song copyrights is like owning good land: the value
keeps rising. But that wasn't the gig, and mid-level management wasn't
my style.

Neither, I thought, was pure promotion, which is what Atlantic Records, a hip little label specializing in rhythm and blues, had to offer.
Ahmet Ertegun and Herb Abramson, the guys who ran the place, also
wanted me to run their publishing company, but nothing in production
or A&R. I'd known Ahmet, Herb, and Nat Shapiro, their current promo
man, through the jazz clubs and postwar jam sessions; I considered
them among the most cultivated cognoscenti in the city. At the same
time, I felt I'd be uncomfortable working for friends, and told them so
(anticipating events to come nearly a quarter-decade later).

"Well, what *would* make you comfortable?" asked the urbane Ertegun.

"Being your partner."

He laughed, and rightfully so. I'm not sure where I got the balls to ask for equity. After all, Atlantic was already in motion. They'd hit with "Drinkin' Wine Spo-Dee-O-Dee," Ruth Brown's "Teardrops from My Eyes," Joe Turner's impossibily beautiful "Chains of Love" (written by Ahmet himself), in addition to having just signed a young, blind blues singer named Ray Charles. Where the hell did I come off asking for a piece of their pie? I wasn't surprised when Ahmet turned me down.

I *was* surprised, though, when a year later he came back to me. Herb Abramson, the president, was going into the Army for a two-year stint, and Ahmet needed someone to help run the company.

"I still want to be a partner," I told him.

"Fine," he said.

And that's how it started.

IN A
FAMILY
WAY

Shirley and I always wanted kids. We wanted a baby as soon as we got back from Kansas, but it didn't happen. We went through the whole drill—fertility clinics, pills, temperature taking.

I might be having lunch at Lindy's with the boys when I'd hear the page. "Jerry," Shirley would say on the phone. "*Now!*"

I'd hurry down to the subway, rush home to the little apartment we had in Elmhurst, Queens, do my duty, and dash back to work. It took some time till our rhythms finally meshed, but in even-patterned succession—1951, 1953, 1955—we had our three children, Anita, Paul, and Lisa.

In the best sense, Shirley was a wonderful music-business wife. In every sense, she was my intellectual peer—and then some. She and I were in continual discussion, not only about music and books but about business. A superb adviser, she was also a good hostess and at a moment's notice could accommodate a couple of guests.

"I never minded," said Shirley, "because Jerry had this capacity for rounding up the most interesting characters in the business."

Alec Wilder was one such. He and our mutual friend Mitch Miller were frequently over for dinner. Like Mitch, Alec was a graduate of the Eastman School who displayed a phenomenal range of musical interests and talent. A number of his compositions—"While We're Young," "I'll Be Around," "It's So Peaceful in the Country"—had become popular in the forties and eventually became standards. He wrote tunes and arrangements for Mildred Bailey and Red Norvo. Sinatra himself was crazy for Alec's music. His classical compositions defied categorization. A genuine eccentric, Alec lived for decades in a room in the Algonquin

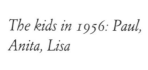

The kids in 1956: Paul, Anita, Lisa

Hotel. His commitment to bachelorhood and to High Art was absolute, his taste in music and literature impeccable. Among his distinguished prose writing are the scholarly *American Popular Song* and *Letters I Never Mailed*, a work of fabulous whimsy. At a moment's notice he'd pack his satchel and head for Grand Central. He was a train fanatic, an addicted reader of schedules, a rider of rural routes who made connections on little-known spurs of railroad lines far into Illinois or South Dakota, South Carolina or the Texas hill country. For Alec, riding the trains was a Zen meditation, the sound of churning wheels a never-ending mantra.

I placed Alec in my private Pantheon of Great Men alongside John Hammond, Hammond's colleague Goddard Lieberson (another patrician who, like Alec and Mitch, studied at Eastman and, as head of Columbia Records, brought grace to company management), Paul Ackerman, Studs Terkel (a writer both lofty and down-to-earth, he also managed Mahalia Jackson, working as her roadie on tour), and Mitch Miller.

Alec and Mitch were such close friends, in fact, that it seemed as though they assisted in the birth of our first two babies. They were having dinner with us in Queens when Shirley's water broke, and within no time Anita was born. Two years later, Shirley and I were sitting next to Alec at Town Hall when Mitch was playing one of Alec's chamber compositions. Again, the cosmic call came; the water broke, and that night

our son, Paul, came. We avoided Mitch and Alec when Shirley was pregnant with our second daughter, Lisa, fearful that their presence might
lead to premature birth.

The birthing process had an impact on me, no doubt. I was especially close to my firstborn, my daughter Anita. "Jerry repeated the pattern of his mother favoring him," observes Shirley in an analytical frame
of mind. "He was a favored first child and so was Anita. He was so crazy
about her our friends joked he was breast-feeding her."

I'm afraid I was also starting to feed another compulsion—extra-
curricular activity. The pattern begins here in the early 1950s—ironically, at the time when Shirley and I were starting our family and I was
starting my record-producing career. My first fling was with a professional woman who worked in Manhattan. Though attractive, she was not
particularly sweet or ingratiating. Ours was a liaison of lust and lust
alone. Love was not an issue. Instead I saw myself living a James M.
Cain / John O'Hara fantasy. This woman and I didn't make love; we
fucked ferociously. We met in the afternoons, we met in the mornings,
we couldn't resist the heat. We raged on for a couple of years.

"Jerry's behavior betrayed him," says Shirley. "When some men have
affairs, they're consumed with guilt and act obsequiously at home. Not
Jerry. He'd become withdrawn and angry, often nasty, his temper likely
to explode at any little provocation. I'd confront him, but he'd deny the
truth. The reckoning came on March 15, 1952—the Ides of March. I
was home when the phone rang. It was Jerry. He called to arrange a
rendezvous, only he'd dialed the wrong number. He thought he was talking to his lover, not his wife."

I realize this could be read as the classic Freudian mistake, the man
who wanted to be caught. I'm not sure. I am sure, though, that I did *not*
want to lose Shirley. I ran home and begged forgiveness.

"Jerry said he'd jump off a bridge if I didn't take him back," Shirley
remembers. "I took him back. I loved him. I knew he loved me, and at
that point I was not willing to face reality, the reality of Jerry's emotional
makeup. I went along because there were things that I wanted too—our
kids, our future. Like his mother, I believed in Jerry's potential.

"In some sense, we were a typical upwardly mobile family of the
fifties. The harder Jerry worked, the more I assumed the responsibility
of parenting. This became especially clear with our second child, Paul.
Early on, Paul had motor-skill problems, which proved to be transient.
But Jerry could be impatient and rough with him, and I intervened. I

made Jerry see a psychologist with me, who stressed that Paul should not be struck under any circumstances. 'Fine,' said Jerry. 'You deal with him. I'll stay away.'"

It's true that I didn't bond with either Paul or my younger daughter, Lisa, until they were practically adults. They suffered, as my brother Arthur had, from parental neglect. I'm not proud of this fact. I wish I had been more understanding, that I'd spent more time with them. But my blood family was not my only family. From that first morning I walked through the office door at 234 West 56th Street, Atlantic Records claimed my heart and soul.

CHARTING
THE
ATLANTIC

I was scared, though I'm not even sure I knew it. I certainly wouldn't have admitted it, but at work it was fear that fueled my engine—fear of being exposed as an amateur, fear of not selling records, fear that my co-workers would drop the ball, fear of failure in every form. Commingling with fear, though, was the bravado that enabled me to demand equity. And on top of that was strong pride in the quality of my partners, who, after all, had the foresight to start this remarkable operation six years earlier.

Ahmet Ertegun is the stuff of myth. He was and is the chief architect of Atlantic Records. For two decades, even though you could never call us competitors, I gave Ahmet a run for his—or our—money in producing music and profits. Then I dropped out while Ahmet led Atlantic onto the battlefield of World Rock, a war Ahmet won. Over six murderously competitive decades, from the forties through the nineties, he has proven himself to be the savviest and suavest executive in the history of American recorded music.

When we first met in the postwar jazz joints of hipsters and hopheads, he'd already developed his own brand of cool. Always impeccably and conservatively dressed—he'd discovered bespoke tailoring early on—his style was a paradox of enthusiastic involvement and droll detachment. Behind tortoiseshell glasses, his heavy-lidded, half-closed eyes could be inscrutable. Yet there was also an eagerness about Ahmet, a sweetness that endeared him to both friends and musicians. Moreover, his pranks and practical jokes assumed mythic proportions. In his appreciation of jazz, he was, along with many of us, a classicist, a connoisseur of the highest order and deepest knowledge. But unlike the rest of us—

street kids from the city—his background read like a fairy tale, peopled with princes, kings, and foreign diplomats.

Ahmet was born in Turkey, his father a lawyer who became ambassador to Switzerland, France, England, and finally the United States. Before Ahmet was a teenager he spoke three languages fluently.

"My role model, though," says Ahmet, "was not my father but my older brother, Nesuhi. It was he who loved fine clothing, he who had developed this taste for American jazz. At age ten I saw Duke Ellington at the London Palladium. This was my first encounter with black people, and I was overwhelmed by the elegance of their tuxedos, their gleaming instruments, and their sense of style. But mostly it was the music. I was accustomed to the sound of scratchy phonograph records, so to hear the purity and power of that orchestra in a live setting was overwhelming. I fell under the spell of black music. A new world opened up for me."

He came to the New World when he was eleven.

"My parents were horrified at the prospect," Ahmet explains. "I was delighted. America meant gangsters and cowboys and, best of all, red-hot jazz."

He lived in the Turkish embassy in Washington. Through the janitor, a black man named Cleo Payne, Ahmet found a window on the neighborhoods that interested him most. His acquaintances soon became medicine men, strippers, tap dancers, hustlers, and jazz players. He picked up Nesuhi's copy of Hugues Panassié's *Le Jazz Hot* and committed it to memory. His scholarly proclivities were honed at private institutions—St. Alban's, the Landon School. At St. John's in Annapolis he followed the program, plowing through the Great Books of Western Civilization while amassing a collection of twenty-five thousand 78-rpm jazz records. He and Nesuhi hired out the Jewish Community Center for concerts with Lester Young, Sidney Bechet, Johnny Hodges, Benny Carter, and Teddy Wilson. By the late thirties he was traveling to New Orleans to hear Kid Ory and to Harlem where, in a rapturous epiphany, he sat under a cloud of marijuana while listening to the incomparable stride piano of James P. Johnson. Ahmet's obsession with black culture was as powerful as my own, his ear bent by what he called their "secret language."

Ahmet's own language was extraordinary. He affected a small continental stutter, an accentless, East Coast–flavored, nasal-toned English with a faint hint of the exotic extraction of his childhood.

When his father died in 1944, Ahmet's adulthood began in earnest.

He did not return to Turkey with his mother, nor did he accompany Nesuhi to California. Instead he hung around Waxie Maxie Silverman's Quality Music Shop at 7th and T streets in Washington, D.C., and learned what music black people were buying.

Ahmet had eyes to make records. He also had ears and tremendous taste. His taste led him to a suite at the Ritz Carlton when he came up to New York to see about getting into the business. His taste also drained his meager finances. Counter to what many believed, he did not have an inheritance of any consequence. What he did have were his instincts, and they led him into a friendship with Herb and Miriam Abramson. I also knew Herb and Miriam and respected them both; they were a culturally evolved couple with a righteous feeling for hip music and left-wing politics. Herb was a blues expert, especially well versed in the Delta school. He'd also gone to dental school and worked for National Records, producing great sides with Joe Turner, Pete Johnson, and the Ravens. He'd begun his own gospel label, Jubilee, and jazz label, Quality. Though short-lived, they gave Herb experience. He was someone Ahmet admired, and in 1947 they formed a partnership. They were advised by Waxie Maxie and Jerry Blaine, a record promoter and close friend to Ahmet. With financing from Dr. Vahdi Sabit, a Turkish dentist, they started Atlantic.

I'd started noticing Atlantic's early releases with Professor Long-hair's "Hey Now Baby," "Hey Little Girl," and "Mardi Gras in New Orleans." Fess—as the Professor was called—was a revelation for me, my first taste of the music being served up in Louisiana in the late forties. There were traces of Jelly Roll Morton's habanera-Cuban tango influence in his piano style, but the overall effect was startlingly original, a jambalaya Caribbean Creole rumba with a solid blues bottom. In a foreshadowing of trips I myself would later take to New Orleans, Ahmet described the first of his many ethnomusicological expeditions.

"Herb and I went down there to see our distributor and look for talent. Someone mentioned Professor Longhair, a musical shaman who played in a style all his own. We asked around and finally found ourselves taking a ferry boat to the other side of the Mississippi, to Algiers, where a white taxi driver would deliver us only as far as an open field. 'You're on your own,' he said, pointing to the lights of a distant village. 'I ain't going into that niggertown.' Abandoned, we trudged across the field, lit only by the light of a crescent moon. The closer we came, the more distinct the sound of distant music—some big rocking band, the rhythm exciting us and pushing us on. Finally we came upon a nightclub—or, rather, a shack—which, like an animated cartoon, appeared to be expanding and deflating with the pulsation of the beat. The man at the door was skeptical. What did these two white men want? 'We're from *Life* magazine,' I lied. Inside, people scattered, thinking we were police. And instead of a full band, I saw only a single musician—Professor Longhair—playing these weird, wide harmonies, using the piano as both keyboard and bass drum, pounding a kick plate to keep time and singing in the open-throated style of the blues shouters of old.

"'My God,' I said to Herb, 'we've discovered a primitive genius.'

"Afterwards, I introduced myself. 'You won't believe this,' I said to the Professor, 'but I want to record you.'

"'You won't believe *this*,' he answered, 'but I just signed with Mercury.'

Ahmet recorded him anyway—"I am many men with many names who play under many styles," Fess used to say—and jewels from that first session remain in the Atlantic catalogue today, over four decades later.

The early catalogue was eclectic. There were Eddie Safranski's Poll Cats; Stan Kenton band members like Art Pepper, Shelly Manne, Pete Rugolo, and Bob Cooper. There were guitarist Tiny Grimes; Swing Era jazzmen like Rex Stewart; vocal groups like the Delta Rhythm Boys, the Clovers, and the Cardinals; pianists Erroll Garner and Mal Waldron; boppers Howard McGhee, James Moody, and Dizzy Gillespie; scat singers Jackie and Roy; Sarah Vaughan; blues legends Leadbelly and Sonny Terry; Mary Lou Williams; clarinetist Barney Bigard; café society singers Mabel Mercer and Bobby Short; Billie Holiday–based Sylvia Syms; boogie-woogie virtuoso Meade Lux Lewis. In short, there was everything.

At the same time, nothing was selling big except for that single Stick McGhee hit—"Drinkin' Wine Spo-Dee-O-Dee"—and some Ruth Brown and Joe Turner. In spite of a noble attempt to represent a broad spectrum of jazz and jazz-tinged music, it was rhythm and blues and rhythm and blues alone that paid the rent—a situation that wouldn't change for a long time to come.

So when I came along, the agenda was already set. Ahmet ran it down to me in no uncertain terms. "Here's the sort of record we need to make," he explained. "There's a black man living in the outskirts of Opelousas, Louisiana. He works hard for his money; he has to be tight with

Wex, Miriam Abramson, Ahmet

a dollar. One morning he hears a song on the radio. It's urgent, bluesy, authentic, irresistible. He becomes obsessed. He can't live without this record. He drops everything, jumps in his pickup, and drives twenty-five miles to the first record store he finds. If we can make that kind of music, we can make it in the business."

It's interesting that Ahmet's decree makes no mention of cross-over—the notion of selling black music to whites. That idea wasn't yet in the air. When I started working at Atlantic, I certainly had no such notions. I knew that the postwar rhythm-and-blues phenomenon had been spearheaded by independent labels. The war had caused a scarcity in shellac, and the majors were recording only their big-selling white acts and very few blacks. Thus black buyers' demand for black records was great. That's the slot the indies filled in the forties. And to a large extent, in the early fifties that was still the deal.

The deal I made with Atlantic was terrific. Shirley conducted the negotiations, perhaps because she had more confidence in me than I had in myself. For $2,063.25, I was handed 13 percent of the company. (Later, Herb, Miriam, and Dr. Sabit were bought out, and my ownership increased to 30 percent.) Ahmet took that $2,063.25, though, and put it towards a green Cadillac convertible, a company car, which he gave me. Wexler from Bennett Avenue—in a Cadillac with fins! Back then all record execs drove Caddies, and I was happy to dump my old fluid-drive Dodge.

My salary-plus-expenses draw came to three hundred dollars a week. On my first morning at work, Miriam dumped the mail on my desk. From that moment on, in a way that felt both natural and inevitable, I fell into the role I'd play for the next fifteen years—I ran the candy store. I got there early and I left late. I worried like crazy. I scrutinized bills, pored over details, supervised, and screamed when someone fucked up. That's not to say I was a good executive; I wasn't. I couldn't delegate, and operated with a divine disbelief in the competence of the staff. Consequently my modus operandi drove my employees nuts, though my brand of incessant demands might have contributed, as the company expanded, to our success. My goals were short-range and limited; tactics always, strategy never.

No enlightened book on the techniques of modern management could include a chapter by me. This was a grits-and-grease label, and we ran it like a mom-and-pop dress shop. Given the competitive climate of New York City and the ferocious nature of the music business, my street sense of survival might well have been what Ahmet found attractive about me. He certainly wasn't averse to having a workhorse partner in the office. Only a few weeks ago I was looking at *Jazz on a Summer Day,* the documentary of the first Newport Jazz Festival in 1958. I was digging Anita O'Day's timeless "Sweet Georgia Brown" when a random camera shot picked up on Ahmet, Mr. Fine himself, perfectly tailored in a blue blazer and grooving lightly and politely on Anita—while I was back at the office licking stamps.

If I was a plodder, Ahmet was an artist. He moved and managed by inspiration. A night owl, he maintained musicians' hours, coming into the office in the afternoon and stalking the clubs till the wee hours of morning, combing the city for singers. He had phenomenal instincts, not

Ahmet, Waxie Maxie Silverman, Miriam, Nesuhi, Wex

simply as a talent scout but as a producer and songwriter as well. Deep within his soul, he too may been feeling those fears the cutthroat industry excites in nearly everyone trying to sell records. But Ahmet has an inbred gift of cosmic cool. His cool is his very center. He's unflappable. Fortunately, we complemented one another. Like a good rhythm section, we swung as a unit. Despite differences of sensibility and habit, we fell into a rock-steady groove that deepened with time. Ahmet's imprint is ingrained in me to this day.

The scene of our early successes was the two top floors over Patsy's Restaurant at 234 West 56th Street. The man who made the most of that space was engineer Tom Dowd, a twenty-year-old wunderkind, the visionary architect of the Atlantic sound. He studied the physical configuration of 234 like a scientist.

"The building itself," says Tom, "was a wood-framed brownstone from the late nineteenth century. The shipping room was on the fourth floor and we were on the fifth. The floor sagged and creaked, and the sloped ceiling had a skylight in the middle of it. The whole office wasn't more than nineteen feet by twenty-eight. The walls were treated with plywood. Jerry's desk was next to Ahmet's. There was no studio. The office *was* the studio, and I had to make do.

"When it was time to record, we'd stack the desks and push furniture into the halls. We'd wing it. I had a technical and musical background at City College and Columbia, and when I started recording in the late forties I was light-years ahead of the hand-me-down radio equipment being used. By default, I suppose, I became an innovator. The early Atlantic sessions—when I was still a freelancer—had me experimenting like a madman. I had no choice. Jerry and Ahmet were sticklers for a clean, crisp sound, and I was determined to get it.

"The whole operation was marked by a curious mixture of determination and improvisation. Jerry arrived in the morning and hit the phones. He'd stay on the phone so long and hard it seemed the instrument was growing out of his ear. He'd run down bills, chase after distributors, promoters, disc jockeys, managers. Jerry was a tiger and a terror. Ahmet was a threat to come in at noon, but he often wouldn't show up till three, talking about some great talent he'd heard the night before. Of course Ahmet worked the phones as well, and Jerry also scrutinized talent. Lines of authority were blurry, but the two bosses would compare notes and thrash out differences. They kept the aisles and files clear. From time to time, though, they'd decide to organize. That was always a joke. There was always talk about saving money, but budgets were never established.

"I remember one meeting when Ahmet and Jerry insisted that we work the studio faster and develop more precise methods of operation. They asked for suggestions. I suggested that Ahmet and Jerry be fired for having absolutely no operating methods themselves. They busted up laughing. So much for procedural discipline."

Even though Tom was just a kid, this eager and exceptionally bright engineer was one of my teachers. Our gig was to get the music played right and righteous in the studio; Tom's job was to capture it on tape. It was up to him to find a true mix of timbres, bass, treble, and midrange; to load as much volume as possible without distortion. Tom pushed those pots (the volume controls) like a painter sorting colors. He turned microphone placement into an art. Most of all, in those days of mono, he was responsible for catching the right mix on the fly. There was no "We'll fix it in the mix." Single tracking was get-it-or-gone.

Tom also knew the music. He actually taught me how to count bars. In the studio, he became my mainstay and later one of my best co-producers. When it came to sound, he displayed an exquisite sensibility.

"Two musicians," he said, "made me super-sensitive to the art of recording. They were both pianists and they were both blind. Until I worked with George Shearing and Ray Charles, I was walking around with cotton in my ears. They offered me whole new insights into the communication between artist and control room. They operated on a higher plane than anything I had previously imagined."

Like Tom, I found myself inspired by the artists who, through an unlikely happenstance, I was actually producing. I was in awe of those people. I was also scared shitless they'd discover I didn't know my elbow from my ass. And though I was presumably their overseer, they were my instructors. These were the artists who made my career and changed my life, infusing the business blues with a joy transcending all earthly matters.

WHAT'S
BLACK
AND RED
AND BLUE
ALL OVER?

It happened before," I wrote in an essay for *Cashbox* in 1954. "It happened in the twenties when Perry Bradford and Spencer Williams were as hot as Irving Berlin; it happened when Bessie Smith and Ethel Waters sold their records into millions of white parlors. Now it's happening again. The blues will get stronger before the blues get weaker. Regardless of its impact on the pop field, the blues will surely go on."

I was talking about the present state of rhythm and blues and the beginnings of rock 'n' roll. In significant numbers, white people were listening to, buying, and playing black music. Atlantic's black-and-red label carried the slogan "Leads the Field in Rhythm and Blues," but it was clear that our market, once exclusively black, was expanding.

The first hint came when my friend Howie Richmond called to say that something new was happening in the South and Southwest. They were calling it "cat music," the pre-rock-'n'-roll handle for rhythm and blues selling to whites. Immediately I glommed on to the name, and we started a "Cat" subsidiary label. That had two advantages: first, I hoped the name would pick up on the trend; and secondly, another label allowed us to use other distributors in major markets. (We usually made exclusive agreements with a single distributor in each city, when in fact there were any number of excellent distributors.) We had black artists on Cat—Little Sylvia Vanderpool (later of Mickey and Sylvia), Mike Gordon and the El Tempos, and the Chords, whose record of "Sh-Boom" would be copied (and buried) by the Crewcuts, a white group.

A picture was beginning to emerge: Kids, especially kids down South, were taking newly invented transistor radios to the beach. White Southerners, I believe, in spite of the traditional aura of racial bigotry, have always enjoyed the most passionate rapport with black music, itself a Southern phenomenon. And in the fifties, white Southern teenagers started the charge towards ballsy rhythm and blues. As the Eisenhower decade became more conformist, the music became more rebellious, more blatantly sexual, climaxing in the remarkable persona of Elvis Presley, a Memphis boy raised on the pure sounds of the black South.

In the wake of postwar prosperity, teenagers were becoming a market of their own. Their buying power was real, their emotional needs immediate, their libidinous drive no longer reflected by the dead-and-gone fox-trots of their parents. Suddenly there was another force at work—old but new, primal yet complex, a music informed by the black genius for expressing pent-up frustration, joy, rage, or ecstasy in a poetic context marked by hip humor and irresistible rhythm.

Ahmet had already anticipated this evolution, the best example being his seminal work with Joe Turner. Big Joe was the blues-shouting bartender from Kansas City whom I'd heard back in my student days. A mountain of a man, his voice was among the most powerful in the history of the form. History had placed him in a niche with Pete Johnson, his boogie-woogie-piano-playing partner, and Count Basie, whose band he'd joined when Ahmet caught him at the Apollo in the early fifties.

"Joe took Jimmy Rushing's place," says Ahmet, "but unlike Jimmy, Joe didn't fit. Musically, he and Basie were fighting each other, and it was depressing. The crowd didn't like it, Joe didn't like it, and afterwards I found him in a bar where he told me Columbia had dropped him from the label. Joe really had the blues. 'I think you're the greatest blues singer in the world,' I told him. 'All you need is fresh material. Sign with Atlantic and we'll make hits.'"

Ahmet's "Chains of Love" hit the charts in 1951, followed by "Sweet Sixteen," "Honey Hush," and "TV Mama." It was "Shake, Rattle and Roll," though, that opened the floodgates for Joe. The song was written by Jesse Stone, a brilliant black arranger with roots back to Jelly Roll Morton. Jesse's musical mind had as much to do as anyone's with the transformation of traditional blues to pop blues—or rhythm and blues, or cat music, or rock 'n' roll, or whatever the hell you want to call it. Jesse was a master, and an integral part of the sound we were developing. He had the unique gift of maintaining a hang-loose boogie-shuffle feel in the context of a formal chart. Jesse was a record producer's dream come true. I always felt he viewed me with a slightly jaundiced eye, as though I might sign the checks but was in on a pass, not knowing shit about the music. Jesse seemed to know everything.

He'd written hits for Jimmy Dorsey. He'd written "Idaho," whose sophisticated chord structure became a favorite vehicle for the bebop-pers. In "Shake, Rattle and Roll," under the pseudonym of Charles Cal-houn, he also wrote, "You wear those dresses, the sun comes shining through, I can't believe my eyes, all that mess belongs to you"—one of my favorite images of erotic poetry. In Bill Haley's white cover, whose sales outstripped Turner's version, the sex was stripped off, the lyrics bleached clean. No matter; Joe's reading remains a gem.

Highly imitated as innovators, Jesse Stone and Howard Biggs (an-other fabulous arranger, whom I mentioned earlier for his work with the Ravens) were absolutely essential to the good rockin' feel of our early-fifties hits. Howard is gone, but Jesse is still with us. In his eighties, he is living in Florida, alert and in full possession of all his faculties.

In the studio, I lost my maiden with LaVern Baker. I'm speaking musi-cally, of course. In spite of my wandering ways, I never had an affair with anyone I produced. I considered that bad business, though a successful Southern producer once expressed surprise and dismay. "I could never get over on a record with a dame unless I fucked her," he said. "That's what it takes to get their juices flowing. And mine."

Bullshit. Getting to the kernel of emotion, to the core of the artist, doesn't require sexual seduction. The heat between producer and singer is hot enough without confusing matters. When the current was flowing from me to a fine female vocalist, the result was euphoria.

With LaVern, I was far too much a novice to meaningfully influence her music. I was just glad to be around. In that first session we cut "How Can You Leave a Man" and "Soul on Fire," songs I co-wrote with Ahmet and Jesse Stone. Necessity was the mother of invention. Faced with a dearth of good material, we often found ourselves composing on the spot, putting together formula ditties matched with lyrics not likely to rival Cole Porter's. LaVern's delivery, however, could rival anyone's. I loved her because—like Ruth Brown, Ahmet's discovery through Waxie Maxie, and Atlantic's first female hitmaker—she stood smack dab in the middle of the great tradition of Ma Rainey and Bessie Smith. There was no compromising LaVern. We tried to keep the material current, but the basic delivery was undiluted.

Sixteen months later we brought LaVern back into the studio with Sam "The Man" Taylor on tenor. She recorded the timeless ballad "Tomorrow Night" (made legendary by Lonnie Johnson), along with the soulful nursery jingle "Tweedlee Dee"—the song that pushed her up the pop charts, in spite of the dogged reluctance of white radio to play black music. Her Nibs Miss Georgia Gibbs did a Caucasian cover which, true to form, outperformed the original (LaVern's reached #14, Georgia's #2.)

In the months just before I arrived on the scene, Ahmet recruited a vocalist whose influence, like Sam Cooke's, would shape a whole generation of soul singers in the sixties, from Smokey Robinson to Marvin Gaye to Ronnie Isley to Curtis Mayfield to Aaron Neville. I'm talking about Clyde McPhatter.

In the early spring of 1953, Ahmet fell by Birdland to catch Billy Ward and the Dominoes, mostly to hear Clyde, a member of the group, sing "Have Mercy, Baby." Ahmet considered this an R&B classic and loved it for the flutey silk of Clyde's high lead tenor.

At the Birdland show, though, Clyde was missing. Ahmet made inquiries backstage. The Dominoes were managed by an entrepreneur named Rose Marks. (It was not uncommon in those days for rhythm-and-blues groups to be run by shrewd Jewish ladies; Deborah Chesler, for example, would have great success with Sonny Til and the Orioles.) Rose and Ward ran the Dominoes like an infantry squadron, with fines for any number of infractions, ranging from tardiness to unshined shoes to wrong notes to backtalking the leaders. Clyde had broken a rule. "I fired his ass," Ward told Ahmet.

Ahmet ran to the phone. An hour later he was in Clyde's furnished room uptown planning a new vocal group. Reserved, shy, and more than a little cautious, Clyde was accustomed to the intrusive ways in which Syd Nathan, czar of the King label, had run recording sessions. "Just one thing, Mr. Ertegun," he said. "I hope you're not going to play drums on my sessions."

Neither Ahmet nor I played so much as a finger cymbal behind Clyde. Ahmet did, however, write a great song for him, "Whatcha Gonna Do?" I helped Clyde write "Honey Love," and Ahmet, Tom Dowd, and

I wrote "Warm Your Heart" (during a trip to the Savoy one spring evening when one brother greeted another with the words "Hold my hand and warm your heart"). Nearly four decades later, Aaron Neville would sing the song and title his Linda Ronstadt–produced album *Warm Your Heart*.

We wanted a cool name for Clyde's new group and spent hours on the subject. "Clyde McPhatter and the Drifters" had a disconcertingly bucolic ring for us, on the order of "Bob Wills and the Texas Playboys," but Clyde wouldn't budge: "Drifters" it was.

As a rule, vocal groups were not rehearsed. Most of the doo-wop producers—Hymie Weiss, Leo Rogers, Morty Craft—lined up their groups in droves and pushed them in front of the mike to do their songs in one take. There were no arrangements, and the band—standard three rhythm, plus tenor—hadn't even heard the tune and certainly not the key. As soon as one group finished two sides, another would be shoved forward on the assembly line. If one of the musicians presumed to inquire about lead sheets or keys, Hymie would yell from the control room, "We don't study keys, motherfucker. Play the music!" This is now known as the golden age of a capella.

I'm glad to say we went our own way. We broke the mold and rehearsed. We even scrapped the first session. Neither the material nor the group members were worthy of Clyde McPhatter.

Clyde set out and found a new quartet—one of many to come, but to my ears the best: Willie Pinckney, bass; David Baughan and Gerhart Thrasher, tenors; and Bubba Thrasher, baritone. David sounded uncannily like Clyde, and, a bit later, so would Johnny Moore (the great lead on "Ruby Baby" and "Under the Boardwalk"). By summer we were ready to record. We went through the usual drill, stacking our desks, Tom setting out camp chairs and mikes, me and Ahmet squeezing into a makeshift control room the size of a small closet. A small RCA portable four-position mono-mixer served as console.

The singing was like nothing I'd ever heard. The three- and four-part harmony was pitch-perfect, with Clyde indicating the various parts. The gospel feel was real. We cut Jesse Stone's "Money Honey"—the breakaway hit—as well as "Gone," "Whatcha Gonna Do?," and "Boogie Woogie Roll."

Those first Drifters were together for a year, until Clyde went into the Army. By then we'd recorded two dozen sides, including "Honey Love," "Such a Night," and the Ravens-inspired "White Christmas," which I mistakenly feared Irving Berlin's people would never approve. They loved it.

The Drifters floated in and out of the history of Atlantic for the next thirteen years, always adding a sense of diversity and distinction to our label.

Those first couple of years at Atlantic had me flying high. With the aid of Miriam Abramson, who shared my zeal for the nitty-gritty of daily detail, the business side was clean-cut and straight-ahead. Ahmet was cooking in the studio, and I was at his side soaking up the make-it-up-as-you-go-along recipes.

Luckily, my arrival came at that fortunate point in American music when the lines between black and white were starting to fade. Things were getting blurry in a hurry, and Atlantic both benefited from and contributed to that breakdown. Hip disc jockeys—white guys who talked black—were starting to play black music to an audience that was increasingly white. Cats like Zenas "Daddy" Sears in Atlanta, George "Hound Dog" Lorenz in Buffalo, Hunter Hancock in Los Angeles, Bob "Wolfman Jack" Smith in Shreveport and Del Rio, Ken "Jack the Cat" Elliott and Clarence "Poppa Stoppa" Hamman in New Orleans, Gene Nobles and John Richbourg and Hoss Allen in Nashville, not to mention a man destined for national prominence, Alan "Moondog" Freed in Cleveland—these were all white guys who broadcasted black, speaking with the timing and rhyming of the ghetto. Both in the existential sense of Norman Mailer's term ("The source of Hip is the Negro," he wrote, "for he has been living on the margin between totalitarianism and de-mocracy for two centuries") and in the sense of pure entertainment, these were White Negroes. Their significance cannot be overempha-sized. These sons-of-bitches not only pointed to the future of American popular music but were also the makers and the breakers of our records.

The black style represented a diverting departure from the mid-fifties blahs. You could segregate schoolrooms and buses, but not the airwaves. Radio could not resist the music's universality—its intrinsic charm, its empathy for human foibles, its direct application to the teen-age condition.

The hip of my generation, who were teenagers in the thirties, had always been drawn to black culture. In fact, I had always known White Negroes, not pretenders or voyeurs but guys who had opted to leave the white world, married black women, and made Harlem or Watts their habitat. These guys *converted.* Clarinetist Mezz Mezzrow—of the famous joints—was the most colorful example; Teddy Reig, the three-hundred-pound soul man who managed Count Basie and Chuck Berry and produced Charlie Parker, was another. Symphony Syd, jazz voice of the night in New York City; Johnny Otis, pioneering rhythm-and-blues band leader, creator of "Willie and the Hand Jive," discoverer of Esther Phillips and Etta James in Los Angeles; Monte Kay, bebop impresario, manager of the Modern Jazz Quartet, whose kinky coif might have been the first Jewfro in hair-fashion history—these were all friends.

I dug cross-cultural collaborations and craved commercial success, which is maybe why Ahmet and I got on so well. We could have developed a label along the lines of Blue Note, Prestige, Vanguard, or Folkways, fastidious documentarians of core American music. Bobby Weinstock, Alfred Lion, Moe Ash, Orrin Keepnews, Manny Solomon, and the other keepers of the flame were doing God's work. Ahmet and I, however, didn't feature ourselves as divinely elected. We weren't looking for canonization; we lusted for hits. Hits were the cash flow, the lifeblood, the heavenly ichor—the wherewithal of survival. While we couldn't divorce ourselves from our tastes and inclinations, neither could we deny our interest in income. Nor could we stand still; we believed to our souls that the way of the independent label was either growth or death. Every month, it seemed, another indie would hit the dust. Our competitors in commercial black music—Lew Chudd at Imperial, Sam and Hymie Weiss at Old Town, Syd Nathan at King, Art Rupe at Specialty, Don Robey at Duke/Peacock, Jules and Saul Bihari at Modern, Bess Berman at Apollo, Herman Lubinsky at Savoy, Phil and Leonard Chess—weren't exactly pushovers. If we slipped, these sweethearts would be right behind us picking up the pieces. This was a pushy, get-to-the-distributor, get-to-the-deejay, get-the-goddamn-song-on-the-air business.

Consequently, the term "commercial" was not a pejorative for me—wasn't then, isn't now. If "commercial" meant a song with a strong hook, an inviting refrain, melodic variety, and a rhythm pattern with a walloping bass line—well, give me commercial and lots of it. The merry jingle of cash registers was music to my ears. As a kid, I might have been cavalier about money. But this was a different deal. I had a family to support; people were working for me. Fear of bankruptcy was always around the corner—deep-depression, nothing-to-eat, nowhere-to-sleep

fear. Given my high level of chain-smoking anxiety, I still wonder that I
didn't develop ulcers early on.

Yet the tonic wasn't money; it was music. Substantial financial re-
wards wouldn't come until well into the sixties. In the precarious fifties,
my fascination with the glories of the music seemed to push me beyond
my own limitations. If now and then Ahmet or I might begin to worry
during a session, unnecessarily afraid that LaVern or Ray was getting too
hoarse or the drummer was dragging, the natural abilities of our artists
would eventually pull things together. We also had the benefit of Dowd's
engineering talents, arrangers like Jesse, and a large pool of New York
City session musicians, many of whom—drummers Connie Kay and
Panama Francis, tenor men Budd Johnson and Sam Taylor, pianists
Hank Jones and Dick Hyman—were jazz musicians of the first order.

A further benefit was the out-of-town trip. This might have been
another reason I didn't go crazy behind the routine of business all day
and recording sessions all night. Now and then I escaped. And with Ahmet as a constant and constantly witty traveling companion, my adventures inevitably took unexpected turns.

ON

THE

ROAD

*M*y *family* has temporarily receded in this narrative, but I'm afraid that's the way it was. I was a hardcore worker, and even though we had three babies by 1955, I couldn't stay away from the office, studio, or road long enough to be much of a father or husband. My affection for Shirley, Anita, Paul, and Lisa was real, but my time was given to the gig.

"As time went on," says Shirley, "Jerry became more difficult. He was hyper—hyperintelligent, hyperconscientious about his work, hyperanxious about controlling details. His temper got worse. Maybe that's one reason I never complained about the inordinate time he spent at work. If he was in a cross mood, or a meal wasn't to his liking, his presence could be more troublesome than his absence. On the other hand, I was tremendously committed to his career and the great progress he was making. It was exciting to watch Jerry grow, and as Atlantic continued to prosper, there were wonderful times when all was right with our world. We had much in common. We both loved the theater, for example, and I don't think we missed a single Eugene O'Neill, Arthur Miller, or Tennessee Williams play on Broadway."

The city's culture was pervasive, and I thrived on it; but I also thrived in certain other places whose music I found especially funky.

Long before I saw *A Streetcar Named Desire*—in fact, ever since I'd heard Jelly Roll Morton—I'd longed to experience New Orleans for myself. I knew the city to be the source of both the jazz I'd loved as a teenager and the rhythm and blues I was recording as an adult. In the early fifties, though, getting to the Crescent City was no picnic. Those twin-engine Convairs would be bouncing over clouds and dropping in air pockets, my stomach in my throat, while Ahmet was unperturbed, either dead to the world or his head buried in Kant's *Critique of Pure Reason* or the latest issue of *Cashbox*.

We'd hit town and he'd be ready to roll. I'd be ready to crash. While he posed in front of the mirror selecting ties, I'd be in bed. The next thing I knew, it was morning and Ahmet was just getting in, brimming over with tales of incredible encounters. Whether by design or by destiny, Ahmet Ertegun attracts existential happenings. Refreshed by sleep, I'd dress quickly and we'd run around visiting retailers, distributors, and disc jockeys. Given the fancy black-iron grillwork of the French Quarter, the swampy humidity, the nonstop two-beat jazz on Bourbon Street, the aroma of Cajun cooking, I was forever stoked. Nothing, however, stimulated us like back of town—across Claiborne Street, the Berlin Wall dividing black and white.

Like the city itself, even the cabs were segregated: a "white" taxi wouldn't cross the line, and a "black" one couldn't carry us. So we'd get our white distributor to drop us off, with noticeable reluctance, in the black neighborhoods. He'd keep his foot on the clutch and then, tires screeching, take off like a bat out of hell.

We loved the old-time frenchified hotels—the Monteleone, the Jung—with their European facades and enormous armoires. We also loved the old rooming houses and hotel bars, the greatest of which was Frank Pania's Dew Drop Inn. Frank was a tall, good-looking Creole with smooth hair and twinkling eyes. He also proved to be a kind and considerate host. I learned as much the first night I fell by his place, when I got so shit-faced I couldn't make it back to my hotel.

Frank made it easy. He put me up in his best room and provided two "Miss Fines" to keep me warm. When morning came, I stumbled downstairs to find Big Joe Turner in his undershirt, suspenders dangling. Joe had recorded "Honey Hush," a big hit for us, and "Crawdad Hole" at Cosmo (née Cosimo) Matassa's famous studio, using Pluma Davis's band—Fats Domino on piano, Lee Allen on tenor, Red Tyler on baritone—all without a shred of help from Ahmet or myself. I was glad to see him sitting there, eating R&B spaghetti for breakfast, with Smiley Lewis and Lloyd Price. Before long, Lloyd went to the piano and Joe started singing "Wee Baby Blues." Still foggy, I felt like I was dreaming. I also felt safe and comfortable. I knew I was in the sure-enough House of the Blues.

"Wexler," said Frank as he brought me a steaming mug of Louisiana coffee, "the only other white man who slept over in the Dew Drop was Lash LaRue," referring to the loopy cowboy star.

There'd be other trips, just as heady. In December of 1953, we recorded Joe ourselves, returning to Cosmo's studio, where we cut the bulletproof "Midnight Cannonball." Joe just kept getting stronger, better, bigger in every way.

In addition to orchestrating record sessions, Ahmet also ran little comic vignettes in which I played cooperating second banana. One day, for instance, we're in New Orleans and we're fresh out. We're at a one-stop distributor—a guy who carries the hit records on all the labels—and he takes us next door to a hock shop to cash a check. Ahmet writes a thousand-dollar check, and the pawnbroker doles it out in a stack of twenties and a stack of singles.

"You take an inch from here," Ahmet instructs me, pointing to the singles stack, "and I'll take an inch from there," indicating the other pile.

"That's fair," I say, playing along.

"No it ain't," the pawnbroker tells me. "This guy's robbing you."

"He'd wouldn't do that," I assure him. "He takes care of me."

"He's fucking you!" he cries, exasperated.

Indignantly, Ahmet takes out his wallet and throws it at me.

"Are we talking leather?" I ask, then remove a shoe and lob it at Ahmet. "Now we're straight," I tell the pawnbroker. "I told you we split everything fifty-fifty."

I walk off with my stack of bills, Ahmet walks off with his; the guy thinks we're both nuts—and we are. (We'd borrowed this little riff, by the way, from Alva Johnston's *New Yorker* profile of the legendary Wilson Mizner, the fabulous bon vivant and impresario.)

One time, we frequent this blues bar run by the Mob. The girls drink colored tea, sell watered-down champagne, and wind up charging guys eighty-five bucks for practically nothing. We scrutinize the scene for a few afternoons until one of the owners pretends to take Ertegun for a mark. "Why don't you let one of the girls buy you a drink?" he says.

Suddenly the Turk runs amok. "Motherfucker!" Ahmet shouts, grabbing the guy by the collar. "They tried serving us some of that piss yesterday, and if you ever ask me again, you'll wind up in the alley with your cock stuffed down your throat!"

I'm ready to run. So effective, however, is Ahmet's delivery that the wiseguy's rolling on the floor, laughing. For the rest of the evening we're drinking nothing but Martell's Cordon Bleu, courtesy of the management.

New Orleans is filled with legends living, dead, and supernatural, a collision of cultures and primal forces—Caribbean, French, Cuban, Creole, Cajun, and Southern-fried Afro-American blues.

Another year, another session at Cosmo's studio, Rampart and Dumaine, scene of some of Fats Domino's earth-shattering sessions with Dave Bartholomew, the extravagantly talented R&B maestro. Tonight it's time for the blues. For years, Ahmet and I have been waiting to record Guitar Slim, whose perfervid preach-shout had such a telling impact on Ray Charles—who'd directed Slim's hit on Specialty, "The Things That I Used to Do," a timeless anthem of rue, reform, and regret. Just before that record was made, I thought I had Slim signed, but he slipped away and wound up on Specialty. That relationship proved short-lived, and we finally got Slim's name on the dotted line. Tonight's the night of our first rehearsal. Tonight's also the night Slim's nowhere in sight.

Eight o'clock comes and goes. Nine, no sign. Ten, I'm nervous as a hen. Eleven . . . eleven-thirty. We're about to give up when suddenly a wave of humanity comes washing over the street—kids, men, women, and couriers. "Here comes Slim! Slim's on the way!" A fleet of three red Cadillacs pulls up, and here's the man himself, emerging in a bower of red-robed beauties, dressed to match the Caddies, plus a retinue of courtiers, janissaries, mountebanks, and tumblers. "Need to change into my singing pants, gents," says Slim.

The small hall fills to bursting with his excited public, so when he finally appears, we urge Slim to get rid of the rooters, needless distractions. Slim nods gravely, plugs in his trademark hundred-foot-long guitar cord (an accessory that allows him to roam the streets outside the clubs he plays, corralling customers), and invites his sidemen to kick off the blues in B-flat. The cats vamp as Slim circles the room, addressing each of his admirers one by one, saying/singing how he hates to see them leave. But leave they do—except for the ladies in red, the most pulchritudinous of whom identifies herself as a shake dancer scooped up by Slim in Vegas only last month.

"Know that thousand-dollar advance you gave him?" she asks.

"Sure," I answer.

"Well, I got it all," she winks, her face a portrait in dimples. "At three hundred a week."

But by then Slim's already getting down, singing the blues and picking up a storm on his guitar.

The next day, at the recording session at Cosmo's, it's hot and humid as hell, maybe 103 degrees, and the tiny studio's packed solid. Wearing an overcoat, a head rag, and a wide-brimmed fedora, Slim's drinking mineral oil from a bottle ("to clear my throat") and complaining about the temperature: it's too cold.

The session is murder. When it's time to solo, Slim runs up the gain on his guitar so high that he blows out the tubes in the tape machine. Though we beg him to come down, Slim is bewitched by his sound and turns up the volume again and again. Every time the tubes blow, Cos, who runs a truly plain operation, has to send a kid down to Canal Street for extras. The process is agonizingly slow.

Slim's singing "There's Plenty Good Room in My House," a gospel-tinged thing, but keeps forgetting the words. We write up a lyric sheet, but now Slim's jumping from the first verse to the bridge, skipping over the second stanza.

We try to explain: "You have to go from here to here," I point out. But Slim is adamant. "When I get there, my natural soul brings me to *here*."

We get an idea. Leaning against a wall, there's a big cardboard placard announcing a R&B show at the San Jacinto Ballroom featuring the Spiders, Tommy Ridgley, and Sugar Boy Crawford. We turn it over, rip it into sections, and separately print the lyrics for the verses, bridge, chorus, and coda. We appoint someone to hold the appropriate section—and that section only—as Slim makes his way through the song. Slim, though, is unhappy with the holder. We try a second holder, and a third, and a fourth. We finally get to the tag—and Slim skips it.

"Slim, you missed the coda."

"Motherfuck the motherfuckin' coda," he says. "I'm here to sing 'There's Plenty Good Room in My House.'"

New Orleans produced a powerful school of R&B laureates. But if the Nobel committee ever decides to give a prize in funk, as well it should, I pray they have the wisdom to first elect Professor Longhair, the illustrious Henry Roeland "Roy" Byrd. He belongs in that rare company with Louis Armstrong, Sidney Bechet, and Jelly Roll Morton, other Crescent City innovators whose contributions to our musical culture are immeasurable. His immortality is ensured not only by the records he made but by the few men who mastered his style, the apostles who carried the pianistic gospel according to Fess to the world: James Booker, Fats Domino, Huey Smith, Allen Toussaint, Art Neville, and Mac Rebennack. Longhair is the Picasso of keyboard funk.

When Ahmet and I recorded him in New Orleans in 1953—his second session for the label—I was surprised that beyond his standard stock of ten or twelve tunes, he had no material. Later Mac Rebennack would explain: "During gigs he'd take a calypso, combine it with some cornball tune like 'A-Tisket A-Tasket,' add some boogie-woogie, mash it all together, and come out with something weird but funky as the devil. That was Fess's way of writing."

Right then and there, Ahmet and I pitched in by suggesting that he make up something along the lines of "Tra La La" or Smiley Lewis's current R&B hit, "Tee Nah Nah" (the same Smiley whose "I Hear You Knocking" became a bonanza for Gale Storm). The nonsense titles were supposed to refer to reefer; we thought that something along those lines would do for a Fess song. We went to work, searching for secret and alluring code words, pasting together a phonetic concoction that became "Tipitina," a group of yodeling honky-tonk sounds strung together: "Tipitina oo-la-malla-walla-dalla try-my-tra-la-la"—"try-my-tra-la-la" being an invitation to smoke? Perhaps. The music was an eight-bar blues, the form so favored in New Orleans, with roots going back to "Stagger Lee." The song wasn't a hit, but it has lived on in the liturgy.

The other tunes from that session—"In the Night," "Ball the Wall," "Who's Been Fooling You"—were hatched in the same way: on-the-spot improvisations. "Ball the Wall," for example, was how Fess interpreted our suggestion to put something together "off the wall."

If Professor Longhair was the George Washington of New Orleans, then Champion Jack Dupree was its Thomas Jefferson, a wonderful writer, pianist, and singer whose Okeh sides from the early forties— "Chain Gang Blues," "Cabbage Green," "Bad Health Blues"—impressed me so deeply that when I had the chance to record him in the fifties, I jumped at it. Back then it took chutzpah to call the album *Blues from the Gutter.* I put Jack with Pete Brown, whose salty alto swung between the Eddie Condon Dixieland axis and low-down Newark R&B.

Like Fess, Champion Jack, a former prizefighter, had had a mighty influence on young Antoine Domino in the famous 1950 session which signaled the start of modern New Orleans funk. Fats took Jack's classic "Junker's Blues" and put the "Fat Man" lyrics to it. Where Fats was smooth, though, Jack was metrically eccentric, punctuating his blues with half-measures and extended bars. He was rough, and ready to be recorded, in my estimation, with minimal adornment. The album still stands as a study of the Crescent City's fabulous roots, running back to "Junker's Blues," "Frankie and Johnny," and "Stack-O-Lee." He was a sly rogue; in "Bad Blood" he managed to combine lubricity with medical advice: "Come here, baby, the doctor gonna give you a shot, climb up on the table and show the doctor what you got." Jack emigrated to Switzerland, where he died in 1992.

New Orleans was one scene, Chicago another. Ahmet and I are in a cab, cruising down Maxwell Street on a brisk, sun-splashed autumn afternoon. A mixture of deep Harlem ghetto and Yiddish Lower East Side, the neighborhood is dense with pushcarts overflowing with fabrics and fruits, tin cans and newspapers, junk, jewelry, shoes, corsets. Bearded merchants with skull caps and thick accents mingle with black men from the South—a few shoot craps, others sit on stoops and sing the Delta blues.

"Let's get out and dick around," says Ahmet, elegantly dressed in gray slacks and double-breasted blue blazer. He tells the cabbie, who can't quite figure us out, to follow along. We're meandering aimlessly when something catches Ahmet's eye: a pit barbecue rib joint, the kind with globules of grease running down the window. First he asks the proprietor if reservations are required, then discusses the menu for a dinner party for a dozen. "As far as wine, we'd like a Bordeaux of a decent year, perhaps a Pomerol. . . ." Ahmet rattles on for the next few minutes before ordering ribs while waving at the cabbie to join us.

Later that afternoon, on the way back to the Drake, in a different cab with a black driver, Ahmet switches gears into authentic street jive. I reply in kind, completely baffling the cabbie. But before the end of the ride, Ahmet's back in a High Anglican frame of mind. "I realize you signed all the important artists to the company last year, Jerry, and I know you added two million to our gross. But I was the one who fished you from the gutter. I took you from a bum to a star. Paying you five thousand a year is really more than you deserve."

"Oh, please," I beseech him, "you're taking three grand a week. With my wife and three kids, man, I gotta deserve—"

"You deserve my gratitude, and you're welcome to it. But not a penny more."

Not until we arrive at the hotel does the outraged cabbie finally cut loose. "Forget this motherfucker!" he shouts. "You're the one bringing in the bread. You got the smarts. Fuck him. Quit and go for yourself!"

That night, Ahmet and I finally get serious. We're in the control room at Universal Studios, cutting Big Joe Turner in a new setting, the Windy City, the Chess brothers' turf.

Even though Phil and Leonard Chess are our main competition, they're also our friends. They've arranged this session for us, recruiting Elmore James, the great Robert Johnson–influenced bottleneck Mississippi guitarist, and pianist Little Johnny Jones to back up Big Joe. Leonard and Phil come by that night, and I'm glad to see them.

They've already attained something of heroic status in the business. Polish Jews who immigrated to Chicago, where they drove a junk wagon with their father before peddling records out of a car trunk, they opened a bar and grill back of town, saw the intense interest in black music among their customers, and started cutting records—first on Aristocrat, then on Chess, Checker, and Cadet. Some view them as crass; some are put off by their Yiddish-inflected speech and their sell-sell-sell sensibilities. Personally, I love them. They're not polished producers; but after all, they're putting out blistering sides by Chuck Berry and Bo Diddley celebrating the blues present and the blues past. Their roster is spectacular: Willie Dixon (the musical brains behind the operation), Muddy Waters, Memphis Slim, Sonny Boy Williamson, Little Walter, Howlin' Wolf, and, somewhat later, Etta James. By the time the decade is over, Chess will have created the finest blues repository in history, contributing more significantly to our national treasury of Delta blues than any label before or since.

"I have an agreement with Muddy Waters," Leonard says that night. "'Muddy,' I tell him, 'when your stuff like "Hoochie Coochie Man" and "Mojo" stops selling, you can come over to my house and do the gardening.'"

"Funny, but I got a different kind of deal with Turner," Ahmet says as Big Joe is getting ready to sing. "If his records don't sell, I can be *his* chauffeur."

We ruminate a bit about royalties. Leonard thinks we're crazy to pay our artists as high as 5 percent, as high as the majors, and believes firmly in a cutoff point, regardless of sales. I argue that straight accounting makes good business, but Leonard counters that there are virtually no defections from Chess. "They're just happy to be making records," he says. "The records get them club work."

Though Leonard's tough-nosed about business, he's also naive and susceptible to Ahmet's wicked humor.

"You're doing us this favor tonight, Leonard," Ahmet says, "but I did you an even bigger one."

"What's that?"

"Well," explains Ahmet, "I was in Atlanta last week, and when I got to the hotel I turned on the radio. Man, I always listen for your music, and I couldn't believe it when I didn't hear one song on Chess."

"You kidding me?" asks Leonard, hooked.

"All afternoon I listened. I didn't listen for an hour or two, but all day. For five straight hours, my dear Leonard, I'm digging Daddy Sears's show. I hear Atlantic. I hear Imperial. I hear Specialty. I hear Herald and Ember records, but no Chess. I picked up the phone and called the disc jockey. 'Hey, Daddy, how come I don't hear no Chess records?' 'Who is this calling?' 'Never mind who's calling. This is Chess Records, motherfucker, and I'm calling you for my friends up there in Chicago.'"

"Come on, man, you didn't!" Leonard cries. "Now I got trouble in Atlanta."

I start to explain that Ahmet's just putting him on, but Elmore and little Johnny are already pounding out "Oke-She-Moke-She-Pop," Joe's version of "Nov Shmoz Kapop," the syndicated comic strip about the little hitchhiker. "I'm from the country, baby," Joe sings, "just blowed up into your great big town, I know you, you from Oke-She-Moke-She-Pop, well, it ain't no city, it's a little ol' whistle stop . . ."

It's our attempt at an up-to-date R&B dance hit, but it's also a poignant piece of poetry, Joe expressing all the excitement of the cultural transition from backwoods to big city, contrasting those days of courting his girl on the back of Grandpa's mule with the modern world of hot-rod cars. "Step into my Roadmaster," he invites her, "this time we going to ride in class, we gonna talk about the future and forget about the past."

It's an instant classic, and a few minutes later that same country girl is given still another modern twist. This time she's metaphorically linked to the craze for "Our Miss Brooks" and "I Love Lucy"—she becomes "TV Mama, the one with the big wide screen." With Little Johnny Jones's rollicking boogie-woogie background and Elmore's by-now-patented "Dust My Broom" guitar licks, Joe paints the picture: "She's got great big eyes and little bitty feet, and in the waist she's so nice and neat. . . ."

"GOOD GOD, LET ME TOUCH RAY CHARLES!"

Rainy night in Florida: distant thunder, lightning streaking the sky, open fields fragrant with wildflowers. I'm out in the boondocks, in Hallandale, a little country town south of Fort Lauderdale, having just watched Ray Charles perform in a show that includes a number of other R&B stars of the early fifties—Lowell Fulson, Pee Wee Crayton, Roy Brown, LaVern Baker.

Ray takes my arm as I lead him down from the bandstand, then a middle-aged black woman rushes up. Her words tumble out—like a prayer, a gospel chant—in a breath: *"Good God, let me touch Ray Charles!"* As she touches his arm, her eyes widen.

Ray stands still, allowing the moment, before nodding, indicating he's ready to move on.

Even in a dilapidated shack of a dance hall with sawdust on the floor and chickens out back, even on a bill with a host of other powerful performers, Ray Charles bears special distinction. Of all the artists I've worked with, only three rate the appellation "genius," and he was the first.

When I met him in 1953, he was twenty-three. I was thirty-six, and in spite of my conflicted feelings of anxiety on one hand and need for control on the other, I realized that the best thing I could do with Ray was leave him alone. He needed a producer like Ray Kroc needed a hamburger. Musically, Ray had everything. It was a privilege to watch him work, to see how he—and American music, for that matter—evolved through his own unique instincts. Our main job was to make certain the studio was ready when he was available and once having recorded him, to present him to as large a public as possible.

Our first encounter was in our office over Patsy's Restaurant. I was struck by his physical presence: strong, broad-shouldered, and barrel-chested, his rhythms simultaneously quick and cautious. Though led by an assistant, once inside a room Ray took no time to suss out the configurations, thereafter moving as one who'd seen all along. His speaking voice, like his singing voice, was deep but ever-changing, sometimes sounding old beyond his years, sometimes filled with youthful ebullience, sometimes sullen and withdrawn. His dark glasses were a symbol of his mystery, an emblem of some secret pain.

He once came to our house for dinner, but he and I had few personal conversations. Our business dealings were straight-ahead, not a single argument between us, yet I couldn't say we were close. I doubt that anyone was. Only later—through things Ray said or wrote, including his autobiography, *Brother Ray*—did I get the full story.

Born in the east Florida backwoods hard by the Georgia border, he lost his sight at age six. Nine years later, his mother died, leaving him alone at the St. Augustine School for the Blind. (Ironically, the place was segregated, no matter that the kids themselves couldn't discern black from white.) Ray had no family, no money, nothing save a keen intelligence and an extraordinary musical gift. At home his primary lessons had been learned at the Shiloh Baptist Church and from Wiley Pitman, a two-fisted hometown pianist in the boogie-woogie vein, the technically complex style that first impressed Ray. At school, where he learned Braille and classical music, Ray became a proficient reader and writer of music. With Artie Shaw as his model, he took up clarinet. On piano—well, Ray wrote, "I couldn't even carry Art Tatum's shit bucket." He also heard and loved "The Grand Ole Opry" on radio. "Jimmie Rodgers, Roy Acuff, Hank Snow, Hank Williams, and later Eddy Arnold—they all made an impression on me." He sponged up everything.

Fortunately, his mother had imbued in him a stubborn independence and the fierce conviction that he could do anything he pleased (a maternal attitude not unlike Elsa Wexler's). Rather than being a handicap, Ray's blindness motivated him to outperform the sighted. His early performances were checkered—indifferent to quite good. He began his professional career in 1946, after his mother died, quitting school to test his mettle in the real world. Even at fifteen, his sense of the contradictions and counterpoints of American music was unusually perceptive.

"I knew about Big Boy Crudup, Tampa Red, Blind Boy Fuller, and Tampa Red," he says. "I knew all about race records. I loved that stuff and could play it to death. I also played a lot of music that had been recorded by blacks and reinterpreted by whites. Good example was Freddie Slack's 'Cow-Cow Boogie,' or another popular song, 'Pistol Packin' Mama.' They were white hits, but based on black sounds and black rhythms going round years before. Those tunes got dark all over again—and in a hot hurry—when I got my hands on them. It wasn't that I was angry at those white cats for taking from blacks. I've always said, just 'cause Alexander Bell invented the phone don't mean Ray Charles can't use it. I gave the ofay boys credit for having good ears. Besides, I played with a white hillbilly band myself."

Ray's referring to the Florida Playboys. It's amazing to think that in the segregated South of 1948 he integrated a country-western band. "I could do it 'cause I could play the music right," Ray explains. "I could play that music with as much feeling as any other Southerner. But I also have another notion why I was left alone: A lot of the black/white thing in the South is caused by white men worrying 'bout black cats fucking with their women. Since they saw I couldn't see—I couldn't be checking over their little ladies—I wasn't a threat."

Paradoxically, Charles, hailed as a great original, was an absorber and an adapter. A pure artist and a commercial-minded survivor at the same time, Ray maintained himself in the early years by covering the Charles Brown and Nat Cole hits of the day in small clubs. In a typically gutsy move, he set out for Seattle in the late forties, sight unseen—he wanted to get as far away from Florida as possible. In Washington he formed a drummerless King Cole–derived group—piano, guitar, and bass—and called it the McSon Trio. Down in L.A., he cut a few sides for Jack Lauderdale's Downbeat/Swingtime label, and one of them, the Charles Brown–sounding "Baby, Let Me Hold Your Hand," was a medium-sized R&B hit in 1951.

The crucial moment came in 1952, when Ahmet bought his contract from Jack Lauderdale for $2,500. Slowly but surely, Ray began his ascent. His first two Atlantic sessions were mediocre. He was following the current trend in R&B, singing behind post-swing, big-beat charts. But soon the arrangements were simplified and the first mini-jewels were chiseled. Take, for example, the echo-chambered, bone-chilling blues "Losing Hand," written by Jesse Stone, an after-hours balm in excelsis; or Lowell Fulson's stark "Sinner's Prayer"; or the whimsical "It Should Have Been Me."

On balance: because Ray didn't write the songs and only lightly influenced the arrangements, and because the band was a for-hire studio cadre, these initial records are important only for Ray's stirring performances and the fact that Ahmet Ertegun wrote him a stomp, "Mess Around," that's part of the literature today.

I first "worked" with Brother Ray in New Orleans during the same trip we recorded Joe Turner's "Midnight Cannonball." We ran into Ray at Cosmo's studio and he asked whether we'd have time to record him and his pickup band. Hell, yes!

Fresh from his success with Guitar Slim, Ray's mind was on writing and arranging. His spasms of struggling seemed behind him. His musical vision was coming into focus. His band—still pro tem—was a group of erstwhile hard-boppers whose cards had been earned on the tin-shed R&B circuit. Since Cosmo was booked, we ran over to radio station WDSU and worked the better part of a night, the agreeable result being "Don't You Know." It was Ray's tune, Ray's chart; and while the side didn't sell big, it contained a jazz-funk riff that was immediately adopted by the hippest players of the day, from Horace Silver to Cannonball Adderley. Even Miles took note.

Looking back, it was a landmark session because of Ray's increasing involvement in every aspect of production. His voice had also lost almost all traces of Nat Cole and Charles Brown. Instead, there was a startling cry—direct, raw, riveted with feeling. The emerging sound was unmistakable, brand-new yet ancient as the woods, the country church of Ray's childhood. The breakthrough was close at hand.

It came eleven months later, in November of '54, in Atlanta. Ray had summoned us down to hear his new band, which was playing the Peacock Club. We arrived in early afternoon. Except for Ray and his group, the place was deserted. Ray counted off and they hit "I Got a Woman." I was staggered.

Ray had been living in Texas, where he'd picked up two saxists, Donald Wilkerson (who soloes on the recorded version of "I Got a Woman") and David "Fathead" Newman, who would be Ray's alter ego on tenor (also doubling on baritone and sometimes playing alto) for the next decade.

"My theory was this," Ray would expound. "If I could find cats who could play jazz, I could fix it so they could play my other little items— the rhythm-and-blues things. If a guy can handle jazz, that means he's a good musician, and it's easy for him to switch over to less demanding styles. Each of my horn players had to be able to stretch out on jazz tunes, play complicated figures if needed and also have that basic, bluesy down-home sound. Sometimes the band would be burning, sometimes it'd be moaning."

The next day we were both moaning and burning, recording at WGST, the Georgia Tech radio station, stopping every hour so the engineer could read the news over the air. It was a bizarre but brilliant day, the sound of a new music ringing in our ears. Besides "I Got a Woman," Ray set down "Greenbacks," "Come Back Baby," and "Blackjack." Finally he was full-fledged, the pattern set and near perfect: the band laid out except for the rhythm section while Ray sang a phrase. At the end of the phrase, he filled on piano, like Lloyd Glenn or Amos Milburn. But here's the kicker: Ray's band doubled the piano figure, voiced to Ray's prescription. The band was two trumpets, baritone sax doubling on alto or tenor, a second tenor sax, drums, bass, piano, and, eventually, no guitar. "I Got a Woman" would prove to be the first Ray Charles smash and also the archetypal Ray Charles song, a sanctified series of sixteen-bar gospel chord progressions. This was a radical departure for the blues-based repertoire of black popular music.

Ray had been singing spirituals since the age of three, and hearing blues for just as long. Those were his two main musical influences. And it was perfectly natural for him to blend them. Many of those first compositions were adaptations of gospel he had sung in quartets back in school. "You Better Leave That Woman Alone," for example, was originally called "You Better Leave That Liar Alone." Using church for pop purposes was immediately controversial and popular, though Ray was harshly criticized for "desecrating God's work" and was even anathematized in church during Sunday sermons. "I really didn't give a shit about that kind of criticism," he told me.

The concerns of the pious quickly faded as Ray's records hit. The public went crazy for his sound. For the next half-decade he made a slew of hits, mostly his own songs and the arrangements he dictated to that gem of a seven-piece band which had become an extension of his own voice, his own soul. His mining of the gospel lode resulted in "Hallelujah, I Love Her So," "This Little Girl of Mine," "Ain't That Love," "Tell All the World About You," and a host of other church-to-pop made-over originals. It didn't take long for more mainstream artists—Peggy Lee, Harry Belafonte, Elvis Presley—to record his songs.

In the studio, I was still more observer than participant. My aim was to learn from the maestro rather than weigh in with my jejune two cents' worth. Years later, however, I was tickled by Ray's observation that "Wexler and Ertegun could pop their fingers to the music on two and four." When he was recording "Ain't That Love," one of the church girls singing background was having a tough time following the stop-time beat on tambourine, and Ray was bugged. Ever cocky about my rhythm sense, I grabbed the tambourine and hit the lick myself.

"Who's that?" he asked.

"Me," I said.

"You got it, baby."

So it was Wexler on tambourine all the way through—sweating blood for fear of missing a beat.

And that's about all Ray ever needed from me in the studio. He was the first self-produced artist I'd ever known, and the model for people like Marvin Gaye and Stevie Wonder, whose independence wouldn't show up until the early seventies.

Observing Ray—on the road, cutting records, during rehearsals—I couldn't help but acknowledge his addiction. He himself has written openly about the heroin habit he didn't kick until the sixties. His knees would shake, his head would bob, his body would endure mini-convulsions. He was obviously hooked. At the same time, though, there wasn't an instance where his addiction interfered with his work. He was assiduously prompt and prepared. When he came to record, his arrangements were written out with painstaking precision. As a bandleader and producer, he was more than conscientious; he was meticulous and demanding, ready to reject the least instance of faulty intonation or rhythm. His own singing and playing were beyond reproach, his writing a paragon of art and commerce combined. When it came to Ray's professionalism, there could be no grounds for complaint. He worked his ass off.

He also continued to upgrade his band. In addition to Donald Wilkerson and Fathead Newman, both sterling saxists in the big-toned Texas tenor tradition, in Memphis he found Hank Crawford, who became to Charles what Billy Strayhorn was to Duke Ellington—an extension of his musical mind, who with the slightest indication could create arrangements with the same sensibility and voicings as the master himself. Hank's first stint was on baritone, but when Ray hired Leroy "Hog" Cooper from Dallas—one of the most underrated bari players of the modern era—Hank switched to alto, where his piercing, full-throated style would influence generations of saxists to come, most notably David

Sanborn. Had he concentrated on alto instead of piano, Ray admits, he would have wound up sounding like Hank. As an alto player, he loved Hank's dirty drawers.

In the beginning, Ray would sit there and dictate the arrangements, and Hank was so overcome that his hands shook as he made notes. After a while, though, he began anticipating Ray and soon copped his arranging style. Ray wanted seven pieces to sound like fifteen, and ultimately Hank got the knack. He became musical director. I compare those charts to those of the small Ellington groups with the idiosyncratic, personalized voices of Johnny Hodges, Barney Bigard, Lawrence Brown, Cootie Williams, and Ben Webster. I also think of the great John Kirby Sextet in full flight at the Onyx Club on 52nd Street.

Other exceptional musicians, like trumpeters Marcus Belgrave and Philip Guilbeau, added to Ray Charles's mix; but the heart of the matter, the men closest to the maestro, were finally Hank and Fathead, who would both become Atlantic recording artists in their own right.

Three female voices also became a vital part of the mix. Ray remembers hiring the Cookies away from Chuck Willis, another important singer on our label, but my recollection is different. The Cookies, with their gritty go-tell-it-on-the-mountain lead singer Margie Hendricks, were signed to Atlantic and had a good-selling record called "In Paradise." In 1956, Ray came to New York and felt the need for female harmonies while recording Doc Pomus's riveting "Lonely Avenue." I came up with the Cookies. Next thing I knew they hit the road with Ray, metamorphosed into the Raeletts, and became a permanent part of his entourage. Ray's innovation—carrying gospel-sounding background singers—became the norm, in both live performances and the recording studios, for everyone from Elvis to Dinah Washington. From then on, the "amen corner" became an institution in pop music.

Ray was as much a perfectionist with the girls as with his musicians. He'd give them their notes and hone their harmonies. I remember one atypical session when the Raeletts were having such a bad time hearing their parts he sent them home. With some skillful engineering by Tom Dowd, Ray sang his own four-part harmony in falsetto on "I Believe to My Soul," accompanied by his back-alley Fender Rhodes licks. (Ray was also first to turn the electric piano into as funky a vehicle as T-Bone's electric guitar.)

In the same session, Ray recorded his first country song, Hank Snow's "I'm Movin' On." He wanted me to hire Chet Atkins to play pedal steel guitar. Ray's instincts were good: he was thinking of the right ax, but the wrong player; Chet didn't play pedal style and, as it happens, wasn't available anyway. But Charley Macey, a New York City session guitarist, fit the bill perfectly. The song was on the flip side of "I Believe to My Soul" and never sold as a single, though it served as an important omen of cross-currents to come. And listening to the opening of "I'm Movin' On" today, I hear an inversion of a Ray Charles lick that became the underpinnings of "What'd I Say," the song that propelled him to the top of the charts.

Ray tested his tunes on the road before recording. When he was ready with fresh material, he'd call for studio time. Brother Ray's all business, and these phone conversations were short and sweet. He never hyped his own stuff—except once. Calling from out of town, he told me a tune he'd been trying out in the clubs was getting a strong response. It might, he said, be something unusual. For Ray, this was an extravagant rave.

He had written "What'd I Say" as an ad-lib filler to kill time at the end of a set at a midwestern dance club. He was the first to admit that he wrote out of not inspiration but need—the need for material. This time his invention was cosmic, a churchy call-and-response groove ground to the sounds of rapture and orgasm. The song was banned at a few stations, but the publicity probably helped, and Ray was in orbit.

For all his pioneering, though, he never considered himself a founding father of rock 'n' roll. His music is definitely on the grown-up side. Examine the songs—words *and* music—of Chuck Berry and Little Richard. Tunes like "Johnny B. Goode," "Sweet Little Sixteen," "Long Tall Sally," and "Good Golly, Miss Molly" were targeted for teens. Berry was writing for white adolescents out of a country bag, and his diction is unalloyed white middle America. As a composer, Ray was indifferent to market concerns. His sensibility is attuned to the rhythm and blues of the late forties, to sophisticated blues crooners like Charles Brown. But without taking aim, "What'd I Say" reached out and grabbed the dance-crazed youth market; Ray hit the jackpot with a song whose sexy hump-and-pump spirit horny teenagers found irresistible.

Soon this same live spirit swept over a concert, on May 28, 1959. In Atlanta, my pal Zenas "Daddy" Sears (the black-talking deejay who'd emigrated from New Jersey) filled Herndon Stadium with a bill featuring Ray, B. B. King, Buddy Johnson, Ruth Brown, Roy Hamilton, Huey Smith and the Clowns, the Drifters, and Jimmy Reed. With a single

Backstage with Brother Ray

microphone in center stage, Sears recorded the proceedings in order to cull a few spots to include in a radio promotion for his next Ray Charles concert. When he sent me a tape of three minutes of music, I got the chill bumps. The sound was clear as glare ice. I couldn't wait to get Zenas on the phone and ask how much more there was. He had the whole damn thing on tape.

Twenty-four hours later, UPS put it in my hands. I remember it was one of those muggy Manhattan nights in June, boiling hot, the air conditioner crapped out, my mind fried with a hundred screaming phone calls, stale cigarettes, black coffee, and studio messes. I was dead. I put on the tape, and suddenly the sound of Fathead's sax levitated me over the city's towers right down into Georgia. His opening licks on "The Right Time" signaled the start of one of the era's great concerts. Ray was in blistering form, matched by Margie Hendricks's spittin'-tough take on "Tell the Truth," screaming—miraculously in tune—as he's never screamed before or since, rendering a drawn-out "Drown in My Tears" with the hallucinatory vision of a fallen angel, his vocal falling out at the precise moment Fathead's tenor falls in, the two of them ham-and-egging it, cooking up a sorrowful storm, the Hank Crawford–voiced septet a marvel of stripped-down harmony, the crowd crazy for the blind man's truth bleeding from the stage, Zenas shouting at the climax, "The high priest . . . the high priest!"

Ray Charles in Person became a classic, overshadowing his live concert at the 1958 Newport Jazz Festival, which was excellent nonetheless, and especially significant in demonstrating to the jazz community—and to the elitist jazz critics—Ray's ability to swing in several directions at once. It was, in fact, at another jazz festival that Leonard Bernstein began moving toward jazz. "Those were great blues drums you played on that number," he complimented Shelly Manne. " 'Blues drums'? Tell you what, Lenny," said Shelly, "you stick to the Bach and we'll take care of the boogie-woogie."

Ray Charles took care of it all; simultaneously, he was a bopper, a bluesman, a gospel shouter, and the initiator of a back-to-the-roots jazz/ soul movement. Ray saw past categories and simply played what he felt. As his R&B singles sold throughout this period, though, we urged him to tend to his pure jazz side. Not that Ray required much convincing: he was a believer, as were Ahmet and myself. Jazz was our first passion, our obsession since childhood, and as vital a part of the label as R&B. To give real insight into the growth of Atlantic's fabled jazz catalogue, however, I must introduce another remarkable Ertegun.

BROTHER,
BROTHER

Ahmet looked upon Herb Abramson as a brother, and the deterioration of that relationship was painful for all of us. When Herb returned from the Army in 1955, Ahmet and I had enjoyed two years of unprecedented success. Ray Charles, LaVern Baker, Joe Turner, Ruth Brown, the Clovers ("Lovey Dovey"), the Robins ("Smokey Joe's Cafe"), Clyde McPhatter and the Drifters ("Money Honey," "Such a Night," "Honey Love")—the hits kept coming. We'd developed the roster as a team, more often than not working in the studio together. Rather than break up the combo, we were convinced that giving Herb his own label, Atco, was the best way to assure him his own niche. After all, he'd been producing long before either Ahmet or me.

He seemed pleased, but things never worked out. First of all, when Herb returned his marriage to Miriam was over, straining the atmosphere in the office. Moreover, ever since Atlantic's inception, Herb had been president. Even during his Army stint he retained his title and drew full salary. We wouldn't have had it any other way. Early on it looked as though certain acts under the Atco domain—the Coasters and Bobby Darin—would prove profitable. But there were personality problems, and finally the partners decided that Ahmet would be company president. When he got the news, Herb stalked out and, after protracted deliberations, received $300,000 in a stock/bonus buyout. Being cash poor—the chronic ailment of an independent label—we painstakingly raised the money to buy back Herb's stock, and eventually the stock belonging to Miriam and the silent partner, Dr. Sabit. By the end of the fifties, the company was wholly owned by three people—myself, Ahmet, and Ahmet's older brother, Nesuhi, who would play a vital part in re-shaping the company's image.

Nesuhi Ertegun had the temperament of an autocrat, the style of an aristocrat, and the sensibility of a scholar. He was a man I loved. I had met him, along with Ahmet and Herb, as a jazz hound in the late forties. Thereafter he'd gone to California, where he began his career, and was still there when I joined Atlantic in 1953. Among the cognoscenti he was already a legend. He had gone to the Sorbonne, lived in the same building as Sartre, and broken bread with Camus. When it came to knowledge of New Orleans music, Nesuhi was formidable. He was responsible for a Kid Ory revival, having arranged for the trombonist to appear on Orson Welles's coast-to-coast radio program in Los Angeles for a month of programs. He had his own label, Crescent City, and also worked with Lester Koenig, owner of Contemporary Records, on a Dixieland subsidiary, Good Time Jazz. When Nesuhi visited us in New York, Ahmet and I were fascinated to learn he was teaching the history of jazz at UCLA, the first course of its kind for college credit. That such a subject was grist for the academic mill seemed implausible, even hilarious. "Let me suggest a final exam question," I proposed to Nesuhi. "'How much did Mezz Mezzrow charge Louis Armstrong for an ounce of grass?'"

Between Nesuhi and myself a mocking pseudo-ironic tone evolved as camouflage for the abiding affection we had for each other. I would rag him for his cosmopolitan bias—soccer, six-day bicycle races, European boxing, cabaret, and talismanic names such as Letourner, Cerdan, Guitry, Cochet, and Django that evoked his coming of age in the capitals of the Old World. If I countered with the likes of Reggie MacNamara, Jake LaMotta, Eddie Lang, Lee Wiley, or Bill Tilden, he'd snort derisively at my parochialism, closing the discussion by slapping the table with a heavy Byzantine hand: *"Finita la commedia!"*

One of our great running disputes revolved around fiddlers. He was partial to Frenchman Stéphane Grappelli, and I to Joe Venuti, Stuff Smith, and Eddie South, the Dark Angel of the Violin. I always felt Grappelli's roots went back to the great Western swing fiddlers, whom I admired tremendously. My guys, though, played with the syncopation of pure jazz. Nesuhi would have none of it: for him, Grappelli was the Alfred de Musset of violinists, the great lyrical romantic poet, the jazz stylist par excellence.

In 1955, Nesuhi announced something shocking: he was about to go to work for one of our chief competitors, Lew Chudd, owner of Imperial Records. While in California, Nesuhi had never seemed threatening to us; after all, he'd been working in jazz esoterica. But this was different. With its roster of New Orleans–based artists like Smiley Lewis, the Spiders, and especially Fats Domino—and with Ricky Nelson lurking in the wings—Imperial was an established firm. In fact, Chudd was one of the guys Ahmet enjoyed needling most. Only a few weeks before, with Fats's "Ain't That a Shame" climbing the charts, Ahmet had called Lew from his bungalow at the Beverly Hills Hotel, disguising his voice with the dark accents of the Deep South.

"Hey, Chudds," said Ahmet.

"This is Mr. Chudd. Who is *this*?"

"This is Fats's uncle, Chester Domino."

Chudd, a humorless man who looked the part of a funeral director, took the bait. "How can I help you, Mr. Domino?"

"I been knowing Fats since the day he was born. Dangled him on my knee. Raised him myself. Taught him everything he know."

"Yes?"

"Well, I just got to L.A. and I see this is one mighty expensive city."

Lew's losing patience. "I'm a busy man, Mr. Domino."

"Me too. And hungry. I could use a taste."

"A taste of what?"

"Look, Chudd, I know you been beating my nephew out of his royalty bread, and I figure the least you can do is lay a little something on me."

"That's outrageous!"

"No more outrageous than you screwing my boy out of his bread."

"I'll have you know, Mr. Domino, that all our royalty accounts are kept on IBM machines and audited according to—"

"I don't give a shit about no I, B, and M or no B, M, and I. I want what's right."

It took another five minutes for Chudd to figure out that Ahmet was on the other end. The shirttail to this story is that Ahmet then went over to Imperial's offices, announcing up and down the halls that everybody had the day off.

Now it was Nesuhi telling Ahmet—no joke—that Imperial wanted him to head up a jazz line and develop a catalogue of LPs. The long-play, 33⅓ format was gaining popularity. Phonograph equipment was evolving; the customers wanted better-quality recordings, and the majors, with their deep pockets, were forging ahead in album production and packaging while independents like us were struggling to stay even.

And so Ahmet, who adored his older brother, insisted that he come in with us, and I was delighted that Nesuhi agreed. In 1955 we each kicked in stock and made him a partner. Nesuhi's focus was on the development of superb jazz. In addition, all album packaging, including R&B, became his special domain—artwork, photography, liner notes, sleeves—and in a very short while the Atlantic logo graced a line of exceptionally tasteful and distinctive covers. Within those covers were extraordinary records. The catalogue he amassed, starting in the fifties, reflects not only his taste and discernment but his understanding of the cataclysmic changes jazz was undergoing.

He brought from Los Angeles the breezes blowing over the West Coast scene—the subdued sounds of Shorty Rogers, Shelly Manne, Jimmy Giuffre, Conte Candoli, Lou Levy. Since Miles Davis's famed "Birth of the Cool" session, the kicked-back reaction to Bird's bop had burgeoned. Other artists whom Nesuhi supervised, such as altoist Lee Konitz and pianist Lennie Tristano, had a soft approach as well—brilliant, cerebral, progressive. Nesuhi also had the ears to hear not just the leaders of the countermovement—the East Coast hard-boppers (Art Blakey's Jazz Messengers, for instance) who disdained the breezy Californians for their limpness—but the bold avant-gardists like Ornette Coleman and, later, John Coltrane, who went to the edge and in some cases jumped off. In a far more conservative direction—and interestingly enough, in spite of his many marriages and bon-vivant lifestyle, Nesuhi was a conservative man—he also cultivated the careers of mainstream artists such as Herbie Mann and Les McCann.

His most important collaboration was with the Modern Jazz Quartet. Ahmet and I were friendly with the MJQ's managers, Monte Kay and Pete Kameron, and helped bring the group to the label. It was Nesuhi, though, who championed and produced them. They became the first concert-hall chamber group in jazz—the Budapest String Quartet of the postbop movement—and their music was an intriguing mirror of the intelligence, charm, and complexity of Nesuhi himself.

"When I began with the Modern Jazz Quartet," Nesuhi told the BBC in their excellent documentary on the history of Atlantic, "it was clear that the jazz audience, unlike the R&B market, was more white than black. It was also clear that this all-black group was typical in absolutely no way. Their two dominant personalities were in marked contrast to one another. John Lewis, the musical director, was the consummate professional, always controlled, with a strong sense of classical music, a man who could play Bach as well as anyone. Milt Jackson, the vibist, was certainly one of the most fluent improvisers of the last forty years and essentially a blues player. Then, of course, bassist Percy Heath and drummer Connie Kay built a richly supportive rhythm base for the soloists. *Fontessa*, a small suite inspired by the Renaissance commedia dell'arte, was their first Atlantic album, and quite successful. The MJQ possessed unusual dignity without sacrificing an iota of swing. They were elegant dressers, eloquent speakers, and their presence on the great concert stages of America and Europe upgraded the image of the jazz artist, much as Duke Ellington had done in his day. The MJQ and I recorded over twenty albums together. Without question the group became the backbone of our jazz catalogue."

Nesuhi relished the refinement of the MJQ, but he also loved the fire of mad shaman Charlie Mingus, one of the most important and revolutionary performers and composers of the period. Mingus was on a revival tear when he came to our label with his Jazz Workshop, ferociously digging up the gospel roots of modern music and constructing works of contradictory genius, at once moving forwards and back, his screaming explorations into a jet-fueled future executed with a wide-eyed, breathless, backwoods wonder. He inspired his cohorts—Jackie McLean, John Handy, J. R. Monterose, Booker Ervin, Eric Dolphy, Jimmy Knepper, Horace Parlan, Mal Waldron, Dannie Richmond—into herculean feats of daring; and many of his records produced by Nesuhi—*Pithecanthropus Erectus, Oh Yeah, The Clown, Blues and Roots*—endure as undaunted and supercharged works of art.

Among Ahmet, Nesuhi, and myself, there were never any discussions as to what profits jazz contributed to the company. Jazz didn't sell a fraction of what rhythm and blues did—not then, not now. If a representative Mingus side sold twenty thousand to thirty thousand copies in the fifties, my guess is that were it first released today, it would sell about the same. All the partners would have relished a jazz hit on the order of Dave Brubeck's *Jazz Goes to College* or Erroll Garner's *Concert by the Sea*—"gold albums" that sold over five hundred thousand copies. That was not to be, but we were satisfied if our jazz line paid its way. And it

My man Nesuhi

delighted Nesuhi to record the likes of Carmen McRae and Mose Allison, the singer, writer, and pianist, whom I considered the William
Faulkner of Southern blues.

Nesuhi was the man; he produced hundreds of wonderful jazz albums. Only on a couple of occasions did Ahmet and I help out. I collab-
orated with Nesuhi on Betty Carter's *Round Midnight*. Earlier, Ahmet
and I had contributed to Chris Connor's long and lush George Gershwin
set. Along with June Christy, Jerri Southern, Helen Merrill, and Julie
London, Chris with her smoky style exemplified the cool school of singers founded by Anita O'Day, herself a student, as all jazz singers are, of
Billie Holiday.

Ours was not a company that proceeded according to any precon-
ceived plans. Terms like "marketing" meant nothing to us. We were
trying to sell records we enjoyed making. Like the music we admired
most, we were improvising the business as we went along. I was hard-

core about accounts receivable, about staying on our distributors and pressing plants, about hustling the deejays and plugging our product. But what really knocked me out was when Nesuhi suggested that we record a series of Ray Charles *jazz* albums, highlighting the keyboard side of his personality. The result was the *Soul Brothers* and *Soul Meeting* albums with Milt Jackson, remarkable sessions of subtle and expansive small-group blues, complemented by guitarists Skeeter Best and Kenny Burrell, bassists Percy Heath and the unforgettable Oscar Pettiford, drummers Connie Kay and Art Taylor, saxist Billy Mitchell. Dialoguing like long-lost friends, Milt and Ray were soul brothers indeed— relaxed, chatty, honest, respectful of each other's time, patient listeners with nowhere to go except further into the landscape of their pasts and the sorrowful joys of their songs. The emergence of albums in the mid-fifties further added to our good timing. Five or six seven-minute stretched-out jazz blues was the perfect menu for an album's worth of material. Ray loved it. He even blew his back-alley alto on a couple of numbers, and his piano playing was never more satisfying.

Earlier, Ahmet had produced a marvelous trio date with songs such as "Dawn Ray" and "The Man I Love." You could hear Bud Powell in Ray's piano style. "Everyone was talkin' 'bout Bud back then," says Ray, "but I actually preferred Hank Jones. I liked his touch, and I had a great feeling for his solo work. With all his wonderful taste, he reminded me of Nat Cole."

The sessions for which we arranged the personnel were fine—Ray was a paragon of musical flexibility—and it should be noted that a very young Quincy Jones wrote precociously sensitive arrangements for several songs, among them "Hornful Soul," "Joy Ride," "Doodlin'," and "Ain't Misbehavin'," with Fathead's lovelorn son-of-Lester take on Fats Waller's sweet melody. At one point I suggested that Ray improvise a piano solo on the sixteen-bar gospel changes of "A Fool for You," and called it "Sweet Sixteen Bars."

But for airtight fly-right all-night listening, there's nothing like Ray Charles/Hank Crawford charts performed by the self-contained Ray Charles band, whose first instrumental album Nesuhi and I supervised. Titled *Fathead: Ray Charles Presents David Newman*, it contains "Hard Times," Fathead's alto-articulated theme, a haunting anthem still being played at righteous blues bars throughout the land.

There are critics who consider *The Genius of Ray Charles* a breakthrough. I can't disagree. "Swanee River Rock," "I Had a Dream," "Yes

Indeed," and a score of other singles were sparkling miniatures, marvels of invention. But the *Genius* album set a pattern from which he'd rarely deviate for the rest of his career—singing in front of large ensembles. The double-edged concept afforded Ray something he'd long desired: accompaniment by a full-sized, brass-bristling big band on one side, and fully orchestrated strings on the other.

Even though I'm listed as co-producer, Nesuhi took the lead from Ray's original idea. I'd been sending him some of our new releases, and on one of them, a Chris Connor album, he was particularly taken by the string charts. He asked me who did the arrangements, and when I told him Ralph Burns, he recognized the name from Woody Herman's band. One of Ray's favorite charts was Burns's "Early Autumn."

It was 1959, and Ray was ready to make a stylistic move. He'd lived with the idea long enough, he told us, and wanted to make a big-band album. One side would be ballads with strings; the other, uptempo numbers with horns. He selected the tunes: "Am I Blue?"; "Just for a Thrill"; "Come Rain or Come Shine"; a Louis Jordan song called "Don't Let the Sun Catch You Crying"; an old Charles Brown number, "Tell Me You'll Wait for Me"; and "You Won't Let Me Go," a Buddy Johnson song Ray had heard as a kid.

On the other side of the album, Ray decided to incorporate his own small band into the larger one, and hired Quincy, his buddy from Seattle days, to write the charts. The material included "Two Years of Torture," a tune by his pal Percy Mayfield, and another associated with Louis Jordan, "Let the Good Times Roll."

The ballad session went smoothly and has been compared with Billie Holiday's *Lady in Satin* or Sinatra's *In the Wee Small Hours* for time-capsule consideration. The tenderness with which Ray caresses the melodies and lyrics is astounding.

The big-band double date, though, was no picnic. Both musically and literally we were going into uncharted territory for Ray. The truth is that Quincy was supposed to have written all the charts, but hadn't. He gave Nesuhi the bad news on a Friday before the Monday date. In a flash, Nesuhi hired Al Cohn, Ernie Wilkins, and Johnny Acea to write over-the-weekend scores, which were still coming in Monday morning—and still being copied—while the players assembled in the studio. As the cats were playing one song, sheets of papers noting the next song were flying everywhere, and special couriers were arriving on motorbikes with last-minute changes.

I was sweating bullets. We'd recruited an all-star cast of star sidemen from the Ellington and Basie bands. The session was the most expensive in Atlantic history, and disorder ruled; panic was in the air, and everyone on edge. Trumpeter Ernie Royal wanted to hit a high A that hadn't been written. He asked for Quincy's approval.

"I'd like it better," said Ray, "if you hit your high G, so we'll have the tonic on top. It'd be tighter that way."

Ernie turned to Quincy and asked, "Is that all right?"

Ray intervened. "I ain't gonna tell you wrong, baby."

That broke the ice. Laughter rang out, and despite the whirlwind of frenzy in which we worked, the session was a killer, the big band swinging to the heavens, Ray singing his ass off.

The only other memorable band date I worked with Nesuhi had involved Joe Turner. In a similar vein to the Ray Charles move, we'd wanted to indulge ourselves and change Joe's groove for one album. His seminal rhythm-and-blues hits—"Shake, Rattle and Roll," "Flip Flop and Fly," "Corrine Corrina"—were great, but we thought it time to revert to the style of Joe's John Hammond productions with boogie-woogie legend Pete Johnson on piano. John gave me Pete's number. He was living in Buffalo, not in the best of health. But Pete came, and Ernie Wilkins wrote the charts for a Basie-based octet (including Joe Newman, Lawrence Brown, Frank Wess, Freddie Green, and Walter Page). The tunes were straight-ahead killer Kansas City shuffles—"Cherry Red," "Roll 'Em Pete," "Low Down Dog," "Wee Baby Blues"—and the arrangements mean and lean, Joe's vocals salty and strong. The result, *The Boss of the Blues*, is *sub specie aeternitatis*.

*N*esuhi brought Atlantic into the age of the long-play album. Singles were no longer the story, although they continued to pay the bills. We entered the epoch of the 33⅓ rpm with a tony style typical of the Erteguns. There were instances, though, when Nesuhi's cosmopolitan manners were less than efficacious. Just imagine this: Chicago, heartland of America, where the nation's hungriest and horniest businessmen loved to flock, leaving their wives and children back home while they, the family providers, attended conventions and meetings marked by widespread depravity—overeating, overboozing, and various forms of sexual frivolity.

This was the general atmosphere in which we had our first sales meeting with our distributors, in 1959. We were gathered in one of the better hotels along Lake Michigan. The group we assembled was typical of the industry, streetwise salesmen focused on profits. Our idea was to shake their hands, give them a good breakfast—the cost of which we shared with Chess—and present them with a quick and enthusiastic overview of our new releases. Maybe we didn't have a fancy floor show with MGM's Connie Francis or Decca's Carmen Miranda wearing fifty dollars' worth of fruit on her head, but we did have hot records to hype.

We also knew that the night before, at a well-attended party, many of the boys had gotten blasted. Their heads were hurting, their attention spans waning, and only a fast-paced, easy-to-digest presentation would serve. All went well until Nesuhi took the podium. His job was to explain our new venture into albums, primarily jazz, but also compilations of singles by our best-selling R&B artists. Somehow he never made it past the jazz albums.

Nesuhi's erudition never failed to impress me. I was delighted when he suggested I read Balzac's *La Physiologie du mariage* or André Breton's dialogues with Marcel Duchamp. I like to think that occasionally I may have had similarly hip tips for him. But this was different; here was Nesuhi in front of a room of jukebox roughnecks limning the historical influences on little-known pianist George Wallington or the frolicsome interplay between low-registered clarinetist Jimmy Giuffre and the Modern Jazz Quartet. The audience yawned; I squirmed; Ahmet broke into a sweat. Yet Nesuhi droned on. But before he drove the guys into irreversible catatonia, Ahmet started hissing at his older brother the Turkish epithet *"Pezevenk!"* Others missed the meaning, but finally— and it took maybe ten minutes more—Nesuhi terminated his thesis.

NEED, GREED, AND ALAN FREED

We all had our faults. I had my temper, my inherent disbelief in my employees' abilities. I was a despot, semienlightened. Ahmet was sometimes prone to panic. Occasionally he'd be tempted to give up on an artist when, in fact, the big hit was just around the corner; I, too, was capable of similar haste.

In the final analysis, we balanced each other. I'd want to make an instant decision—say, whether to sign a singer—and Ahmet, who avoided the office for long periods, wouldn't be around for the deliberations. I'd go crazy looking for him, insisting that we had to go one way or another. "But Jerry," he liked to reply, "time's on our side. Let's let them wait. Let them come around to us." Sometimes he was right; sometimes he wasn't. I never quite adjusted to his procrastinating style, and I don't think he ever fully adapted to my compulsiveness. But we worked it out, not just because we respected each other's intelligence but, more to the point, because the records kept selling. Until one day they didn't.

During my first four years, 1953 through 1957, we grew at a satisfying, mostly exhilarating clip—cash poor, but we lived well. In 1956, Shirley, the kids, and I moved from our rented house in Bayside and bought a large house with a big yard on Sycamore Drive in Great Neck. I'd finally made it to the suburbs, even though, except for business dinners to which I brought associates, I used the house mainly as a bedroom; I was always in the city, always in motion, either in the office or at the recording studio. My yearly income was probably up to fifty thousand dollars. I was aware of missing my kids, but I really didn't try to remedy the problem. I was on the fast track—rushing artists into the studio, rushing advance acetate copies to deejays—and unwilling to lose a beat. To increase my efficiency, I even hired a driver. "The funny thing about that," remembers Shirley, "was that Jerry got so frustrated directing the driver—telling him which routes to take and what cars to pass—that he wound up behind the wheel himself. Jerry drove the driver."

I drove myself hard. I don't know if this was the legacy of Elsa, but what I did know was that the mortality rate in the music business was scary. The rise of R&B and rock 'n' roll fairly parallels the fall of the independents. The more money youth music made, the more the big labels loomed. Though there were exceptions, the trend was clear, even at the time. By the late sixties—and certainly in the decades to follow—the pattern of failing independent labels was irreversible and, according to some, insidious.

Survival was a devilish feat, due to both the caprices of consumer taste and the difficulty of getting your records on the radio, the crucial marketing move. You had to meet the distributor, the deejay, or the program director in person. Essentially, you had to go to the station and pay for the favor of getting your single played. Back then there were no laws against pay-for-play. In fact, you'd have to be a fool, or wildly self-destructive, not to have paid the piper. I neither objected nor moralized. We were paying for advertising, plain and simple. Many of the personnel we paid, especially deejays, were woefully undersalaried in proportion to their importance. They deserved what they got. Not all payments were cash. Payment might be a cheap sweater, a bottle of rye, or—at certain times, and usually at conventions—the introduction to a companionable lady. After a while, though, we got disgusted with pimping and stopped cold.

Atlantic's reputation in the music industry was—and remains—several cuts above the norm. While some of our competitors fucked their artists outrageously, denying them proper royalties, we were considered honest and fair, neither mobsters nor cheats. But neither were we candy-asses when it came to competition. We played to win. And had some goddamn good belly laughs along the way.

In 1956, in the dead of winter, Ahmet and I, feet frozen and bone tired from a bumpy prop-plane ride, taxied through Memphis, Tennessee, to WHBQ, where Dewey Phillips's "Red Hot and Blue" was on the air and on a roll. Dewey was one of those black-voiced Caucasoid poets, a dazzling technician at the turntable, directing comments into the mike for

public consumption and, a nanosecond later, off-mike for the delecta-
tion of the hangers-on in the control room. "Spinning this out for all the
Little Richard fans," he announced, before covering the mike and adding "and raunchy motherfuckers" while reaching for the ringing phone.

In the middle of this daredevil deejay act we were listening to "Rip
It Up" while waiting for a break in the action. When it came, I used my
best Southern chops and politely introduced myself.

"I'm Jerry Wexler from Atlantic Records," I said, holding out my
hand, "and this is my partner Ahmet Ertegun."

At that moment, the song ended and Dewey was back on the air.
"Got a couple more Yankee record thieves in the studio tonight, folks.
They in here to loot and steal us blind, but 'fraid they're a little late. Ol'
Leonard Chess been here and gone. Done cleaned us out."

General laughter. After the show Dewey took us over to the Variety
Club, where Elvis Presley was in the corner having a beer. Dewey had
broken Elvis's early singles on Sam Phillips's Sun label by playing them
nonstop. In fact, not long before this encounter in Memphis, Sam Phillips had Elvis's contract up for sale, and we bid up to $30,000. I loved
his singing—that incredible fusion of stone country and deep black soul
delivered in a gorgeous, melodic voice almost operatic in its breadth and
timbre. He combined hillbilly and rhythm and blues, the harmonious
marriage of two tough styles destined to coexist for decades to come.
That's not to say I had any inkling that he'd emerge as the Jesus of rock.
I simply dug his voice. If I had had foresight about the staggering profits,
I might have found a way to outbid RCA (whose $40,000 offer was un-
derwritten by Gene Aberbach of publishers Hill & Range). As it was, we
didn't think much about it and, if truth be known, might have been relieved that the final price was over our heads. If Elvis had accepted our
offer, we would've had to scramble even to come up with the thirty
grand.

But Elvis wasn't to sing that night at the Variety Club. Ahmet was.

"Tell me," Ahmet asked Dewey, each of us fortified by a few bour-
bons and branches, "when Leonard Chess came through town, did he
sing our latest Ray Charles release?"

"What you talking about, man?"

"I want to know if Leonard did a rendition of 'Hallelujah, I Love
Her So'?"

"You can't be serious," Dewey replied. "What for would he do that?"

"For the same reason," Ahmet said, pausing to clear his throat, "that

I sing Muddy Waters's 'I'm Your Hoochie Coochie Man.' I push his tunes wherever I go. You mean to say he doesn't do the same for us?"

With that, Ahmet stood at the table and sang "I'm Your Hoochie Coochie Man" from beginning to end, copying Muddy's best licks. Knocked out by the sight of a Turkish dude blowing the nasty blues, Dewey fell off the chair—and from that moment on, Mr. Red Hot and Blue was our hoss.

I loved Dewey, and not simply because he played the shit out of our records. Here was a guy who began by playing records over a loud-speaker in a Memphis department store. His jive was so strong he wound up the hottest radio jockey in town, second to none at making hits. His lexicon was unique. He referred to everybody, including himself, as "Elvis." "Elvis," he'd tell me on the phone, "this is Elvis. Elvis is coming to New York." The real Elvis dug him, and so did Sam Phillips. He soon became the beneficiary of the Presley cornucopia. Limousines, private jets, Vegas, showgirls—Dewey's life transformed from the simple to the baroque.

Then came the problems. An ulcerated sore on his shin refused to heal, and the painkillers that were prescribed are what finally did him in. He lost the "Red Hot and Blue" show and hung around Memphis unemployed. All through his decline we were in touch. It broke my heart to see him going from town and town (me often fronting the car-fare), losing one radio gig after another. Sam Phillips, though, took care of Dewey until the day he died.

*O*ur roster had been expanding. In 1956, we signed Chuck Willis, having courted his managers for over a year. I admired his songwriting as well as his singing. After Elmore Hope, Chuck was the second black R&B act to sport a bejeweled turban. The emcees introduced him as "Sheik of the Shake," and he was especially popular in his home territory of Atlanta, where he'd been discovered by Daddy Sears.

Soon after he'd written his first hit on Atlantic, a gorgeous ballad called "It's Too Late," he proposed to record a standard. I expected something like "Body and Soul" or "Tenderly," but got "C.C. Rider" instead and was delighted that Chuck viewed the old Ma Rainey blues as a standard. The record still gives me chills: Tremoloing marimbas set the mood. Chuck tells the story with utter conviction, the (clearly) Caucasian backup group weighing in with clean, strong backgrounds and Gene

"Daddy G." Barge blowing a tenor sax solo that sets the stage for King Curtis, who would later be such an integral conveyor of the Atlantic sound. In fact, I cannibalized pieces of "C.C. Rider," using the same tenor lick on LaVern Baker's "I Cried a Tear" and Chuck's "What Am I Living For?" (Using the elements of one record to bolster another was common practice, and we were adepts.) The lick itself, which still lives in the tradition, deserves notation:

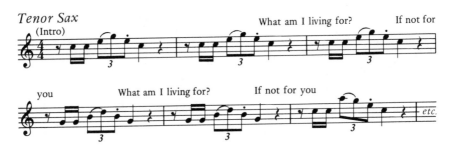

On the strength of the rhythm pattern of "C.C. Rider," Chuck's first pop hit, Dick Clark anointed him "King of the Stroll," a made-up dance popularized on "American Bandstand." In early 1958, Chuck recorded "What Am I Livin' For?" backed with "(I Don't Want to) Hang Up My Rock and Roll Shoes," a poignant and unknowing augury of his death three months later from a bleeding ulcer. Chuck died on the operating table in Atlanta, barely thirty years old. For the posthumous release of *I Remember Chuck*, the album cover displayed his headstone, his birth and death dates, and a dozen roses strewn across his grave. The critics deemed it tacky, but I think it's lovely. If it was kitsch taste, it was *my* kitsch.

I place Ivory Joe Hunter alongside Chuck. They were both sweet balladeers leaning towards country singing—Ivory Joe a touch more than Chuck. I believe Ivory Joe, together with Ray Charles, set the stage for the merger of black blues ballads and white country music in the sixties—and singers like Solomon Burke, Arthur Alexander, Betty Lavette, Dorothy Moore, Joe Simon, and Clarence Carter.

Dig deep into the roots of both modes—blues and country—and you'll find a common thread. The bottom of the Southern agrarian ladder society is the locus of America's pain and misery. You can hear it, for instance, in the Delmore Brothers' anguished thirties plaint "Blues Stay Away from Me," which I recorded in the seventies with Doug Sahm,

Signing Ivory Joe Hunter

Bob Dylan, and Dr. John. As a kid, without a frame of reference, I'd heard Vernon Dalhart's "The Prisoner's Song." Not even knowing it was a country tune, I was touched to tears: "If I had the wings of an angel, over these prison walls I would fly." I picked up on Riley Puckett's "Ragged but Right," Gid Tanner and his Skillet Lickers' "Ida Red," Milton Brown's "Hesitation Blues," and any number of other Western swing classics from the mid-thirties by people like Bob Wills and W. Lee O'Daniel, who went stumping with his band and made governor of Texas.

In 1950 Ivory Joe, a prolific tunesmith, recorded "I Almost Lost My Mind," first an R&B hit for Joe, then a pop smash when Pat Boone covered it six years later. After we signed Joe in 1954, he made any number of tough sides—"A Tear Fell," "You Mean Everything to Me"—but it wasn't until "Since I Met You Baby," a spinoff of "I Almost Lost My Mind," that he crossed over. We were overjoyed. Ivory Joe was a love, a game hunter from Monroe, Louisiana, who at Christmas would mail me a haunch of venison; it would arrive dripping blood, unrefrigerated and pungent.

"Since I Met You Baby" was recorded at a session Ahmet and I supervised. It was satisfying to see our ideas—and borrowings—working so well. The truth is that we lifted the arrangement of Pat Boone's steal of Joe's original "I Almost Lost My Mind." Ray Ellis wrote the light vocal backgrounds. We also put in a turnaround from "Santa Fe Blues" which has become a standard.

At the break, alto saxist Leon Cohen, noted for his pure tone, played the unadorned melody against the humming vocal group, a device we lifted from Boone's cover. Ivory Joe sang it straight, and the thing went through the roof—an ironic instance of the imitated imitating the imitator.

For all our cleverness, though, after Chuck Willis and Ivory Joe, our records suddenly stopped selling, and we started to panic.

Until that point I'd been making regular payments to an Alan Freed contact. The first Monday morning of the month we would meet in the cloak room of the Brill Building, where I'd hand him a paper bag with six hundred dollars in cash to keep Alan happy. It was a purely defensive move. The baksheesh didn't guarantee play for any particular record; we were only buying access.

By then Freed was the most powerful deejay in America, the one ofay playing black music who took it much further than anyone before him. I have to give him credit for that. His story is well known—an eccentric obsessed with Wagnerian opera (he named one of his daughters Sieglinde), black jive, and rhythm and blues. He started out in radio in New Castle, Pennsylvania, playing symphonic and chamber music, passed through Akron, and wound up in Cleveland on WJW, the big white-audience station broadcasting the Indians' baseball games. That's where he became the madman "Moondog," a gravel-voiced charmer, tireless concert promoter, and hard-drinking enthusiast who hooked a whole city on the sounds of a black nation. His defenders said he lived every note of the music, loved it to the depths of his soul. He was far from the first black-sounding white deejay, but Alan led untold legions of whites to R&B like nobody else before or since. It's as though he lit the fuse that exploded R&B into full-bore rock 'n' roll—a term, incidentally, that he himself popularized.

When he arrived at New York's WINS, he was managed by Morris Levy, Birdland owner and mobbed-up music mogul, had more power than anyone realized, and reportedly was making $75,000 a year. He'd been good to the Chess Brothers in Chicago—they couldn't have conquered the Midwest without him—and I soon realized he was someone with whom I had to work. Through connections in the industry, I also realized that Alan dealt with two categories of record people—those who were in on a pass and those who weren't. We weren't. The free riders were either Alan's impoverished cronies, hanging on by their teeth in the record business, or wealthy wheeler-dealers like Morris with whom Alan was in business. He viewed the Erteguns and me as marks, paying customers. I was happy to be in the ball game at all; it meant that I had access. The accretion of his power and the brashness with which he wielded his influence meant that, through mere indifference, he could do tremendous harm. In addition to his powerful radio show, his rock 'n' roll concert promotions at the Brooklyn Paramount became institutions in themselves. As it happened, they often featured Atlantic artists.

When hard times set in for us, I felt sure Alan would be sympathetic. I went to see him, hat in hand. I had to tell him that the Atlantic partners were on virtually no salary and were borrowing money to keep the ship afloat. Remember that Alan and I had the same affinity for the music. He adamantly played original black versions, not white covers. Although there was no personal bond between us, I assumed there was some mutual respect. So I bit the bullet and asked him to carry us for a couple months.

"I'd love to, Wex, but I can't do it," he answered. "That's taking the bread out of my children's mouths." With that memorable declaration, he took us off the radio.

Later in the decade, a chill passed over the industry when the district attorney began probing payola. When Atlantic was subpoenaed, I was elected to face the music. Our lawyer had advised us to open our books—bring all checks, present all proof—and I did. There was nothing to hide, and I've always been a pragmatist. At Christmas you tip the doorman not to celebrate the birth of the sweet infant Jesus but for damage control in the coming year; fail to acknowledge the deejays and pro-gram directors and you were out of business. But I knew goddamn well how these investigations could twist the facts, so I sat there in the DA's waiting room, knees knocking, stomach in knots. Fortunately, we were asked only to sign a consent decree, a way of saying, "We didn't do it—and we ain't gonna do it again." Leonard Chess had the balls not to sign such a document, and he was right. In the end, there were no conse-quences—for Leonard or for us.

Alan Freed had no such luck and began a long, tragic decline. He became the fall guy, blackballed and broken when he pleaded guilty to bribery in 1962. In 1964, he was indicted for tax evasion, but, exiled in Palm Springs, he died of heartbreak and drink before the trial could start, his power long vanquished. Other deejays, fair-haired gentiles with squeaky-clean images, were just as involved in questionable publishing, record pressing, concert promotions, and game shows, and Congress and the networks gave them a clean bill of health. Freed, on the other hand, was incapable of curbing his arrogance. He self-destructed even as he changed the course of American radio.

*M*eanwhile, two records got us back in the game. These tunes were so winning, so widely popular, so immediately irresistible, no one could keep them off the air. Ironically, they were consecutively numbered, one right after the other, in our master log. The first was "Yakety Yak" by the Coasters; the second, Bobby Darin's "Splish Splash." Each sold well over a million. At wholesale, that meant $400,000 or $500,000 in revenue.

MR. DISORDERLY CONDUCT AND THE MAN FROM ANOTHER PLANET

Jerry Leiber and Mike Stoller blew in like a fresh breeze from the Coast. The comic spin to their musical vignettes, their reflections on black American life, their witty lyrics, gritty syncopations, and brilliant productions made an inestimable contribution to Atlantic's success. Creators of fantastic characters, they were characters themselves. Their place is secure in the annals of pop, their roots a combination of barroom blues and the radio programs of their late-forties childhood—"The Shadow," "The Lone Ranger," "Gangbusters," "Amos and Andy," Jack Benny, and Fred Allen.

Nesuhi discovered them in Los Angeles, where they'd written "Smokey Joe's Cafe" for the Robins and "Ruby Baby" (produced by Nesuhi) for the Clyde McPhatter–less Drifters, both released on Atlantic in 1955.

"Earlier in the fifties we'd written hits," says Leiber. "We were still in our teens. Charles Brown recorded 'Hard Times,' Little Willie Littlefield did 'K. C. Lovin'" (later called 'Kansas City'), and Big Mama Thornton sang 'Hound Dog' three years before Elvis, who also sang our 'Jailhouse Rock,' 'Treat Me Nice,' 'Loving You,' and 'King Creole.' Later we started a little label called Spark with our friend Lester Sill. Lester was one of the great California R&B pioneers, but we couldn't get a record past the Rocky Mountains. Nesuhi appeared as something of a savior."

Leiber, Mr. Disorderly Conduct, was a charming mess—extravagantly verbal, always in a flamboyant dither. He had grown up poor in Baltimore, where his widowed mother ran a grocery store. Delivering food and coal oil to the black part of town, Jerry witnessed the miss-meal cramps and the sure-enough blues. He was hooked for life. With his Robert Oppenheimer visage—the huge forehead and penetrating eyes—Stoller was the taciturn virtuoso, an enigmatic keyboard wizard who looked as though he'd just arrived from Venus or Jupiter. He had formal music training and a taste for jazz piano. Both Mike and Jerry had impeccable taste, especially for jazz and blues.

We made a distribution deal, and it was instant magic. One after another, master tapes of those beautiful satirical mini-operettas would come in from California, each one more surprising than the last. In 1957 they showed up in New York, and from the minute Ahmet and I met them, the rapport was right. They were conversant with the right stuff—modern art, modern literature—and thrilled when we whisked them over to Birdland to hear the Modern Jazz Quartet. But it wasn't jazz that bonded us; it was their unique pop confections, their use of singing groups to enact songs Stoller called "playlets."

"Creatively, we had to play around," says Leiber, the lyricist. "We had to amuse ourselves. If Stoller laughed, I had it made. To get him to crack a smile was a minor miracle.

"Even though we were white, we didn't play off a white sensibility. We identified with youth and rebellion and making mischief. We thumbed our nose at the adult world. We crawled inside the skins of our characters, we related to the guys in the singing groups, and the result was a cross-cultural phenomenon: a white kid's take on a black kid's take of white society. Color lines were blurred, but the motif was always absurdity. We were putting a twist on Caucasian traditions, turning folk heroes on their heads—Paul Bunyan, John Henry, the Northwest Mounties."

The classic Coasters hits are the cream of the Leiber and Stoller oeuvre. As with Ray Charles, our main contribution was staying out of the way, and I very rarely went to their sessions. Jerry and Mike proved to be ideal producers of their own material. They wrote records, not songs.

"We may have been the first independent A&R men in the business," says Leiber, referring to the traditional artists-and-repertoire function—finding the artists and matching them with the right material. (For the first two decades, Ahmet, Nesuhi, and I went it alone. It wasn't till the early seventies that I set up A&R as a discrete department.)

L&S, as we called them, were as crazy as we were. As my late friend Arnold Shaw wrote in his R&B bible, *Honkers and Shouters,* Jerry and Mike used "every resource of intonation and instrumentation to poke fun at palpable targets: TV Western heroes in 'Along Came Jones,' phony exotic dancers in 'Little Egypt,' middle-aged hipsters in 'Shoppin' for Clothes,' tourism in 'Down in Mexico.'"

The main Coasters were Billy Guy, Carl Gardner, Cornell Gunter, and Dub Jones (bass voice of the irrepressible Charlie Brown). The ingredients were perfectly blended. Beginning with "Yakety Yak," a number-one hit in 1958, King Curtis's lickety-split barnyard tenor sax sets the riotous tone for virtually all their productions. Lyrically, the message is peppered with salty teenage defiance, the same indignant spirit that informs "Charlie Brown," the follow-up smash about the bad boy archetype who, thirty-five years later, continues to be a staple of hip-hop in the form of rough-and-tumble rap. Leiber and Stoller dealt with the generation gap a decade before the term was ever coined.

"We used humor to take off the edge," explains Leiber. "We'd have the Coasters in hysterics. After reading the lyrics, Billy Guy would predict, 'Man, they're gonna hang us in Mississippi from the highest tree.' The material was potent, the metaphors sometimes hidden, but the hook always dramatic. As actors the Coasters should have won Oscars."

Leiber had a flair for theatrics. In fact, in another era, he could have made some fantastic white-boy rhythm and blues on his own. The demos, on which he sang lead, were terrific. He had a great growl of a voice, and it's clear that Billy Guy, his black surrogate, was his musical alter ego.

Through the late fifties, the hits kept coming, culminating in "Poison Ivy," a lighthearted, easy-rocking metaphor for crabs and the clap. "She'll really do you in," the song goes, "if you let her get under your skin." The cure? "You're gonna need an ocean of calamine lotion."

"Before the recording of 'There Goes My Baby,'" wrote British scholar Colin Escott, "a new era was dawning. Primitive, booting rock 'n' roll was losing ground in the marketplace. Elvis Presley was in the Army, Little Richard was in the ministry, Jerry Lee Lewis was in disgrace and Buddy Holly had died a tragic death. Leiber and Stoller themselves, who had played such a prominent role in the genesis of rock 'n' roll, were developing twin fascinations for orchestral coloration and Latin rhythms."

"We had a thing for the South American *baião* rhythm," says Stoller. "We were always fascinated with percussive variations. We loved exotic drums. We'd go to Carroll's Broadway music store and rent whatever struck our fancy—tom-toms, congas, marimbas, and this monster we called the African hairy drum. One way or another, those sounds set off the Drifters."

In the sixties, Leiber and Stoller continued successfully down this new path. They had picked up the Drifters, who without Clyde Mc-Phatter had been floundering for years. Ahmet and I had tried to revive the group once or twice before, but nothing came of it. If Jerry and Mike can make magic with the Coasters, I thought, why not with the Drifters? I got George Treadwell—their trumpeter-manager, and at one point Sarah Vaughan's husband—to find a new group. He took the Crowns, led by Ben E. King, and dubbed them Drifters. Leiber and Stoller turned them into stars.

The kickoff song turned me off. When I first heard "There Goes My Baby," I pronounced it dogmeat. I hated the muddy swirling-string sound. There's an apocryphal story about my throwing a tuna fish sandwich against the wall—that's how pissed off I was supposed to be.

"No doubt," says Stoller, "Wexler hated it. We were going for a different effect than anything we'd tried with the Coasters. It was an extravagant mode, what I call a Caucasian melody, a Rimsky-Korsakov–Borodin pseudo line."

To me it sounded like a radio caught between two stations, neither one totally tuned. The timpani was hitting a note that ran contrary to the chords, resulting in an awkward mess. "That out-of-tune timpani," argues Leiber, "made the record."

"Ahmet wasn't crazy about it either," says Stoller, "but somewhat less negative than Wexler. After all, Ahmet is a diplomat and Jerry a hothead. While Jerry was menacing, Ahmet was conciliatory. He gave us two hours to mix the song with Tommy Dowd."

I gave the record the back of my hand and refused to put it out for over a year. When it was finally released, it shot to number one, sold over a million, and became one of the biggest hits in our history. Hey, what did I say?

The half-decade marking the second stage of the Drifters' success—1959 through 1964—is remarkable for the productions of Leiber and Stoller, the lead singing of Ben E. King, Rudy Lewis, and Johnny Moore, and, of course, for the songs themselves; the material soared.

"Wexler kept a wary eye on the ballooning recording budgets," says Leiber. "But in the early sixties, the Drifters were carrying the label. How could he complain?"

I couldn't. The good thing was that Leiber and Stoller were detached enough to understand that their own material was too tongue-in-cheek and sassy for the romantic Drifters. Mike and Jerry sought other songs, getting the best the Brill Building had to offer. Doc Pomus and Morty Shuman's "Save the Last Dance for Me" is perhaps the most sterling example. If the music industry had a heart, it would have been Doc Pomus.

"The minute I heard the first four bars of 'Last Dance,'" Leiber remembers, "I knew it was a hit. I loved the story: Doc—one of the great writers, hipsters, sweethearts of all time—had been confined to a wheelchair most of his life, and there he is, going out with his wife, a gorgeous blonde. He's watching her dance, he's being cool, but he's also living the lyrics. He's saying, 'Save the last dance for me.' It's really a poignant piece of personal poetry."

The same could be said for Doc and Morty's "This Magic Moment," with Ben E. King selling the song, the fabulous King, who left the group and went solo with us in 1960, hitting hard with back-to-back classics, "Spanish Harlem" (by Leiber and Phil Spector) and "Stand by Me" (by King and Leiber and Stoller). A third gem, "Don't Play That Song," was co-written by Ben and Ahmet, with Ahmet producing.

Carole King and Gerry Goffin added to the Drifters' luster with "Up on the Roof" and "Some Kind of Wonderful," sensational vehicles for Rudy Lewis, who along with Clyde McPhatter and Ben E. King was one of the three stellar Drifter leads. The songwriting scene was loaded with talent. In fact, it was at a Drifters session that Burt Bacharach, who'd written "Please Stay" for them, discovered the young backup singer Dionne Warwick.

I made a few discoveries of my own. I'd found "Under the Boardwalk" in 1964, five years after "There Goes My Baby." I felt certain it'd work for the Drifters. I tried to convince the group, but they weren't buying. Neither was their new producer, Bert Berns. I didn't care what anyone thought. I said, "Tell you what, fellas—do this one and you can pick the rest of them. Otherwise there ain't no session."

The night before the session I got a call: lead singer Rudy Lewis had been found dead in the hotel with a needle in his arm. I tried to cancel, but the union said no go; it was a costly string date, and players had already been hired. The most I could get was a twenty-four-hour delay. There wasn't even time to change keys for Johnny Moore, now slated to sing lead. But Johnny pulled it off, operating in a register lower than his norm.

I worked the record like a demon, breaking it out in boardwalk cities like Asbury Park and Atlantic City, hyping it to deejays along the Jersey shore and, in fact, the entire littoral down to the Carolinas. "Under the Boardwalk" went top ten and stayed there all summer. Chances are you'll hear it next summer.

The Drifters straggled on for years after the demise of Rudy Lewis, but the magic was gone.

If the songs—"This Magic Moment," "Stand by Me," "Save the Last Dance," "On Broadway" (with Phil Spector's guitar flourishes), "Under the Boardwalk"—meld together in your mind, it's understandable. A certain feeling was in the air, a synthesis of heady romance and the Cubano-Ricano rhythms of Broadway. Every Monday Mambo Night at the Palladium, the magic of Machito, Tito Puente, and Eddie Palmieri was propelling everyone onto the dance floor. Another seminal figure was the great Cuban trumpeter Mario Bauza, a graduate player-arranger from Chick Webb's great band of the thirties; he was the phenomenon who bridged the worlds of native American Negro dance music and this salsa, this Hispanic import. Concurrently, modernist Dizzy Gillespie was absorbing the Cuban cross-rhythms of Chano Pozo, master conga player, thereby introducing polyrhythms into bebop. A little while later, Charlie Parker jammed and recorded with Machito on Norman Granz's Clef label.

The heavy influx of Latins from South America and the Caribbean started in the thirties, abetted by Vito Marcantonio, an Italian-American U.S. representative from Harlem who virtually singlehandedly cajoled Congress into opening the gates. By the late forties, salsa had spread like wildfire through the burgeoning Latin communities. When the Palladium went salsa, the conflagration reached into the boroughs and started the historic bridge-and-tunnel trek to Broadway. Young Jewish hipsters were especially attracted. Seduced by the sensuality of the music, nubile Jewish chicks flocked in droves to the Latin dance halls. They came to be known, with lubricious irony, as "bagel babies."

The phonograph record's King of Salsa was George Goldner, a Jew-boy from the Bronx who came downtown to the Palladium, converted to a mambo freak, and married a Latina. Among his artists were Tito Puente, Tito Rodriguez, and Eddie Palmieri. His labels—Gee, Rama, End, Gone—are in the books, and so are his hits: Frankie Lymon and the Teenagers' "Why Do Fools Fall in Love"; the Chantels' "Maybe"; the Flamingos' "I Only Have Eyes for You"; Little Anthony and the Imperials' "Tears on My Pillow" and "Shimmy, Shimmy, Ko-Ko-Bop."

In the early sixties, the scene was sizzling, the characters—the Brooklyn songwriters, the Harlem singers, the Jewish and Turkish label owners—breaking their backs to stay afloat in the music maelstrom. It was in this mix of hustlers and geniuses that I met and, for a hot New York minute, worked with the most enigmatic hustler/genius of them all.

"I CAME FROM CALIFORNIA TO MAKE HITS"

Lester Sill of Spark Records fame called from Los Angeles. "I found another one. He went to Hollywood High, same as Jerry and Mike. He's a child prodigy—plays guitar, sings, composes, and arranges."

Phil Spector came to New York with one hit under his belt, the Teddy Bears' "To Know Him Is To Love Him." We gave him the run of our office, little suspecting that he would soon be sleeping there at night, setting up a scam with the switchboard operator to make long-distance calls home. When we found out, we figured he was worth it.

Wiry, short, relentlessly intense, Spector was convinced he knew as much as—or more than—anybody at Atlantic. Without a cachet, he comported himself as a peer. We went along, or at least tried to, because we knew about his ears.

Without being either civil or subtle, Spector was terribly talented. Unfortunately, there was never any benefit to Atlantic. The fact is, in the early days I didn't fully understand Phil's peculiar prowess. There was no getting past our personality biases. When we were laying out a song, or trying a chord sequence or tempo change, Phil's truculent response to anything I suggested would be "Fuck that, man, I came from California to make hits."

The scene was Belltone Studios, where Phil and I were recording the Pearls, an epicene male duo, singing a song I thought had hit potential, "Twist and Shout." Bert Berns, the composer, was there, but I stashed him in a guest viewing room in the mezzanine, where he could listen but not partake. Phil and I went at it with unrestrained ferocity. In the end we managed to fuck up a natural hit. When Bert objected, I invited him to shut up.

Months later, Ahmet and Phil flew to California to meet with Bobby Darin, who was to become Atlantic's first pop star. For all of Phil's fiery independence, he was mesmerized by Ahmet. Ahmet Ertegun was his god. It wasn't enough for Phil to emulate the exquisite European manner; he went so far as to appropriate Ahmet's slight stutter.

"Bobby Darin was quite temperamental," Ahmet recalls, "but I had my own way of handling him. His musical ideas were brilliant, but not always, and I tried to be very diplomatic with him. I had a notion that Phil, with his own inventive ideas, could help me produce Bobby's next record.

"The setting was terrific. On a tranquil Saturday afternoon we pulled up at an imposing mansion. We were admitted by a butler who took us to a beautiful backyard, where Bobby and his wife, Sandra Dee, were both in bathing suits, sipping cold drinks by the pool. I introduced Phil as my assistant. After some small talk, Bobby began singing us some songs he'd just written. I never liked to discourage Bobby. My policy was to listen to all his material and then praise those with the most commercial potential.

"'Good,' I said after the first song. 'Good,' I repeated after the second. 'Fine,' I commented after the third. 'Interesting,' I remarked after the fourth.

"'What?!' Phil broke in. 'Are you fuckin' crazy or am I? He can't record these songs. These songs are pure shit!'

"'Who is this guy?' Bobby wanted to know. 'Get him the fuck out of here.'"

Eventually I came to like Phil and consider him *the* producer of the era. The affection grew—*after* he'd left us, after he'd done the Crystals' "He's a Rebel" and "Da Doo Ron Ron," after the Ronettes' "Be My Baby," after Darlene Love's "The Boy I'm Gonna Marry," after the Righteous Brothers' "You've Lost that Lovin' Feelin'" and "Unchained Melody" and Ike and Tina's "River Deep—Mountain High." Phil turned his back on the world after "River Deep" wasn't hailed as the Great American Hit—a slight that I rate as *the* overrated trauma of Western pop culture. Anyway, Phil ensconced himself in a Hollywood castle with a moat, barbed wires, remote cameras, armed guards, and attack dogs. Despite the paranoia, Phil is literate and intelligent, with a keen knowledge and appreciation for jazz. He speaks and writes insightfully. Over the years our correspondence has brought me pleasure. Phil now makes occasional forays out of the castle keep, and I met up with him again in the summer of 1991 at a meeting of the Rock 'n' Roll Hall of Fame nominating committee. Big hugs—he was articulate and charming and had us all in stitches.

It was Phil, I'll never forget, who took in a failing Lenny Bruce—moved Lenny right into his home, then recorded and released a couple of his records. The liner notes of one reprinted a letter I wrote to Phil, in which I described Lenny as someone "who reads Spinoza and does a retrospective analysis of Jewish persecution, finally coming up with the wonderful idea that 'suffering teaches us only that suffering has absolutely no value.'"

Lenny suffered. Phil suffered. They were both weird originals, visionaries who resonated chords that had never even been touched before.

There are three kinds of producers. The first is the documentarian, like Leonard Chess, who took Muddy Waters's Delta blues and recorded them just as Muddy played them—raw, unadorned, and real. Leonard replicated in the studio what he heard in the bar.

I fit into the second category—the producer as servant of the project. Typically, this is a producer who begins as an amateur, an impassioned fan, and somehow finds himself in charge of sessions with no special cachet. His job is to enhance: meaning find the right song, the right arranger, the right band, the right studio—in short, do whatever it takes to get the best out of the artist.

Phil is the prime example of the third category: producer as star, as artist, as unifying force. For Phil, every item in a record—rhythm track, strings, background vocal, lead vocal, instrumental solo—was a tile in a mosaic. The design was solely of his making, not the singer's or the songwriter's. Phil's thing was the massive "wall of sound." Some see it as the greatest concoction since the invention of the wheel; others consider it labored, artificial, and cloying. Rather than develop the singers' careers, he developed himself. Rather than serve the artists—Phil left no legacy of great artists, excepting Bill Medley—the artists served Phil. There is no denying the energy and singularity of his style. He'd use

three pianists, two bassists, four drummers, dictating string lines, grabbing the guitar himself to show what he wanted, certain that every one
of those double-ups, every last eccentric lick, had a place and an impact.
Phil's imprint was huge, Wagnerian. His creations were something more
than megalomaniac self-testaments. Art? I don't know—but monu-
ments of craft for sure.

DARIN'

I was at my desk when I heard the sound of a churchy-bluesy piano. My first thought was Ray Charles, but Ray wasn't in town. So who the hell was it? Bobby Darin was who it was—and maybe you're surprised. Bobby was a bitch of a pianist, and certainly one of the essential players in Atlantic's history.

He was discovered by Don Kirshner (later a hugely successful rock promoter) in a candy store on Fort Washington Avenue and 191st Street on the northern tip of Manhattan, my fabled Washington Heights. Don was a street genius who, with no music experience, got into the business and built an empire of songwriters and singers. He was zealous and jealous and amazingly effective. He put Connie Francis on MGM and Bobby on Decca. Connie hit, Bobby didn't, but Herb Abramson thought Bobby could and signed him to Atco. After several muted releases, Ahmet took over and made the record that launched Bobby's career. "Splish Splash" was written by Darin and—honest to God—the mother of deejay Murray the K. Ahmet cut it as part of a split date with jazz singer Morgana King.

I was alongside Ahmet for "Queen of the Hop." After the date, Dowd and I worked some tape reverb magic, doubling the shuffle rhythm pattern, which became an alluring hook and helped the song go top ten. The Sinatra-styled "Mack the Knife" and "Beyond the Sea" proved that Bobby could swing in styles ranging from rock to big-band jazz. What's more, his supper-club show was dynamite, by all accounts in the Sinatra and Sammy Davis league. Unfortunately, his transition from teen idol to nightclub star began to tarnish his image; in some quarters he was soon perceived as wimpishly Las Vegas. One day I'd see

*Clockwise: Wex, Herb
Abramson, Steve Blauner,
Bobby Darin*

him in the studio recording a marvelous duet album with Johnny Mercer; the next week he was wearing a Western suit, heading out for a tour
of the provinces with his guitar slung over his back à la Woody Guthrie
or Rambling Jack Elliott.

Bobby Darin was our first pop act, and proof of Ahmet's uncanny
knack for what would sell. So Ahmet gets to tell the story of "Mack the
Knife":

"I was having a quiet lunch with Lotte Lenya, the widow of Kurt
Weill. We were in her apartment on Third Avenue—Miss Lenya, myself, and her second husband—when she casually queried, 'You do have
a record company, don't you, Mr. Ertegun?'

"'A small one,' I explained. 'Primarily blues and jazz.'

"'I'd be most pleased if you would record one of Kurt's songs.'

"I smiled and said that while I greatly admired Mr. Weill's work, it
might be difficult to match his material with any of my artists.

"'Promise me you'll try, though,' she urged.

"'Of course I'll do my best,' I assured her, without a clue.

"A few days later I ran into Bobby Darin. He mentioned that he'd
just seen a wonderful Greenwich Village revival of Weill's *Threepenny
Opera,* and how did I feel about 'Mack the Knife'?

"'Great idea,' I assured him.

"I immediately phoned Miss Lenya to report that I had been able to fulfill her request. She was overwhelmed, and so was I. We made a small fortune on the record, which became the best-selling song of the year and won the company its first producer's Grammy."

Bobby was always a bit of mystery. The woman who raised him and told him she was his sister was in truth his mother, something Bobby didn't know until he was in his thirties and a superstar. An honors graduate of the High School of Music and Art, Darin couldn't resist wearing his Mensa button, symbol of membership in the high-IQ society. He ragged me and Ahmet to take the Mensa test, hoping we'd flunk, but we regarded the button as the nerds' badge of honor.

When Coral, a Decca subsidiary, offered him under-the-table money to record under a pseudonym—this after he was under contract to us—he also couldn't resist. "Early in the Morning" was a hit, but we soon found out we'd been euchred and were able to recoup. The little scam, however, cost us at least half of the expected sales volume.

Bobby's first royalty payment was so big—$80,000, comparable to $800,000 today—that I wanted to give it to him ceremoniously. I took the check to the Copa on the night of Darin's opening, sure this would be just the thing to put him in a great mood before he kicked off his show.

"This is it?" asked his manager, Steve Blauner. It wasn't the last time Blauner (we called him Steve Blunder) busted our bubble.

Before long Bobby was gone. He came back to the label in 1966 but never again matched his early run of hits. By then the sounds were changing. I didn't know it, but a new musical era was opening, ushered in by the King of Rock 'n' Soul.

NOTIONS,
LOTIONS,
AND
POTIONS—
ROOTS,
FRUITS,
AND
SNOOTS

*S*olomon Burke could have emerged from a sideshow or carnival. He was at the same time an ordained minister and stand-up vocalist of rare prowess and remarkable range.

Later in the sixties, a decade rich with soul singers, I was grilling steaks in my backyard in Great Neck for Philly deejays Jimmy and Louise Bishop. We got into a philosophical discussion about who the greatest soul singer was—James Brown? Otis Redding? Wilson Pickett? Sam and Dave? Ben E. King?

"Solomon Burke," Jimmy said, "with a borrowed band."

Amen. Earlier in the sixties, before Solomon walked into my life, Atlantic was trying to recover from the double whammy of losing Ray Charles and Bobby Darin. Together they had accounted for at least a third of our business. At the height of their careers, Ray went to ABC and Bobby to Capitol. Both labels were more mainstream and glitzier than ours.

In Ray's case, we did everything in our power to keep him on board. "There were no hard feelings," Ray admitted to me years later, "just a juicier offer from ABC. I hated to leave you fellas because the feeling at Atlantic was so right. Matter of fact, you remember that after I switched,

Tommy Dowd set up my first board in the recording studio I'd built in L.A. Didn't charge me a dime."

Brother Ray and I have different memories of his departure. We frantically tried to chase him down, prepared to match any offer. We couldn't find him, couldn't get a meeting. Ray's version is that he sat down with Ahmet and was told Atlantic couldn't match the ABC money. Either way, he was gone, and so was my peace of mind.

At the same time, the gods were merciful: as Ray slipped away, Solomon slipped in. "There's a Solomon Burke out here," my secretary, Noreen Woods, said over the intercom. "He doesn't have an appointment, but he wants to see you."

"Solomon, have I been waiting for you!" I said, practically leaping over my desk and busting through the door. "You're home. I'm signing you up today." And I did.

My old boss at *Billboard,* Paul Ackerman, had been pulling my coat for years, insisting that I get Solomon Burke. I knew the records he'd cut for Apollo, but I didn't know if his contract had expired. Nabbing him, I knew I had someone who could light a fire under me. By the start of the sixties, I was burnt out.

At various times, exhaustion has hit me hard. Perhaps it's the intensity of the enterprise, or the sheer hours of recording, producing, and promoting. Whatever the cause, certain periods in my career have left me done in and jaded. In the early sixties, with Brother Ray turning out gems for ABC ("Georgia on My Mind," "Ruby," "Hit the Road, Jack"), Ahmet cultivating talent in California, and Leiber and Stoller coasting along with the Drifters, I was caught up in the role of daily op man while supervising staff, hiring and firing. I was bored.

Solomon was the infusion of fresh energy I needed. And the song we needed—the country-and-western "Just Out of Reach"—was also a Paul Ackerman tip. As a black artist interpreting country material with strings added, he also anticipated Ray Charles's "I Can't Stop Loving You," "You Don't Know Me," "You Are My Sunshine," and "Your Cheating Heart."

Physically huge, the King of Rock 'n' Soul reigned over a large body of work. He was a piece of work—wily, highly intelligent, a salesman of epic proportions, sly, sure-footed, a never-say-die entrepreneur.

The best Solomon stories are those he tells on himself. "I was touring the South with a mixed bag of artists—white and black. As an old pro, I was hip to what was happening, but the other brothers on the tour,

Cutting "Just Out of Reach"
with Solomon Burke

guys from Chicago and New York, hadn't been below the Mason-Dixon
line. They thought you could eat anywhere. I tried to warn them, told
them to be prepared, because I was prepared with my own little kitchen
setup. 'Got all the ingredients,' I said, 'and gonna be good enough to sell
y'all sandwiches. A sandwich, soda, and hot dog from me will only be
five bucks—and the potato chips are free.' They laughed until the bus
made its first stop. That's when they got laughed out of the restaurant.
'A sandwich, soda, and hot dog from me will only be six bucks—and the
potato chips are free.' But these brothers were stubborn, sure that at the
next stop they'd cop some food. Sure enough, at the next stop they sent
out Dion, the white singer, to do their dealing. Dion comes back carrying two cardboard boxes full of sandwiches, chicken, and french fries—
so many fries they're spilling over the box—and hot chocolates with
whipped cream all on top, cream pies, ice cream—you name it. The
brothers are so excited and hungry they jump off to help Dion carry the
goodies. When the redneck restaurant owner sees what's up, he goes for
his gun and starts shooting. Dion drops the food all over the ground, the
boys race back to the bus, we barely escape with our lives . . . and I'm
talkin' 'bout a sandwich, soda, and hot dog—nine bucks, and just a dollar for potato chips."

The stories are legendary: Solomon selling popcorn and candy at his own shows at the Apollo; Solomon, (mail-order) Doctor of Mortuary Science, opening funeral homes; Solomon running a limo service; Solomon selling herbal extracts, mojo juice, conjures, peppermint, and snake oil at a drugstore (for which I suggested the handle "Dr. Solomon Burke: Notions, Lotions, and Potions—Roots, Fruits, and Snoots"), the same drugstore where a white-coated Solomon would accept prescriptions and then bicycle over to a real drugstore to have them filled.

But Solomon was a real singing king, crowned by Baltimore deejay Rockin' Robin and hailed as the conqueror wherever he appeared in the early sixties, a glittering gold suit his coat of arms. Once, in the boondocks of the Carolinas, Solomon was performing in a tobacco barn before a crowd of black farmers. It was the end of a grueling nine-week tour, and his trademark suit was badly creased, so instead he donned a black tux, changing in a station wagon parked nearby.

"Stop!" ordered a farmer in the first row, his pistol pointed at the singer's head. "I'm here to see Solomon Burke."

"That's me."

"If you Solomon Burke, where's your gold suit?"

Solomon trudged back to the station wagon, followed by the entire audience. They waited as he changed into the soiled suit.

The farmer relented. "You Solomon Burke all right. Sing the music!"

Solomon came along at a moment when the British invasion was gearing up. We had nothing like the Dave Clark Five or Herman's Hermits, let alone the Beatles. Solomon Burke carried Atlantic by selling a shitload of records—and they were terrific.

Of all the attributes of soul singing, I consider sweetness the most important—sweetness of vocal character, sweetness in reading lyrics, sweetness in shaping melody. Sam Cooke was the great prophet of this school and Solomon its next great proponent. A decade later Donny Hathaway elevated the style, spreading the sweet-sound influence over present-day singers.

Solomon was a joy. His tenor wasn't marred by the growl and the implicit threat of the Pentecostal fire-and-brimstone preacher, an approach with little appeal for me. Like Ray Charles, Solomon was churchy without being coarse, his melisma subtle and restrained, his voice an instrument of exquisite sensitivity.

At our first session, I felt like the producer who'd come in from the cold. It was December of 1960. A blizzard had blanketed the East Coast;

I was in Great Neck, and the date was scheduled for our little studio on West 56th Street. The snowstorm had shut down the trains, and there was no way to get into the city. I finally found a cab driver to take me to Manhattan for fifty dollars. But everyone showed—Solomon, the musicians, arranger Ray Ellis, the background girls. We cut "Just Out of Reach (of My Two Empty Arms)," "How Many Times," and "Keep the Magic Working." The magic worked just fine, and by early evening Solomon had recorded all three songs. We were setting up to hear the playbacks when Solomon put on his coat and headed for the door.

"Don't you want to hear what you did?" I asked him.

"Would love to, baby," he answered, "but I'm running back to Philly before the snow melts. I'm making four dollars an hour driving a snow truck." Only twenty-four, Solomon had a wife and eight kids. He never heard his master take on "Just Out of Reach" until it hit the radio stations in Philadelphia.

The motor that drove Solomon Burke was a complex mechanism. Part artist, part hustler, he was a wit and a wonder, always hitting on me for more money, bigger advances, and anticipated royalties. He knew I knew what was up. And I knew he knew me better than most. We locked horns, but could laugh about it. Our rapport was strong even when the money game was most intense.

In the beginning, Solomon's studio attitude was terrific. He came in fresh and eager to learn the songs. He was always prepared. He studied my acetate demos in advance. With time the hits came—"If You Need Me," "Goodbye Baby," "Got to Get You Off My Mind"—but he started to get lax and a little lazy. He'd show up without knowing the song. Not having learned the melody, he'd skate, bending the notes far out of shape. I called it "oversoul." "If you oversoul this thing any more, Solomon," I'd say, "it's going to turn green."

Unlike Ray Charles, Burke had no eyes to produce. He was content to let the producer pick the song and arranger; mostly he wanted to get in and out as quickly as possible. His great creativity came in interpretation; that's where he delivered the goods. In the fade to "Cry to Me," for example, listen to his ad-lib licks: "cra . . . cra . . . cra . . . cra-cra-cra-cra-cra-crying"—a staccato stutter turn that, in a few years, would become Otis Redding's vocal logo.

The writer of "Cry to Me" was Bert Berns. Bert was an outstanding songwriter and groove doctor. He was also mercurial, and as egocentric and opinionated as I was. He was my first protégé.

THE

BIG

BANG!

$B_{(Bert)}$—A (Ahmet)—N (Nesuhi)—G (Gerald)!

Hey, we were so tight—Berns, my partners, and myself—that we started a young publishing company and later a label (Bang!) as an offshoot of Atlantic. That's how deeply I respected Bert's talent. I'd never made such a deal with an outsider.

Two years before, when Bert Berns first came around, he was working at fifty dollars a week plugging tunes for Bobby Mellin, a publisher friend. "You're gonna love this guy," Bobby promised, and I did. In 1961, the first full year Berns worked at Atlantic, he earned $60,000.

Bert was street, a homeboy. In fact, my father used to wash the windows of his parents' dress shop in the Bronx. Not that Bert had a comfortable childhood. Indeed, he told me that his parents were so intent on making their store successful that they put Bert and his sister in an orphanage rather than raise them. Bert bore the wounds for the rest of his life.

Only later would I learn of his obsession with power. He was intrigued by the wiseguys, loved hanging with hoodlums and trading gangster stories. Bert was also an adventurer who had haunted pre-Castro Cuba, where, he claimed, he'd run guns and dope; he once boasted about owning a nightclub in Havana. All this may have been romantic exaggeration; but his feeling for Latin rhythms was right as rain. His affinity for the Cuban *quajira* was deep, and he practically made a cottage industry on the chord changes of "Guantanamera," written in the nineteenth century by José Martí, the Cuban revolutionary hero. He used those identical changes in "Twist and Shout," "A Little Bit of Soap," and "My Girl Sloopy" (an R&B hit for the Vibrations in 1964), plus a slew of similar songs. The "Guantanamera" progression can be heard everywhere—from "La Bamba" to the bridge of Phil Spector's production of Barry Mann and Cynthia Weil's "You've Lost That Lovin' Feelin'" for the Righteous Brothers to Erma Franklin's "Piece of My Heart." But I was amazed to discover one day that it had first appeared years before in Doc Pomus and Morty Shuman's "Sweets for My Sweets" for the Drifters.

Later in the sixties, after Leiber and Stoller left our label, Berns produced the Drifters singing Carole King and Gerry Goffin's "At the Club," Barry and Cynthia's "Saturday Night at the Movies," and Arthur Resnick and Kenny Young's "I've Got Sand in My Shoes" and "Under the Boardwalk." His productions, as described by rock writer Joel Selvin, "were marked by an ability to balance a large number of elements—background vocals, horns, strings, rhythm tracks—without crowding the arrangements or intruding on the sense of song." His work with Garnet Mimms alone ("Cry Baby") is testimony to the fact that he was one of the first important soul producers.

However, Bert's soul and Solomon Burke's didn't mesh. After their initial successes, they fell out. That didn't surprise me, given their disparate personalities. Solomon was regal, Berns cocky and stubborn. The first time Burke saw Bert—who did look a bit freaky, with his hairpiece cascading down his back—he said, "Come on, Jerry, you gotta be kidding me with this paddy motherfucker." I told him to cool it until we got into the studio. And "Cry to Me" made Bert just a little more agreeable to Solomon.

Not long afterwards, a man named Monroe Golden sent me a tape with eight or nine demos from Detroit, all sung by Wilson Pickett, formerly of the Falcons, whose "I Found a Love" we'd recently distributed. Pickett sounded sensational. I played the songs for Bert. I was especially high on "If You Need Me." It was a hell of a demo. Bert wanted us to release Pickett's version—doubtless a good idea, but I wanted to save the song for Solomon. Unlike a lot of other labels, our primary policy was to build the artists already in house. So I bought the publishing rights for a thousand bucks, Bert and I co-produced "If You Need Me" with Burke, and we put the song in the can.

A little while later, I was having a tranquil morning shave in Great Neck when the phone rang. "It's the Magnificent Montague," Shirley said. Nathan Montague was a pal, a hip black deejay on WWRL, a man of ultrasmooth style ("Are you out there, darlin'? Just touch the radio, just put your hand all over me . . .") and singular erudition. He was a cultural anthropologist whose collection of Afro-American artifacts— books, posters, rare records—was world-class.

Monty was excited. He said his request line was ringing off the hook, all for a record that hadn't even been issued. He was playing the master. The song, he said, was "If You Need Me." Impossible, I told him; we hadn't even released Solomon's record yet.

"This isn't Solomon," said Monty. "It's Wilson Pickett, and it's a stone smash."

When we bought the publishing rights we'd failed to buy the demo rights—my dumb oversight—and now I started to panic. I rushed to the office, found out Harold Logan and Lloyd Price had the master on their little Double L label (distributed by Liberty Records), and invited them over. Atlantic could have the Pickett master, they said, but only if Solomon's version was canned. No deal. They left, Logan muttering threats under his breath. Liberty put out Pickett's version, and I had to run with Solomon's.

The game was on, and it did me good. I'd taken myself out of the promotion business and needed a healthy kick in the ass. I went into orbit. I lived on the phone, pitching every deejay I knew; I hit the road, pulled every string, called in all my markers, bopped till I dropped.

Meanwhile, Harold Logan was touring black radio stations in the South and Midwest, promoting his version with a Louisville slugger. I got calls in the middle of the night, including one from the all-night man in Detroit. Logan was right outside his control room, he whispered, and it was head-breaking time if he didn't play Pickett. My "Solomonic" advice: "Play Pickett till Logan leaves town."

Solomon's version, really the equal of Wilson's, was on the charts for eleven weeks, peaking at #37. Pickett's held on for six weeks and stalled at #67. "Don't fuck with that man," Liberty Records' Al Bennett told a group of people lobby-crawling at the next record convention, "Wexler will bury you." He was also referring to the fact that Doris Troy's original version of "Just One Look" had virtually swamped Bennett's white cover, a nifty reversal. I didn't mind the compliment. "If You Need Me" got me back in the hands-on business of promoting records.

After Solomon fell out with Bert, I called Gene Page, a prolific arranger, to come to New York from L.A. to chart Burke's "Tonight's the Night" and "Got to Get You Off My Mind," a song Solomon told me he'd "unofficially" written with Sam Cooke the week before Sam was shot to death in a Los Angeles motel. I have a weak spot for "Tonight's the Night." The backup girls are angelic, and Eric Gale's guitar obbligato never quits.

*M*eanwhile, Jeff Barry, the songwriter and producer, brought me Neil Diamond. Neil had been signed to Leiber and Stoller's Red Bird label on a fifty-dollars-per-week retainer. Red Bird was dragging at the time, so Neil was being dropped. After he played a few songs in my office—just Neil and his guitar—I was knocked out. I had our counsel Paul Marshall draw up the contract, but before signing time Bert Berns called and said Neil was a friend of his—would I mind if we put him on Bang!?

Since Ahmet, Nesuhi, and I were partners in Bang!, and since the enterprise was newly fledging, I agreed. Bert and I were on a handshake basis, typical in those days. Just as Bert's arrangements were often spit-balled—and brilliantly so—so were our business dealings. Why worry? By now Bert was a proven hitmaker. His production of "Twist and Shout" for the Isley Brothers was a smash; the Beatles made the song even bigger. Bert also had a #1 record with the McCoys' "Hang on Sloopy." And he wrote and produced "Piece of My Heart" for Erma Franklin, Aretha's sister, which was later to become a signature song for Janis Joplin.

Bert had uncovered tremendous talents. In England he'd found guitarist Jimmy Page (then known as "Little" Jimmy Page), whom he actually brought to America in hopes of using him on R&B sessions—the same Page later to lead Led Zeppelin, Atlantic's biggest seller of all time. The first album by Van Morrison, the great Celtic bard, which included "Brown Eyed Girl," was produced by Bert and released on Bang! When he returned from England, Bert had Van's band Them in tow, as well as Lulu, famous for "To Sir with Love," from the Sidney Poitier movie.

Bert was eclectic, a tireless go-getter and hitmaker. But then things started to get funny. He insisted on unjustifiable control over the publishing company. There were signs that he was running with some wise-guys. Next thing, he sued us for breach of contract and the whole deal blew up. We said goodbye to Bert and Bang!—not cost-free. Neil Diamond, Van Morrison, and the McCoys remained with him and were lost to Atlantic forever.

Bert died of a heart condition in December 1967. He was thirty-eight. I didn't attend the funeral.

RASHOMON
AT THE
OAK
ROOM

In 1978, George W. S. Trow, Jr., wrote "Eclectic, Reminiscent, Amused, Fickle, Perverse," an exhaustive two-part profile of Ahmet Ertegun in *The New Yorker.* Like many others, Trow was intrigued by Ahmet's style, and the piece—overwritten, overanalytical, and fascinating—is primarily a study of style. At one point Trow notes the difference between Ertegun's and my own aesthetics as applied to black music: "Ahmet most enjoyed paradox and anomaly and incongruity and excess of style, while Wexler sought instead evidence of that unspoiled energy which, taken together with eccentricity of expression, can be perceived as honesty."

In fact, Ahmet and I had begun moving in different directions back in the late fifties, early sixties. His success with Bobby Darin set him on a new track, introducing him to the California scene, where he would later discover a number of lucrative pop acts. As Ahmet grew older, he grew less judgmental and more interested in a wide range of commercial forms, particularly the exploding white rock 'n' roll. I stayed with what I knew and loved.

Gone were the days when Ahmet and I went off together to explore the back alleys of New Orleans. The business had gotten too big. Domains were separating, demands diverging. We'd moved from the makeshift setup above Patsy's on 56th Street to 157 West 57th, across from Carnegie Hall and the Russian Tea Room, where we'd eat blinis for days. It was a definite upgrade, and I even had my own bathroom and shower. Ahmet and I had always shared an office; but now, though we still faced each other, a sliding door between us could be closed at will. Later, when we moved to 1841 Broadway, we were separated by a long hallway.

Separation led to alienation. At the time of the *New Yorker* profile, I felt very distant from Ahmet. We have since reconciled. There was one quote from that article, though, for which Ahmet apologized to me. The words were not his but those of his wife, Mica. Trow had asked her why her husband didn't see much of Wexler anymore.

"He tried to buy Ahmet out of the company once," she replied. "With Jerry Leiber and Mike Stoller."

Mica was referring to a luncheon in the Oak Room of the Plaza Hotel in 1964, a meeting whose importance—and negative reper-cussions—became clear to me only years later. At the time, I mis-understood the emotional impact of that moment on Ahmet; misunderstanding, I believe, still surrounds the encounter. Before we get to the Plaza, though, some brief background information. A year earlier, Leiber and Stoller had a falling-out with us over money. "Our lawyer Lee Eastman insisted we do an audit," says Stoller, "and it turned out Atlantic owed us eighteen thousand dollars. Wexler, who can be tough and intimidating as hell, put it to us this way: 'You can have the money or you can continue working with our artists.'

"We gave in on the money," Stoller recalls, "but Jerry took the Drift-ers away from us anyway and started using Bert Berns."

"That hurt us deeply," Leiber says. "It was like having a fight with your brothers—Jerry and Ahmet were family to us—and then having the door locked. We weren't allowed back in."

"There was also the matter of credit," Stoller insists. "We wanted to be listed as producers, but Wexler wouldn't hear of it. 'You're listed as songwriters and arrangers,' Wexler would say. 'How many goddamn times does your name have to be on the record?'"

"Wexler and Ertegun could be ruthless opportunists on one hand," Leiber continues, "and enormously generous on the other. They could be lovely or lethal. When it came to grabbing an artist or a song, watch out! Nesuhi was the real gentleman of the group. His behavior was im-peccable."

Mike and Jerry, like me, were not without a streak of avarice. We were all poor boys getting our first taste of real money. Yet I can't under-stand why, given the hundreds of thousands of dollars they earned with us, chump change like eighteen thousand dollars would cause a cave-in. Maybe their beef was justified—and maybe it could have been a tech-nical dispute over returns. Either way, when it comes to audits the rec-

ord company is invariably the villain, and, at least for a while, we were
viewed as such by our friends.

But one break leads to another, and before long Mike and Jerry got
the one break they'd been waiting for: their own label, Red Bird. They
had Ellie Greenwich, Jeff Barry, and Shadow Morton on staff, writing
and producing smashes for the Dixie Cups ("Chapel of Love," "People
Say"), the Jelly Beans ("I Wanna Love Him So Bad"), the Shangri-Las
("Remember [Walkin' in the Sand]," "Leader of the Pack," "I Can Never
Go Home Anymore"), and the Ad Libs ("The Boy from New York City").
Red Bird was red hot while our business had cooled considerably. So
had the differences between Leiber and Stoller and myself—at least
enough to engender merger talks. I was interested, and presumed Ahmet would be too.

The Oak Room cast of characters, however, included two significant
others: the late Lee Eastman and the late George Goldner. Eastman was
the lawyer who initiated the audit that caused the schism (and who later
became Paul McCartney's father-in-law). Goldner, the aforementioned
Mambo King, was an infamous old-time record boss, a natty dresser and
compulsive gambler who'd reputedly lost five labels at the track, all of
them picked up for peanuts by Morris Levy. (Levy, of course, was known
to be connected. He was a mentor of Alan Freed's and owner of Birdland, Roulette Records, and a string of major publishing firms; in his last
years he was convicted of extortion.)

Goldner was a man of many sides. He was shrewd but strangely
naive. Years before the Plaza meeting, for example, Ahmet had phoned
him and, while on hold, got cross-wired into a conversation between
George and his Philadelphia distributor, Ivan Ballen. Goldner was running his Tico label then and personally taking orders for Tito Puente
records. Ballen was ordering "twos and fews" and driving Goldner
mad—two copies of record number 845, one copy of record number
754, and so forth.

"Hurry," said George, "I have to piss." But the distributor was play-
fully laborious and, even worse, stopped ordering to claim that Goldner
was plugging the wrong side of Tito's new single.

The order finally came to an end, but before George had time to run
to the bathroom Ahmet was on the phone. "Mr. Goldner," Ahmet said
with his idea of a Southwestern drawl, "my name's Billy Bob Whitworth
and I got the biggest cotton-pickin' one-stop in Oklahoma City. This

mambo thing is going crazy down here, but I can't get your Tito Puente records to save my life."

"You can now," said George. "I'll take your order. But hurry. I have to piss so bad my eyeballs are turning yellow." Ahmet proceeded painstakingly, number for number, giving Goldner the exact "twos and fews" order just given by the Philadelphia distributor. "I can't believe this," said George. There was a ten-beat pause. "Mr. Whitworth, sir, do you believe in fate?"

"I can't believe," Ahmet replied, "that you're pushing the wrong Tito Puente side."

"What! Who the hell is this?"

"It's Ahmet."

"You're in Philly and you overheard the conversation!" Goldner shouted.

"I'm in New York," Ahmet said. "Call my office if you don't believe me."

Goldner hung up, called New York, and there was Ahmet on the line. "How the hell—?"

"Save it, George," Ahmet interrupted. "Now you know why we stay hot. We know what's going on everywhere."

That day at the Oak Room, neither Ahmet nor I grasped the influence Goldner held over Jerry and Mike. George was running Red Bird, but he was also two-timing them, selling records out the back door.

"We were trying to use Atlantic," says Leiber, "to drive George out. Goldner was involving us with guys with faces you'd see only at fights at the old Madison Square Garden. We were afraid of George and thought of Ahmet and Jerry as executives strong enough to control him. We thought of Goldner as crass and Atlantic as class."

"The Oak Room luncheon got out of hand," Stoller remembers. "First off, Lee Eastman took an adversarial position. Lee knew that a merger would mean losing us as clients. Inevitably we'd have gone with Atlantic's lawyers."

"George," says Leiber, "was not only drunk, he was sabotaging the effort. He wanted to maintain the status quo. A merger would have meant his being relegated to a lower position. He insulted Ahmet and embarrassed me and Mike."

I favored the merger but was put off by Goldner's rude behavior. When Ahmet said the deal held no interest for him, the conversation was over. I thought the entire issue was dead—but I was wrong. On several occasions, in print and in private conversations, Ahmet has claimed that Leiber, Stoller, and I tried to buy him out. Nothing could be further from the truth.

"The idea is preposterous," says Leiber. "We wouldn't dream of merging with Atlantic without Ahmet Ertegun."

"There *is* no Atlantic without Ahmet," Stoller confirms. "He's the company's chief asset. What would be the point of the deal?"

It astounds some people to learn that throughout the years Ahmet and I never discussed the matter again—yet that's the truth. I wasn't aware that the subject was an ongoing sore point for my partner. Perhaps it also turned Mica against me.

I have come to the opinion that Mica changed the balance in my relationship with Ahmet. They married in 1961 and since then have become one of the most written-about couples in café society, their crowd a brew of rock stars, diplomats, financiers, movie stars, and avant-garde artists. A Rumanian émigré, Mica is at once ambitious, attractive, charming, and bright, a talented and successful interior decorator. But she was always an enigma to me.

Clearly Mica wanted a different life for Ahmet. They became a team, much like Ahmet and I had once been. And our lives had verged apart. Shirley and I had three kids and a house in the suburbs where we entertained disc jockeys and promo men at backyard barbecues. They had a brownstone on the Upper East Side. The "social ramble," as Satchel Paige called it, probably helped the company. Ahmet established himself as *the* high-profile record executive, and no one else has ever had his flair for beguiling artists.

Athough tacitly Ahmet and I understood we needed each other, our dealings were becoming more autonomous. From time to time our styles would clash. More than once I'd want to sign an act; Ahmet would be laying up, unreachable, elusive. Occasionally the delays worked in our favor. But now we operated better as separate units—an m.o. that grew more evident not simply in the style of music we produced from the mid-sixties forward but also in the geographic territories we claimed. Though our base was still New York—we'd always be a Manhattan-rooted label—more and more Ahmet orbited in Los Angeles and London while I headed south to Memphis, Muscle Shoals, and Miami.

SOUTHERN

FRIED

In the early sixties, the Drifters and Solomon Burke were carrying us. Brill Building pop was scoring hits with brilliant Brooklyn writers like Doc Pomus and Morty Shuman, Carole King and Gerry Goffin, mostly with teenage tunes spiced with Latin syncopation. Meanwhile, in a distant venue, something radically different was going on. The South was the scene, and the music, later labeled Soul, would change my life. Oddly enough, I was led there—at least in part—not by a singer or songwriter but by the enterprising Joe Galkin.

"You're crazy," I told Joe at the start of his Southern adventure. "That's all they need down there—an obnoxious Hebe like you." Galkin represented the old-guard song plugger, an endangered species in the fifties and extinct by the sixties. Rock 'n' roll did them in. They lived in the past, lamenting the death of "good music"—Rodgers and Hammerstein, Lerner and Loewe—while damning R&B and rock. Joe insisted he was clued in, but I thought he'd be better off with his poker games and his bar in Sunnyside, Queens, where Friars Club types sipped rye and swapped lies about Sammy Kaye and Abe Lyman.

Joe paid no mind. He left New York, vacated his penthouse at the Essex House, and moved to Atlanta, where he lived in a room at the Georgia Terrace Hotel and started all over again, this time as a freelance promoter. He was a tireless worker who proved to be a fabulous friend to Southern disc jockeys, not through heavy payola but by lavishing them with personal attention. Whenever he saw a radio transmitter, he'd stop and shmooze, leaving the deejays with a fifth of Jim Beam or an Orlon sport shirt.

"He'd cruise the South in this big Benz with a phone," says Dickie

Kline, Joe's protégé and later Atlantic's chief promo man. "He couldn't drive long distances because his legs fell asleep—his circulation was bad—so he did it in short spurts. The spurts were nonstop.

"Joe was a funny-looking guy with a bald, pear-shaped noggin. He looked like a gremlin, he drank like a fish and was absolutely adorable. The first time I ran into him was in Dallas, at KRZY, when in the middle of a record being played by deejay Dr. Jazzmo, Galkin picked up the needle, slapped on the single he was selling—'Lavender Blue' by Sammy Turner—and said, 'Play a goddamn smash, will ya? Play a god-damn smash!' "

Joe's conversational style was a muddle of false starts, gumball diction, ellipses, and the mumbles. His m.o. was chaos.

The first record he broke for me was Solomon Burke's "Just Out of Reach." Joe saw the single's potential weeks before I did. He wanted a hundred dollars a week to promote it, so I gave him fifty. Before I knew it we jumped from selling three hundred copies a week to three thousand. Astonishingly, Galkin even managed to slip Solomon onto the playlists of a few white stations. Within no time Joe was making over forty thousand dollars a year; even more impressively, he'd built up a network of program directors and disc jockeys—Shelly Stewart and Diggy Doo from Birmingham, Jockey Jack Gibson from Atlanta, Jivin' Gene from Charlotte, Okie Dokie from New Orleans, Fat Daddy from Miami—and won their respect and affection. They were crazy about this crazy guy, and as a result, he worked a few crazy miracles.

"Gotta smash for you this morning," he said on the phone from Greenville, Mississippi, teasing me by deliberately not mentioning the title.

I ventured the name of every R&B artist I could think of.

"No," said Joe, finally breaking the news. "It's Acker Bilk's 'Stranger on the Shore.' "

Now I knew he was demented. He was referring to a little Dixieland clarinet pastiche we'd acquired from England through the good offices of my buddy Howie Richmond.

The single ended up selling over a million copies. We threw a celebration for Acker, who was reduced to tears when he saw the band we'd assembled, a pantheon of his heroes: Bud Freeman, Vic Dickenson, Bob Wilber, Zutty Singleton. The eminent George Wein was piano man and leader.

But most importantly, Joe Galkin pointed me south at a critical moment when new sounds were exploding—a roots music that seemed to refer to the past, present, and future all at once.

*H*ymie Weiss was—and is—a lovable roughneck, and he was not mobbed up. His Old Town label recorded some great talent—the Solitaires, the Fiestas, Arthur Prysock—and Hymie, unsophisticated as he was, had a good heart. In 1960 he called and said, "Schmuck, you got a hit down here. If I didn't know it was your record, I'd grab it for myself. The fuckin' thing's selling like crazy."

The thing was Carla Thomas's "Gee Whiz." It came out on Satellite, a small Memphis label with which I'd made a distribution arrangement a year earlier. Satellite produced the actual recordings in the studio, using their own facilities and house musicians, then sent us the finished tape, and we took it from there. They bore studio costs; we paid for everything from that point on. We mastered, pressed, fabricated the package, distributed, marketed, and promoted hard. On every record sold they earned a royalty varying from 12 to 18 percent of retail—with no deductions.

I was hipped to Satellite by pressing plant operator Buster Williams, a courtly Southern gentleman whose thick Tennessee accent fascinated me as much as my Bronx brogue amused him. Buster was pressing enormous quantities of "Cause I Love You," a duet with Carla and her father, Rufus, so I flew down to Memphis to pick up the master. Our lawyer Paul Marshall cut a distribution deal with the label owners, Jim Stewart and his sister, Estelle Axton (who would later change their handle to Stax—*St*ewart *Ax*ton). "Cause I Love You" didn't hit, but a year later, when "Gee Whiz" did, I was back in Memphis.

"Jim Stewart was a country fiddler," explains Tom Dowd, who followed me to Tennessee, first as my engineer and then as co-producer. "Jim's a diminutive man who worked in the mortgage department of a bank. That's how he found this old vacant theater—originally for movies, then used for country-and-western shows, then a makeshift church—where his sister set up a record store in the lobby. The heavy in-store traffic gave them a great feel for current music taste. The studio was in the auditorium and Jim did the engineering. And even after their early hits, Jim still held on to his day job. Wexler would try to reach him at the studio but would be given the number at the bank. After going through three secretaries, Jerry finally figured out that Stewart, the force behind these hot black records, was a plain vanilla mortgage clerk."

I liked Jim. He was personable and warm. When he came to New York he'd stay with us in Great Neck. He became family. His sister was something of a Medusa—she was a mover and a shaker, but I respected her strength and made sure we got along.

The Memphis connection, though, started out rocky. When I went down, I was anxious to meet with Carla and Rufus Thomas. Rufus already had a reputation as the city's leading soul man—emcee at the Handy Theater, deejay on WDIA, singer for Sun Records, where "Bear Cat," his witty response to "Hound Dog," was Sam Phillips's first little hit in 1953. I love Rufus. I love his finely honed sense of comic irony, especially on the nuances of race relations. Rufus was sardonic without being mean, ballsy without being bitter. He was hip. His daughter Carla was beautiful and bright, a schoolteacher and singer whose voice suggested sexy, sweet passion.

I wanted to take Rufus and Carla to dinner in a restaurant, but at that time in Memphis there was no place where a mixed party could be comfortable. Reluctantly I agreed that room service would have to do. We picked up Carla, Rufus, and Mrs. Thomas at the radio station, and when we got back to the hotel Jim suggested that we avoid the lobby. Perhaps he was overreacting. I didn't think there would be any trouble, but it was his town, not mine, and we followed his lead. Walking around back to the freight elevator, down the garbage alley, Rufus mumbled, "Nothing changes. Down in the alley with the garbage. Same ol', same ol' shit." Which is what I felt like.

That night, after they'd gone and I was asleep, I thought I was dreaming. But the pounding at the door was a different kind of nightmare. "Vice squad!" they shouted. "You got a woman in there? Open up!"

Like hell I would. I met them in public, down in the lobby. Meanwhile, I dashed off a note to Ahmet, telling him what was happening, and dropped it in a mail slot, just in case. I had visions of these guys throwing me in the trunk of a car and dumping me somewhere in Arkansas. Apparently someone had seen black people leaving my room, and this was their response.

I got the cops' superior on the phone, some redneck lieutenant, and unburdened myself. "Lovely fucking greeting card you send me!" I said.

Despite the racist crap, the music in Memphis was a marvel. Their way of recording turned my head around, especially the work of the remarkable rhythm section.

The rhythm section was the heart of the matter, the chief reason Memphis mattered. The even racial composition of Booker T. and the MG's became a metaphor in my mind for their extraordinary harmony, in and out of the studio. Booker T. Jones, the keyboardist, and drummer Al Jackson were black; guitarist Steve Cropper and bassist Donald "Duck" Dunn were white; and Duck's predecessor, Louis Steinberg, was Jewish. The results were anything but gray. The boys played in red-clay soil, and I was walking into fertile territory. The funkiness of the music— bare-boned, simple, yet razor-sharp—knocked my dick in the dirt.

Once I heard this playing, I realized it was the converse of what we were doing in New York. Atlantic was famous, Ahmet once explained, for our strong, clean rhythm sound, heavy on bass. "We were among the first independents to mike instruments in the rhythm section separately, but to get that rhythmic punch, we found it necessary to use written arrangements. This was a major departure for R&B recordings. Some writers have described the Atlantic sound as R&B with strings or arranged R&B, and there's merit in that."

My rubric was "immaculate funk," to which we'd lately added the Latin kick. But after all the long years of recording in New York City, I was tired. Except for the Solomon Burke sessions, my work was dwindling. I couldn't get out of my own way. The arrangers were out of ideas, the songwriters out of material, the session players out of licks, and I was out of inspiration.

Inspiration was on the boil at Stax. The rhythm section had developed a method of building ad hoc head arrangements. Nothing was written down. Because of my experience with written charts, this was an exciting revelation. And separated from the larger group with whom they'd been playing on the road—the all-Caucasian Mar-Keys—the MG's were magic in the studio: Booker had this great low-down Ray Charles feel; Cropper was a marvel, a guitarist who combined rhythm and lead, an intuitive writer of tremendous breadth; Jackson perhaps the premier funk drummer of the decade; Duck dead-on with hypnotic natural-feel bass lines.

I'd watch them come in the morning, hang up their coats, grab their axes, and start to play. If they didn't have a session or a song, they'd ad-lib, developing chord and rhythm patterns until something blossomed. It was effortless, easy as breathing. Here were four men (with rapport as close as a classical string quartet's) making it up as they went along. The feel was everything; the feel was real, right, and tight in the pocket.

Given my unappeasable rage for approbation, I wasn't displeased to learn these young men associated me with the R&B records that had schooled them. They viewed me as a something of an Old Master. Actually, I'd always felt like an old man of the business. When I joined Atlantic in 1953, I was already thirty-six; in the youth-crazed sixties I was pushing fifty; when I produced Dylan in the seventies I was past sixty. I'd like to think my age was more a help than a hindrance, but combined with my insecurity it gave me a patriarchal stature I couldn't always keep subdued.

Even as Stax started making money for all concerned—William Bell's "You Don't Miss Your Water," Booker T. and the MG's instrumental "Green Onions," and Rufus Thomas's whistling and yelping "Walkin' the Dog" all hit big in '62 and '63—there were disagreements. For example, I often had problems with Stax's mixes; their rhythm tracks often tended to overpower lead vocals. To me, a record comes down to a singer and a song; other elements must be subordinate. "You have your New York ears," Jim would tell me, "and we have our Memphis ears." At times we'd get in each other's way and drive each other nuts.

"The sound situation at Stax," explains Duck Dunn, "was peculiar. The old movie theater on East McLemore, the Capitol, was in the middle of funkytown and renamed Soulsville U.S.A. The studio was built on a downhill slope. The control room was where the screen used to be. We used the original theater speakers and the old tattered curtains for acoustics. We'd crank the shit up, play it back, and let it boom like crazy. Sounded great. The drums were in the middle, the horns would be live, and there was always a delay of the beat. It worked."

Not always. "Early on," Tom Dowd recalls, "just after Wexler made the deal with Stax, we were waiting for a record that was five weeks late. Jerry calls down to Memphis, screaming at Jim, 'What the hell is happening?' Their tape recorder is missing a part that hasn't arrived. 'Get on a plane to Memphis,' Wexler orders me, 'and straighten this shit out.' Stewart picks me up at the airport and takes me to the studio. I see a resistor's burned out and a tube's missing. I get my second engineer in New York to pick up the parts and give them to a stewardess with a ten-dollar tip on the first flight in the morning. That afternoon I have the machine realigned and humming. Stewart's in shock. He can't believe it. By nightfall, Booker, Steve, Duck, and Al have recorded three tracks.

"At first everyone was a little afraid that East Coast technology would mean losing the soul button, but they soon saw we had the same goals. They kept calling for me. After initial reluctance, they welcomed my modernization. They were sweet, beautiful people, the folks in Memphis, and they'd be the first to say they learned as much from Wexler as he learned from them. Jerry would be demanding; he made them less laid back. While they taught him about musical relaxation, he schooled them on concentration and intensity. He showed them that you couldn't go to sleep making a blues record."

Before long, I found myself wide awake and involved, shaken from my slump, moving toward hands-on production down south. My main motivator was a man some called the Midnight Mover.

WICKED

Pickett was a pistol. I called him the Black Panther even before the phrase was political. He had matinee-idol looks, flaming eyes, lustrous ebony skin, a sleek, muscular torso. His temperament was fire, his flash-and-fury singing style a study in controlled aggression, his blood-curdling scream always musical, always in tune. In the mid-sixties Wicked Wilson Pickett mainlined American music with a hefty dose of undiluted soul. Three decades later, his steel-belted hits like "Funky Broadway," "Mustang Sally," "In the Midnight Hour," and "Midnight Mover" have lost none of their tread.

Pickett told me he wanted to be on Atlantic when we met in my Broadway office in 1964. This was only a year after the fight over "If You Need Me"—Wilson Pickett versus Solomon Burke—and I asked if that hadn't pissed him off.

"Fuck that," he said. "I need the bread."

I sent Wilson into the studio with Bert Berns—this was before our falling-out—but all I got back was a single, a seven-thousand-dollar production bill (outrageous for those days), and no hits. Pickett was obstreperous, and Bert abrasive; the chemistry couldn't work. So I took it upon myself to find the songs; but what I liked, Wilson didn't, and vice versa. For a year we did the dance of the fireflies. We couldn't get it together. I knew what a powerhouse singer he was, and it was killing me.

Finally I got an idea—not for a song but for a trip: me and Pickett to Memphis, whose freshness just might give us the edge. And instead of trying to provide material, I urged him—with local genius Steve Cropper—to create his own. I put the two of them in a hotel room with a bottle of Jack Daniel's and the simple exhortation—"Write!"—which they did. When we got in that beat-up old movie theater on East Mc-Lemore, the place was rocking, the speakers nearly blown by the power of Wayne Jackson's punctuated horns. One of the songs was "In the Midnight Hour." I loved the lyric and the gospel fervor; Cropper inspired Pickett's truest passion. Originally from Prattville, Alabama, the Wicked One was back home, raising hell.

I was taken with everything but the rhythm pattern. Jim Stewart was at the board setting knobs, and I was working the talkback, directing the vocal, when I suddenly realized I was on the wrong side of the glass.

"Jerry amazed us," Cropper told Jann Wenner for a piece in *Rolling Stone*. "He ran out of the booth and started dancing."

"The bass thing was Wexler's idea," Duck Dunn said. "We were going another way when Jerry started doing the jerk dance."

I was shaking my booty to a groove made popular by the Larks' "The Jerk," a mid-sixties hit. The idea was to push the second beat while holding back the fourth—something easier demonstrated than explained. The boys caught it, put it in the pocket, and sent Pickett flying up the charts. "Midnight Hour" was a stone smash, Wilson's vocal a cyclone of conviction. The song became a bar-band anthem; the MG's incorporated the little rhythm variation into their playing from then on.

At the same session we cut "Don't Fight It," "That's a Man's Way," and "I'm Not Tired." From the get-go, Pickett's image was unapologetically macho—"I'm a man and a half," he'd later boast in a song by the same name.

A few months later, Wilson was back in Memphis for a second outing, which produced "634-5789." I didn't make the trip, and when I heard the tape in my office I liked the song but not the out-of-tune femme vocals. I happened to look up when one of our acts, Patti LaBelle and her Bluebelles, was walking past. "Patti," I said, "I have a little gig for you and the ladies."

They went into the studio and cut the strongest, tightest, cleanest call-and-response accompaniment I could have hoped for. I place Patti in the highest pantheon of female singers—for power, range, heart and soul—and it's an unfortunate irony that she never hit it big with us. We didn't find her the right material and, even worse, made the ghastly mistake of trying to turn her Bluebelles into the Supremes.

Meanwhile, though, they weren't making mistakes down at Stax. While Pickett was popping, Eddie Floyd (another former Falcon) and Steve Cropper co-wrote "Knock on Wood," a central theme of the Soul

Wex, Wilson, Ahmet

Era. Jim Stewart also tapped the enormous potential of songwriters David Porter and Isaac Hayes (later the orchestrator of *Shaft* fame and a solo singing star). Porter and Hayes were to the sixties what Leiber and Stoller were to the fifties—poets with precisely the right punch. Their catalogue of songs ("Soul Man," "Hold On, I'm Comin'," "When Something Is Wrong with My Baby," "You Got Me Hummin'," "I Thank You," "Wrap It Up") defined the times along with the two great singers they produced for us.

I first heard Sam and Dave in a sweltering Miami nightclub earlier in the decade. The joint was called the King of Hearts, and it was wall-to-wall sisters and brothers boogalooing in hundred-degree tropical heat. Our distributor Henry Stone had hipped me to the act, which as the evening grew more intense had me out on the floor boogying like a fool.

I thought they'd be perfect for Memphis and immediately made an arrangement with Jim Stewart that differed from all the other Stax contracts: I signed them to an Atlantic deal. To benefit from Stax's production, their records would come out on the Stax label. Stax would enjoy the same royalty as if Sam and Dave were original Stax signatories—and Atlantic would pick up their signing advance. Everyone was happy, especially when Jim brought in Porter and Hayes as writers and producers and the hits started happening.

Strange to learn that Sam and Dave were personally incompatible—their feuds were mythic—because musically they were ham and eggs. Their live act was filled with animation, harmony, and seeming goodwill. I put Sam in the sweet tradition of Sam Cooke or Solomon Burke, while Dave had an ominous Four Tops' Levi Stubbs–sounding voice, the preacher promising hellfire.

Meanwhile, for all his success, Pickett was giving everyone fits. He was so difficult—arrogant, demanding, always ready to fight—that Jim Stewart finally barred him from the studio. I was upset, of course; and there were other conflicts between Jim and me. He had cooled to the idea of non-Stax artists like Pickett pulling hits out of his studio. Don Covay's "See-Saw," also cut in Memphis for Atlantic, was bouncing up the charts. For us to distribute and promote his label was one thing; Jim realized that in the R&B field, our contacts with deejays and program directors were tops. But it was another thing to let us use his studio—and, in Stewart's mind, the Stax gestalt—to create hits from which Jim didn't enjoy long-term profits.

There was also the matter of Chips Moman, the guitarist, producer, songwriter, and all-around organizer who once served as Stewart's first lieutenant. Chips is one of the great Southern musical minds, a manipulator and mesmerizer who, under a full moon in deserted parking lots, has been known to con drug-crazed badasses into handing over their guns. I always got on with Moman, but Jim didn't, and at a certain point he began to resent our relationship.

At the same time, the indefatigable Joe Galkin was pulling my coat to a hot rhythm section not far down the road in northern Alabama, where, hard by the Tennessee River and the Wilson Dam, four little communities—Florence, Sheffield, Tuscumbia, and Muscle Shoals—were clustered together. When Joe asked if I was interested, I told him I needed to see if the boys could play.

*R*ick Hall was the Berry Gordy of Muscle Shoals, a po' boy from the bottom of the agrarian ladder, a white man with a strong feel for black blues. A former musician, a souped-up salesman and hard-nosed entrepreneur, he started a label called FAME (Florence, Alabama Music Enterprises) and had a couple of hits (Arthur Alexander's "You Better Move On," Jimmy Hughes's "Steal Away").

For Rick, Joe Galkin was a second father. "I'd stay with Joe when I

Pickett in the studio

was selling records in Atlanta," he remembers. "Galkin was my mentor. He was always talking about Atlantic and Jerry Wexler. He was devoted to them and convinced that Wexler and I needed to get together. He got Jerry on the phone for me, but I didn't know what the hell to say. 'Call me if you find something you're excited about,' Wexler said. Never heard anyone get off a phone as fast as Jerry Wexler.

"A little later my sidekick Dan Penn, who has incredible ears and is a helluva songwriter—him and Chips Moman wrote 'The Dark End of the Street'—brought me this acetate of a tune Quin Ivy and Marlin Greene had produced down the street in Ivy's homegrown studio on a twenty-five-dollar Sears Roebuck discmaker. I heard this thing and couldn't believe it. The first line came pouring out of the singer's heart. The singer was an orderly at a hospital around here. He had a voice like an angel. So I called Wexler."

When he called, I was having a party in Great Neck, one of those casual music-business picnics that Shirley and I liked to throw—steaks on the grill, beers by the pool, record maniacs running around. Over the long-distance wire, Hall said he had something hot. "Send it up," I said. When I heard it, I called Ahmet in Europe and told him I'd found a single that was going to pay for our whole summer.

The song was Percy Sledge's "When a Man Loves a Woman," a transcendent moment in the saga of Muscle Shoals, a holy love hymn that shot to number one and made me realize Galkin was right: I had to get with Hall in a hurry. I did, and I took Wilson with me.

"Pickett was a wildcat," says Rick. "He got off the plane in our little cotton patch of an airport ready to go. He was wearing this houndstooth coat, looking like he just stepped out of the pages of a fashion magazine—hair all slicked back, flashing smile, built like a running back for the New York Giants. I'm thinking to myself, How the hell am I gonna control this guy?"

Rick couldn't. Nobody could. But for a long while it didn't matter, because the magic was in the music and the music was so deeply ingrained in Muscle Shoals—in guitarists like Eddie Hinton, keyboardists like Spooner Oldham, songwriters like Donnie Fritts. Music was in the air you breathed and the water you drank, coming at you so inexorably and naturally that I found myself returning to the place not simply a few more times but on dozens of occasions over the next quarter-century.

More than any other locale or individual, Muscle Shoals changed my life—musically and every which way.

WHITE
ROCK
EFFER-
VESCING

*R*hythm and blues was in a ferment, mirroring the excitement of the times—the civil rights movement, the radicalization of youth, the liberal attitudes toward drugs, the rise of rock 'n' roll. If the music I was producing reflected the nation's growing emphasis on black self-pride and forthright soul, Ahmet was tuning in to other musical strains. Through jazz saxist Nino Tempo—(who, with his sister April Stevens, had a #1 pop hit for us in 1963 with "Deep Purple")—Ahmet signed a couple once called Caesar and Cleo but better known as Sonny and Cher, an improbably commercial pair: "I Got You Babe" went to number one in 1965. There had been other top singles for us—"Alley Cat," for instance, which Nesuhi discovered. Beyond pleasant pop, though, Ahmet was tracking another pattern, pointing to a future that he envisioned far more clearly than I.

"The British invasion," he says, "had tremendous repercussions. The Beatles and Stones changed everything. Jerry considered the music derivative. Most of it surely was; some of it, however, was original. Either way, I wanted to get involved, and I did—with L.A.-area groups such as the Buffalo Springfield, who had three superb lead singers in Richard Furay, Stephen Stills, and Neil Young."

Ahmet signed a number of pioneering rock stars: he brought in Cream, King Crimson, Yes, and, through Robert Stigwood and Brian Epstein, the Bee Gees. I signed Vanilla Fudge. These acquisitions were thrilling, but I didn't have what it took to produce a self-contained rock group. My thing was getting great backings for great singers.

Ahmet's gift for acquiring talent was remarkable. Whether in London or in Los Angeles, his timing was impeccable; he was always in the

With Sonny and Cher

right venue at the right time. His cool was irresistible to managers and artists alike. He loved competing for new bands; once Ahmet learned of an auction battle by record executives for some unsigned singer, he'd fly into the fray and usually emerge victorious.

A case in point was the ferocious fight over the Young Rascals. Sid Bernstein, the promoter who booked the Beatles in America, was big both physically and professionally, a goodhearted mogul and master manipulator. He called me about this group he was managing and showcasing out on Long Island at the Barge, in Westhampton. "If I like them, Sid," I warned him, "I don't want to get into an auction."

Nesuhi and I ran out there and were knocked sideways. These Rascals were blue-eyed soul brothers who could write, sing, and play their asses off. Their songs were dynamite. They sounded fresh and fiery, and I wanted to sign them right away. So did Leiber and Stoller, who were at the gig along with a clutch of attorneys. What's worse, during the break we couldn't get near Felix Cavaliere, the group's leader, and his buddies, Eddie Brigati, Gene Cornish, and Dino Danelli. Jerry and Mike were swarming all over them, blocking our way.

The next day I was on the horn with Sid. "All right," I told him, "we want them. What's the deal?"

"Sorry, Wex," he said. "Other labels are involved. In fact, Phil Spector's flying in from the coast to hear them tonight."

I could see I was going down slow; our only hope was in the cleanup hitter. I called Ahmet at his summer place in Southampton, and that night he showed just as Spector arrived. After the gig Ahmet and Phil sat down with the Rascals in a charm shoot-out. Since Spector had always copped off Ertegun's style, the confrontation was strangely oedipal. Finally, though, it was no contest. With his European charm, his war stories of the R&B fifties, his ability to do the polite white-boy dozens, his put-downs, his praises, his accomplishments, his eclecticism, his hedonism—Ahmet wiped Spector out. The Rascals were ours, and their first rush of releases—"Good Lovin'," "You Better Run," "I've Been Lonely Too Long," "A Girl Like You," "How Can I Be Sure," and especially the classic "Groovin'"—were great music and serious money-makers.

Most of the white groups did not sound as soulful as the Rascals. In the emerging rock guitar style, for example, I heard a clutter of hysterical notes I abhorred. Because I was making the music I loved so deeply—Southern soul—I might have been myopic about the changes in white rock 'n' roll. I might have been myopic about many things.

*F*ear was still my engine, and it was fear of failure that had me pushing for the sale of our label. In 1963 we sold our publishing company, Progressive, but the capital returns were modest. We lived well yet had never enjoyed a cash windfall. I had no savings, no real wealth, and no faith that the record business might not collapse at any moment. Among all the independent record companies born in the forties and fifties, we alone were surviving the sixties. How well I remember those labels and the grizzled infighters who owned them: Exclusive (Leon and Otis Rene), Modern (the Biharis), Imperial (Lew Chudd), Specialty (Art Rupe), Old Town (Hymie Weiss), Herald/Ember (Al Silver), Chess (the brothers Chess), and on and on into the night—memorable logos all. I am reminded of the tribes of the Sinai desert—the Hittites, the Moabites, the Midianites, the Amorites. Gone, perished, vanished from the face of the earth. Only one survives—the Hebrews. Given the turbulence of the decade, who knew how long we'd last? I wanted to cash out. Ahmet was reluctant, Nesuhi less so; but my persistence would finally, and unfortunately, prevail.

THE

WORK

JONES

Once again, my personal life seems to have gotten lost in the musical shuffle. I was lost in my work, thrilled by my work, overwhelmed by my work—and always wanting more.

As a result, Shirley suffered, and so did the kids. In the last half of the sixties my children were teenagers—bright, talented and as much in love with music as I was. In some ways we could relate on that level; yet business came first.

When writer Lita Eliscu came to our house to interview me for the alternative paper *SoHo News,* she got a good glimpse of my home life. "Dinner was an offbeat and quite delicious combination of *haute* soul food and fine French wine," she wrote. "After dinner we all trooped into the living room to listen to stereo tape mixes of Jerry's latest work-in-progress. His children glided in, only staying long enough to deliver an immaculate perception or two about an imperfect horn solo or a bridge still needing work. Jerry listened seriously, considering possibilities."

"Jerry tried to be there for us," says Shirley, "but the house was an extension of the office. We supported him. We listened to acetates; the kids helped select singles and critiqued mixes. Once I convinced Jerry to take Paul on a fishing trip to Shelter Island and the North Fork of Long Island. It wasn't great, because, in his inimitable way, Jerry wound up A&R-ing the trip. He could never get his mind out of the studio or the office."

That trip with Paul, though, reinforced my burning desire to live on the water. Sailing along the Sound, I was moved by the green lawns sloping down to Peconic Bay, the gabled Victorian houses, the expansive pillared mansions. Perhaps I was paying more attention to the scenery than to my son.

"I would dread dinners," Paul remembers, "whenever there were guests. Jerry had this habit of pontificating. He liked to push people's buttons and get into rancorous arguments. It didn't take much to set him off. Once Grandma Elsa said, 'Gerald has the exact same temper as his father,' and that explained a lot. I was also getting lost in the Grateful Dead, another area of contention. Jerry hated the stuff. He'd walk into my room and start screaming about how shitty it was. Two years later he was trying to sign them for their European rights. It took me a long time to figure out that the only way to gain Jerry's respect was to back him down. He had a street mentality. He'd walk over you if he could."

I realized that all the kids—Anita as the oldest, Paul, and then Lisa—had started smoking pot, but I took the liberal position of the times: it was better than booze and had creative properties. Besides, as a long-term recreational doper I had no problems with substances. I'd never get high during the day. I practiced the reward-the-seal-with-a-fish policy: If I was a good boy and did all my work, after hours I might allow myself a joint or, later in the seventies, a snort of cocaine. The kids and I sometimes smoked together—something I naively thought would bring us closer. Our taste in music was already uncannily close.

I remember the night, for instance, I took Anita to see Albert King at the Village Gate. She was deeply into Memphis funk, and there she was backstage, this small teenage girl looking up at a six-foot-five blues-man.

"Nice meetin' ya, hon," said Albert.

"Oh, Mr. King," said Anita, "please promise me you won't get a wah-wah pedal." Steve Cropper had just gotten a wah-wah, and Anita, a pur-ist like her old man, was crushed.

My younger daughter, Lisa, had started hammering out grooves; she'd been banging on tabletops with knives and spoons ever since she was a baby. "There was something about James Brown's 'Cold Sweat,'" says Lisa, "that drove me crazy. I couldn't stop listening, couldn't stop repeating the rhythm pattern."

I'm with Lisa. No one in the world makes me want to dance like James Brown. And seeing Lisa keep such precise time warmed my heart; Shirley and I bought her a kiddie drum set, which not long after was upgraded to the real deal.

Aside from the powerful musical bond, our family situation wasn't

With Shirley, 1970

great. I was conscious of the emotional distance between me and my kids but lacked the know-how, the means, or the drive to remedy the situation. As someone later pointed out, we might have been happier in a big apartment on the Upper West Side of Manhattan. We were isolated in the suburbs. But after a crazy day at the office or a long night in the studio, I craved peace and quiet, a bedroom far from the noise of city streets.

All this took its toll on Shirley. We were not as tight as we once were, although there were moments.

We had planned, for example, to spend a vacation together at the Arizona Biltmore. My heart was set on playing golf; so when, amazingly, it started snowing, we flew to Miami, where we checked in to the Thunderbird and I headed for the links. That night Shirley and I both came down with the mumps. We quarantined ourselves, and the motel manager, anxious to keep our sickness under wraps, sent in all our meals. I was on the phone a good deal of the time with my good buddy Milton "Fat Daddy" Smith, the hottest R&B deejay in town. Fat Daddy couldn't resist spilling the beans about "my man with the mumps," much to the innkeeper's chagrin.

Shirley and I were in that room for a week. You'd think we'd go nuts, but not a chance. We used the time to read all of William Faulkner in British paperback editions. It was wonderful. But it took the mumps for me to give my wife some undivided attention. Shirley savored good writing, and she even prepared an exhaustive genealogy of the characters in Faulkner's fictional Yoknapatawpha County.

And by this time, it was clear that the South held a different sort of magic for me.

SOUL

MEN

I didn't work alone; I rarely do. I like to collaborate. Despite my alternating moods of insecurity and arrogance, I never lost sight of my nonmusicianship.

I sailed under the flag of impassioned fandom, a fanatic for flawless execution, an onlooker, organizer, encourager, and, ultimately, promoter. One of the reasons I was so effective, I'm certain, had to do with the team I'd assembled.

Tommy Dowd is the great sound man of our time. His expertise allowed me to remain—contentedly—a technological cripple. In time, Tom evolved from engineer to co-producer to producer on his own. From the fifties on, he kept Atlantic in the forefront of high tech. He revolutionized the recording systems in Memphis and Muscle Shoals, proving to the good ol' boys that they needn't sacrifice soul for sound.

Back in the fifties, Tommy had put us years ahead when he had us buy an eight-track Ampex. It was Ampex #3: #1 had been used spectacularly by Les Paul in his basement for his historic multitrack recordings with his wife, Mary Ford; #2 was a toy for Mitch Miller's longtime contractor, Jiggs Carroll, in the Woodward Hotel. Thus we were the first record company to go eight-track, enabling us years later to put out sides from the vault in true stereo. In association with MCI—not the megacorporation but a Florida-based high-fidelity outfit—Dowd also helped develop a dramatically improved eight-track in the sixties. Eventually we bought four—two for New York, one for the Criteria Studios in Miami, one for Muscle Shoals, providing electronic compatibility wherever I worked.

In 1963, an additional member of our squad came aboard. "Everybody back home in Turkey knew of Ambassador Ertegun," says Arif

Tommy Dowd, world's greatest engineer

Mardin, who, like Tommy, was a protégé with skills that supplemented my own. "I had studied at the University of Istanbul, gotten a graduate degree at the London School of Economics, but finally wound up at the Berklee School of Music. Jazz was my love, to be a jazz writer and arranger my goal; and it was at the Newport Jazz Festival where I finally cornered Nesuhi. He hired me as his assistant and assigned me vault research, hunting down unreleased John Coltrane and Charles Mingus tracks. Wexler had me do horn overdubs on a Chuck Willis memorial album and may have been impressed with my abilities, but generally I was ignored—until a certain BMI dinner where King Curtis was leading the Atlantic house band. I had established a great relationship with King, who asked me to write ten-second cues for the winning songs at the postdinner ceremonies. The program went extremely well, and Jerry wanted to know who had written the continuity music. 'Your own man,' Curtis answered. 'You have a house arranger and you don't even know it.'"

In no time Arif went from being a "hey, you" in the studio to writing horn sketches and string parts. As I brought him along, he evolved into a fantastic arranger. During sessions—some smooth, others stormy—I was impressed by both his enormous talent and his cool. Arif is a patrician, and no one works better under stress. What Tommy was to engineering, Arif was to arranging, the super pro. What's more, the two could easily switch roles. No producer has ever enjoyed better backup.

The marvelous Arif Mardin

They freed me up to direct, concentrate on the groove, the interpretation, the overall feel. Soul music is nothing if not feel.

When Pickett started recording in Muscle Shoals, I felt apprehensive. I found Rick Hall's supervision far too severe; he was impatient and
treated the musicians like pawns. After observing for an hour, I called
for a change. "You do the engineering, Rick," I said, "and I'll work the
talkback."

Pickett was in great voice—that wasn't the problem. It was Junior
Lowe, the bass player, who wasn't locking on the groove. Chips Moman
let me know that Junior was basically a guitarist, not a bassist, and we'd
do better with Tommy Cogbill. The switch was magical; Tommy tore it
up. So did rhythm guitarist Jimmy Johnson; the sure-footed and naturally inventive Roger Hawkins, especially adept at sound consistency,
especially soulful with the sock cymbal and bass drum; and Spooner
Oldham, the Ichabod Crane–looking keyboard wizard.

In spite of the stellar musicianship on the first tune, "Land of 1000
Dances," we were having a hard time with the double count-off. After
dozens of abortive attempts, I came up with an idea. "Sing the counts,
Wilson," I suggested. "Make the counts part of the intro."

Listen to the song and you'll hear the Wicked One screaming "One, two, three!," then repeat "One, two, three!" before the band hits on the downbeat of this Chris Kenner dance romp. The horns—Wayne Jackson, Charlie Chalmers, Andrew Love, and Floyd Newman—kick Pickett's ass all the way across Alabama.

In later sessions, we cut "Everybody Needs Somebody to Love," a song I'd written with Bert Berns and Solomon Burke, as well as the high-riding "Mustang Sally," the low-down "Funky Broadway," and a motif Pickett and I put together, "Soul Dance Number Three." (Years later, when I was going into the studio with the mighty Tower of Power, their baritone saxist, Steve "The Doctor" Kupka, after being introduced to me, simply winked and whispered, "Soul Dance Number Three." I wanted to kiss him.)

Now all the elements fell into place for Pickett. To the Muscle Shoals mix he added his friend Bobby Womack, who not only contributed tasty left-handed guitar accents and fills but also brought in songs like "I'm in Love," "I Found a True Love," and "I'm a Midnight Mover." A superlative singer himself, Bobby became a key contributor to the overall production.

The musical integration was a joy to hear and to behold. The racial mix was serendipitous. For the past decade, musicians in the Memphis–Muscle Shoals axis, black and white, had found a ready market in the fraternity parties of the great Southern universities. Ever since those early pre–rock 'n' roll "beach" records emerging from the Carolina coast in the fifties, I could see that Southern whites liked their music uncompromisingly black. Despite the ugly legacy of Jim Crow, their white hearts and minds were gripped, it would seem, forevermore.

Credit the reach and power of WLAC in Nashville, which broadcast clear-channel nondirectional into twenty-two states. The white dee-jays—John R, Gene Nobles, and Hoss Allen—were black-talking, blues-loving stars. The records they played influenced at least two generations of fans. From a sales point of view, they were marvelous. The ad spots cost a buck apiece late at night, and in conjunction with mail-order operations like Ernie's and Randy's, we got fantastic sales results throughout the country.

First came the fans, and not long after, the musicians. As Al Bell, later Stax's promo director, pointed out, the collision between openly integrated music and a tightly segregated society created a new kind of energy. You can hear a subtle defiance in the songs. White Southern musicians—unlike their British counterparts, who learned the blues off records—lived the blues themselves, saw them, tasted them, were rooted in the same soil as their black teachers.

I was in my early fifties; the Muscle Shoals players were in their early twenties, a couple of generations younger. Later on, a real bonding took place—we became family. But in the beginning it took some getting used to.

"I remember the first time Jerry called me into the control room," says David Hood, the bassist in what would become the basic Shoals rhythm section of drummer Roger Hawkins, guitarist Jimmy Johnson, and keyboardist Barry Beckett. "Wexler's loud voice—his New York accent—just boomed all over the room. He could stun you with that voice. Man, I was petrified. Later on, we became so tight I asked him to officiate at my wedding. He began the ceremony saying, 'I have no power vested in me whatsoever . . .'"

"After a while," says Jimmy Johnson, "we became Jerry's second set of kids."

"Before Wexler," Hawkins remembers, "things were pretty quiet around the Shoals. Spooner Oldham and Dan Penn had written 'I'm Your Puppet,' which became a big hit for James and Bobby Purify, and there were a couple of other items, but not many. Jerry put the national spotlight on us. When Wexler said he liked my playing, well, that was a big moment in my life."

No bigger than it was for me, because it was the boys in Muscle Shoals who taught me a new way of making records, spontaneously, synergistically. I'd hit town on the weekend. I'd get together with the singer and Barry Beckett, who ultimately evolved into the de facto leader of the group, and we'd rough out the songs which we'd already selected. We'd set the layout and the keys, then Barry would write a bare-bones chart by the numbers. The Muscle Shoals method of arrangements involved numbering—not naming—chords. It was simple—one through six, which might sound musically illiterate but worked like a charm, making it easy to change keys and leaving lots of room for variations.

When the boys came in Monday afternoon, they'd get a copy of the chord chart and would start to pick. They'd play around, maybe lock into a lick, find a nourishing groove, feel their way into a structure. Someone might develop an especially tasty rhythm line—maybe a two-bar syncopated pattern, an outstanding turnaround, or a provocative fill. The arrangement would build communally and organically. The ideas could come from anyone. Pete Carr, for example, another tremendous Muscle

Shoals lead guitarist, made marvelous contributions to dozens of sessions. Pete's thinking was not conventional; his two-bar patterns formed the basis of many a rhythm arrangement.

The bottom line was rhythm. Horn and strings—the icing on the cake—might be added afterwards, or not. The trick was to keep the session open, the creative juices flowing, the improvisatory feeling of on-the-spot, here-and-now creation vital and fresh.

"When Jerry started producing Pickett," says Jimmy Johnson, "he saw that our style allowed him to get involved in the rhythm section. He became part of the rhythm section. He loved that. He loved coming out of the control room and helping us find grooves. Maybe in New York he wasn't so loose with the musicians. He liked our Southern hospitality, and he could feel we were honored to have him down here. The combination worked—his get-it-done personality and our being laid-back. He got us organized—in and out, cut the tracks, do the vocals, mix it down. We gave him the relaxed feeling he wanted, and Pickett gave him hits."

Pickett's records were terrific, and strong examples of the Southern school of recording. But they were not the only examples, and perhaps not even the best. Some argue that distinction belongs to another singer, who, like Ray Charles before him, was himself a producer. I'm talking about Otis Redding.

*W*exler, I want you to finance a session." It was 1963, and Joe Galkin was smoking up a breeze down South; the airplay for Atlantic was fantastic.

"Who?" I asked. Joe was a hustler, but a hustler with good hunches.

"Johnny Jenkins and the Pinetoppers. I'm managing them and I want to record them at Stax. Give me two thousand dollars."

"Never heard of 'em."

"You will. Johnny's a great guitarist, and one of his sidemen can sing. It'll take two thousand dollars."

Galkin was an irresistible pain in the ass. So I put up the dough and they did the session at Stax. The sideman Joe mentioned was also Jenkins's driver, and he drove the band van from Macon to Memphis to do the date. When the instrumentals were completed, there was less than an hour left of studio time. That's when the sideman sang two songs. The first, "Hey Hey Baby," cloned Little Richard—who, like the driver, came

Otis

from Macon—and didn't do much for me. But the second, the ballad "These Arms of Mine," was brilliant. The driver was Otis Redding.

If things had gone according to Hoyle, Otis would have been signed to Atlantic; we had, after all, financed his first session. But Jim Stewart wanted him on Stax, and our arrangement was working so well that I let it pass.

As time went on, I quickly saw I'd been both right and wrong: right because Stax was the perfect studio setting for Otis, and wrong because he was destined to become an international star, and had I stuck to business-only principles, he would have been Atlantic's first international star of the sixties. In the end, I had no regrets. I realized I was lucky to be associated with Otis and blessed to be his friend.

Otis was magic, even if you couldn't tell by his debut at the Apollo, where we first tightened up. I'd picked him up at La Guardia and was surprised to see him standing there alone—no valet, no roadie, no manager. There was something pure about his personality, calm, dignified, vibrant. He'd had a couple of R&B chart hits, but nothing big. I drove him up to Harlem, introduced him to Bob Schiffman, the Apollo's owner, and took him to dinner.

The Otis I saw that night was essentially the same Otis I would always see. Stardom never changed him. He had a strong inner life. He was emotionally centered. His manners were impeccable. His humor was sly and roguish; he relished calling Ahmet "Omelet," and always with a straight face. He had a positive sense of racial identity but resisted the blandishments of militants who tried to turn him against us and his manager, Phil Walden. Redding was one of those rare souls who saw beyond color and externalities; he dealt with you as a human being, not as a white or a black or a Christian or a Jew. His intelligence was keen, his curiosity high, and despite stories to the contrary he was anything *but* the cliché of the backwoods country boy come to the big city. Otis knew what was happening.

At first he was inept on stage. He simply stood in front of the microphone—arms outstretched, body motionless—and sang "These Arms of Mine." (It was the same with Marvin Gaye when he started out, standing stock-still and singing.) Otis didn't move. His stage animation would come later after he'd worked with Sam and Dave. Yet in spite of his inertia, the women at the Apollo loved him, not only for his looks—he was tall, strapping, and handsome—but for his voice and vulnerability as well. Like Pickett, Otis had chops like a wolf; his voice was big and gorgeous and filled with feeling. He also exuded a warmth that tempered the aggressive side of his soul, a porous strain of generous emotion that covered every song he sang: "Pain in My Heart," "Security," "Chained and Bound," "I've Been Loving You Too Long," "Hard to Handle," "I've Got Dreams to Remember," "Love Man."

Otis will forever be associated with Steve Cropper, his chief collaborator in the Stax studio, the man with whom he wrote "Mr. Pitiful," "I Can't Turn You Loose," "Just One More Day," "Fa-Fa-Fa-Fa-Fa (Sad Song)," "I'm Sick Y'All," "Direct Me," and the eternal "(Sittin' on) The Dock of the Bay." Cropper was an innovator, a fabulous songwriter and only the second guitarist I'd encountered who could simultaneously play rhythm and lead (Cornell Dupree was the first). Until then, we required two, sometimes three guitarists to handle those diverse functions.

"The Stax studio," says bassist Duck Dunn, "would light up when Otis came in. He got everyone to play above their heads. He got performances out of us like no one else. He was an incredible creative spark, a life force that wouldn't quit."

"I lived between Otis sessions," trumpeter Wayne Jackson told musicologist Rob Bowman. "Otis was the focus for everybody. You could feel the excitement when he was coming."

The arrangements themselves were perhaps the slickest of the Southern style—loose and tight all at once, horn punctuations replacing background vocals. The horn accents—those unexpected bursts of energy and joy—were largely Otis's invention. Between 1961, when he started out by imitating Little Richard with "Shout Bamalama" and "Fat Girl," and by 1965, when he recorded the album *Otis Blue* after the tragic death of the great Sam Cooke, Redding had become a master. When he sang Sam's "A Change Is Gonna Come," it was clear that the torch had been passed; the tradition was alive.

The big change for Otis came in 1967 when we took him to the Monterey Pop Festival. John Phillips of the Mamas and the Papas and Lou Adler, best known as Carole King's producer, asked me to invite Otis, so I called Phil Walden.

Walden was a college boy from Macon, more Redding's soul brother than his manager. He'd known Otis since high school and was as wildly in love with R&B as any man who has ever lived, a devotee and businessman with whom I would soon begin a subsidiary label, Capricorn Records. (Phil and I share the same astrological sign, a fact that, while a joke to me, had the right ring for a record company in the Age of Aquarius.) In my mind, Walden was the archetype of the thousands of Southern whites who'd got bit by the funk bug.

Anyway, I missed the boat at Monterey. The festival can be seen now—and sharper observers than I saw it then—as a rite of passage, the blossoming of a flower-power scene dominated by hippie musicians, hippie singers, and a hippie audience. My friend at Columbia Clive Davis alertly turned Monterey into a bonanza; he came in and scooped up Janis Joplin (with Big Brother and the Holding Company) and the Electric Flag, putting the label at the cutting edge of rock. I came home light, even though I nearly hooked one big fish.

Things were strange. I remember standing in the wings under the Northern California sky, the air thick with the scent of hemp, when Jimi Hendrix walked up to me. He was about to go on stage. I'd known Jimi since his backup days with the Isley Brothers and King Curtis, and I appreciated the revolutionary overhaul he'd given the electric guitar.

There he was, however, a veteran of the soul circuit, in crazy feathers and psychedelic regalia. He looked at me almost apologetically, knowing I knew where he came from. "It's only for the show," he whispered in my ear before going out there and blowing up the star-spangled night.

Otis was a little apprehensive, a man accustomed to playing before just about any audience—we'd just returned from the triumphant Stax/Volt tour of Europe—but this one. Over fifty thousand acid-trippers were screaming for something Otis wasn't sure he understood. As he stood there backed by Booker T. and the MG's and the Mar-Key horns, he faced the biggest crowd of his life.

"Y'all are the love crowd, right?" he asked. "We all love each other, don't we?"

Love is what he gave them—love and himself. Otis didn't change, didn't bend to the fashion of the moment. Otis simply sang his heart out, sang "Shake" and "I've Been Loving You Too Long" and "Try a Little Tenderness," touching the hearts of the kids in a way that changed his career. He broke through, proving pure soul was strong enough to stand on its own. At that moment, Otis became a pop act.

To Mike Bloomfield, the Jewish Chicago boy with a wicked Muddy Waters guitar style, Cropper was as much a star as Otis. During the festival, Mike was to Cropper as Boswell to Johnson; he followed Steve everywhere he went, hung on his every word, marveled at his every lick. For my part, I was impressed enough with the idea of Bloomfield's Electric Flag to pitch him. Bloomfield, who had a wide-eyed and simplistic manner, was enthusiastic, and said he'd been raised on Atlantic artists. All he had to do was mention my interest to his agent, the inscrutable, eccentric, infamous Albert Grossman.

As Bob Dylan's manager, Grossman was a high-powered operator. We weren't close, but I was certain he'd be interested in having Bloomfield on our label. I was wrong. "Grossman says we can't go with you because Atlantic steals from the niggers" is what Mike said to me the next day, naively quoting his manager.

"Give Albert my thanks," I said. I was pissed. We had a strong reputation for good royalty payments and fair dealing.

That, however, wasn't the end of my Electric Flag saga. A few years down the road they wound up recording for us—but by then their chapter had already been written.

Grossman and I had two other encounters, and the first had happened in 1961, when Peter, Paul and Mary were set to record in our

Broadway studios. I'd recruited them on the strength of their stunning rendition of Pete Seeger's "Where Have All the Flowers Gone?" At the last minute, with musicians standing by, Albert called to say Mary had laryngitis, and the session was scrubbed. In fact, Grossman had been mugged by Artie Mogul, who offered him more money and whisked them down the street to Warner.

Mutual pals like Mo Ostin and Bob Krasnow were always after me and Albert to reconcile. So in the late seventies I had Grossman and Mo and Bob to dinner. The olive branches were exchanged. In return, Albert invited me up to his place in Woodstock. At a bar he owned, a hangout for the local music mafia, I happened to play a Professor Longhair tape over the PA; I was in the process of negotiating a new contract with Fess. Suddenly everything stopped. It was like the Pied Piper, with musicians showing up in droves from every corner of Woodstock—Elvin Bishop and Robbie Robertson and Paul Butterfield. Albert, not much of a blues scholar, thought he'd lucked up on a possible Elvis. Next thing I knew he bought the tape out from under me, his honored houseguest. Of course he never made a dime off it, having mistaken Fess's electric cult music for the mother lode.

A few months after Monterey, on December 10, 1967, Shirley and I just had stepped off a plane at Kennedy Airport, returning from a convention where I'd been named Record Executive of the Year for the third straight time. The hat trick was great for my deplorable ego, but what pleased me most was that the deejays had done the voting. Then I was paged over the loudspeakers. It was a phone call. I've forgotten the caller, but I'll never forget the message. Otis was dead.

Heading for a gig in Madison, his private twin-engine Beechcraft had crashed into a Wisconsin lake. His band, the Bar-Kays, along with the second-string Stax rhythm section, went down along with their leader. Only horn man Ben Cauley survived. Otis was twenty-six. Sam Cooke had died on exactly the same date three years earlier. This was the beginning of a period of death: a week after Otis, Bert Berns died of a heart condition; and a week after that my own father died, played out after a lifetime of toil.

For a long while after Otis I was numb. My brain was full of memories, not just of the magical set in Monterey but of the triumphant Stax/ Volt European tour: Booker T. and the MG's, the Mar-Keys, Arthur

Industry lunch for the Record Executive of the Year

Conley, Carla Thomas, Eddie Floyd, Sam and Dave in their Day-Glo green suits, and the star, the Big O himself—one of the great soul revues of all time. Shirley and Anita had come along, and it was the image of Anita that haunted me. At their first meeting she said to him, "How can you *stand* being Otis Redding?" She had listened to his records one after another, day and night, again and again, obsessed beyond reason, and then Otis had asked her to dance with him onstage in Paris, and called her from Memphis to hear his latest mix. Anita wept uncontrollably at the news of his death, and ended up selecting takes for Otis's first post-humous release, because no one knew or loved his music more than my teenage daughter.

On the plane down to Macon for his funeral, my mind was filled with "Try a Little Tenderness"—the way Otis sang it, the way the chart built, the tick-tick metronome beat, Isaac Hayes's soaring organ, the mystery of infinite grace and finite time. Unbelievably, Otis's time was over. It was wrong, sudden, still impossible.

The city auditorium was overflowing. Thousands of fans had been pouring past his open casket since six that morning. At the start of the service, Joe Simon sang "Jesus Keep Me Near the Cross"; Johnnie Taylor sang "I'll Be Standing By." Booker T. played the organ. When it was time to give the eulogy, I could barely compose myself. My voice cracked; my eyes filled with tears.

"Otis was a natural prince," I said. "When you were with him he communicated love and a tremendous faith in human possibilities, a promise that great and happy events were coming. He was loved the world over. This year he was chosen by the British trade publications as the number-one male singer in the world, replacing Elvis Presley for the first time in ten years."

I mentioned those who had come to pay tribute: Steve Cropper, Al Jackson, Duck Dunn, Isaac Hayes, David Porter, Eddie Floyd, William Bell, Carla and Rufus Thomas, James Brown, Wilson Pickett, Joe Tex, Solomon Burke, Don Covay, Tom Dowd, and Arthur Conley, to whom Otis was mentor, hero, and second father.

"Out of his character and dedication," I continued, "he bought his beautiful ranch in Macon to make his home and base his business operations when he could have chosen any other place in the world. He thought it the obligation of educated or talented blacks to remain in their native South to help open the doors of opportunities for their race. Respect for his roots is another quality of the man whose composition 'Respect' has become an anthem of hope for people everywhere. Respect is something Otis achieved. Otis sang, 'Respect when I come home.' And Otis has come home."

There would be one further irony to Otis's saga, one last poignant chorus. Just before his fatal flight, he had recorded vocals for a song he'd written with Steve Cropper. "Otis told me, 'See you on Monday,' says Cropper. "That's when we were going to add the horns and sweeteners. He never heard the horns or the sound of the surf and the seagulls which we added. He never heard the mix."

That song was "(Sittin' on) The Dock of the Bay." I thought Otis's voice was too far back—my standing argument with Stax—and I insisted they bring down the sea sound and boost the vocal. "I went back and tried to remix it, but I couldn't," says Steve. "I couldn't move a knob. Without saying a word, I put the same mix on another tape and sent it to Atlantic. That's the version—the original version—that saw the light of day."

"Dock of the Bay" proved to be Otis's most enduring record, his only single to reach the top of the pop charts, where it remained for months. That the motif which would prove so commercial was also so deeply meditative is another testament to Otis's genius. His music was changing. He'd been listening to the Beatles (whose *Sgt. Pepper* had come out earlier that year) and experimenting with tempos, lyrics, and moods. Two weeks before his death, he called and asked me to produce his next album. He wanted to move from the Stax sound to the more polished and bigger sonorities of, let's say, Ray Charles. I was flattered out of my mind—but worried to death about the political implications with Jim Stewart.

"No sweat, Jerry," Otis reassured me. "I'll take care of that part of it."

I have a theory that "Dock of the Bay" sold so well because the fans were taken with the mystical coincidence of the song and Otis's death. I think it was spiritually nourishing for them to project him seated in heavenly rapture on some big dock-of-the-bay in the sky. But for me there was no serenity in the posthumous release. The ocean breeze and the washing of waves on shore did nothing to ease the pain of his passing. There has never been the slightest solace in it. Even now, when I hear "Dock of the Bay" I feel a rush of resentment and anger.

"LISTEN
AT
HER . . .
LISTEN
AT
HER!"

*W*hen she was fourteen, Aretha Franklin sang "Precious Lord" in her father's church. The Reverend C. L. Franklin was spiritual leader of the New Bethel Baptist Church, one of Detroit's biggest congregations. The live recording, a favorite of mine, came out on Chess in 1956. The voice was not that of a child but rather of an ecstatic hierophant. Since the days of covering Mahalia Jackson and Sister Rosetta Tharpe for *Billboard,* I'd been a fan of gospel, realizing that the church, along with the raw blues, was the foundation of the music that moved me so much. On Aretha's first recording, her singing was informed with her genius. From the congregation a man cried out, "Listen at her . . . listen at her!" And I did.

From 1961 through 1967, Aretha made over a dozen albums for Columbia. She'd been signed by John Hammond, who called hers the greatest voice since Billie Holiday's. John cut superb sides on her, including "Today I Sing the Blues." Eventually she became the ward of the pop department, which turned out gems like "If Ever I Should Lose You." But as producer Clyde Otis said, "No one really knew what to do with her." There were minor hits such as "Running Out of Fools," but mostly Aretha languished.

I always had my eye on her, although in 1967 there were a million others matters that seemed more important. I was in Muscle Shoals, still dealing with Pickett—which was never easy. As the records got better, Wilson became more obstreperous.

Early one afternoon, we were having trouble finishing a vocal when Percy Sledge walked in.

"You sound good, Pickett," he said. "Man, you sounding like Otis."

"I don't sound like *nobody*," Wilson fired back, "except *me*."

Knowing Pickett's temperament, I shooed Percy out, and we got back to overdubbing. An hour later, we still didn't have the vocal when Percy popped in again. He was a sweetheart but the last person I wanted to see just then. And before I could get him out of there, he said, "It's sure enough Otis in there, Pickett. But now I'm hearing some James."

That was the red flag that enraged the bull. Wilson hated James Brown—for years there'd been bad blood between them over a woman. Suddenly Pickett charged. I stepped between them, a huge mistake. Wilson lifted me—and mind you, I'm no featherweight—and flung me against the wall across the room. He didn't want to hurt me, just wanted to get me out of the way. Percy was dumbfounded, but not afraid; after all, he'd been a professional boxer. I stepped in between them again, and luckily that stopped it.

In the middle of this madness, the phone was ringing. When the combatants finally cooled, I grabbed it. It was Louise Bishop: "Aretha's ready for you," she said. "Here's her phone number." Louise was a gospel deejay in Philly. In those days, Aretha ran with the gospel crowd, and Louise was the mutual friend I'd hoped would bring us together.

I called Aretha that minute and set up a meeting in New York. Her Columbia contract had expired. Within the week, she and Ted White, her husband, sat down in my office—no lawyers, managers, or agents in sight—and we made a handshake deal. It was beautiful.

My first instinct was to offer her to Jim Stewart and have the Stax team produce her. Stax was steaming, and no one figured to produce Aretha any better than those good folks in Memphis. I told Jim that if he went for the $25,000 advance, Aretha could be a Stax artist with Atlantic promotion and distribution, the same arrangement we had with Sam and Dave. Stewart passed. Thank you, Jesus.

That left it to me. Don't get me wrong: I was pleased to produce Aretha; I admired her talent and felt her strength. But at the time of her signing I was swamped, running back and forth between Muscle Shoals and Manhattan. The work was overwhelming. I was not only pushing for the sale of our company but considering moving out of New York altogether. I was toying with a crazy idea that wouldn't go away, the notion of getting a house on the North Fork of Long Island and another place

Working with Aretha

in Miami, with a boat in each backyard—spend the winters in Florida, the summers on the Sound, and break the monotony of the Great Neck grind, maybe even set up a studio down South.

Because I was always doing twelve things at once, I was also always on the lookout for producers for my artists. In Aretha's case, fate, fortune, or the pull of my own passion led me into the studio with her to work in a more involving way than I had ever worked before. John Hammond, more friend than competitor, had encouraged me from the outset. "You'll do good things with Aretha," he assured me. "You understand her musically." Personally, John tipped me, she was enigmatic and withdrawn.

I knew that her preacher father was respected by his community as a civil rights leader and early advocate of black pride. He was a close friend of Martin Luther King, whom he brought to Detroit for the famous 1963 march up Woodward Avenue. He had recorded dozens of sermons for Chess which were rhetorical and metaphorical master-pieces, "The Eagle Stirreth Her Nest" being a classic of the genre. He had the gift of Good Book storytelling, never failing to rouse his church to fevered pitch. Franklin was a national leader, a charismatic character who reputedly took an occasional walk on the wild side. He'd been busted for pot possession and liked to party. Under unexplained circumstances, his wife had left him and their five children—Vaughn, Erma, Cecil, Aretha, and baby Carolyn—when Aretha was six. When Aretha was ten, her mother died. Some say the preacher used his children, especially the precocious Aretha, as props and pawns; others called him a devoted father. Aretha generally avoided the subject.

She started touring as a teenager, an opening act on her father's gospel show along with Lucy Branch and Sammy Bryant. C.L. also sang. In addition to loving religious song, Reverend Franklin loved jazz and R&B. Aretha's early education was formed by both the gospel greats of her day—Clara Ward, the Staple Singers, the Soul Stirrers, James Cleveland, the Mighty Clouds of Joy—and the secular stars as well. On the road and in his spacious mansion in Detroit, Reverend Franklin entertained artists like Art Tatum and Dinah Washington, R&B luminaries like Sam Cooke, Fats Domino, and Bobby Bland. In a world filled with musical and sexual excitement, Aretha heard and saw everything at an early age. By age seventeen, she herself had given birth to two children. And in a twist on the old myth where the preacher wants his child to sing only for the Lord, C.L. helped Aretha go pop. After all, he was something of a pop preacher himself and lived the pop life to the hilt. When members of his congregation objected to Aretha's secular songs, the Reverend set them straight in a hurry.

John Hammond signed her in 1960. "Sam Cooke was desperately trying to get Aretha for RCA," Hammond remembered. "I'm glad I prevailed. I cherish the records we made together, but, finally, Columbia was a white company who misunderstood her genius."

"Genius" is the word. Clearly Aretha was continuing what Ray Charles had begun—the secularization of gospel, turning church rhythms, church patterns, and especially church feelings into personalized love songs. Like Ray, Aretha was a hands-on performer, a two-fisted pianist plugged into the main circuit of Holy Ghost power. Even though we produced Aretha in a way that we never produced Ray, she remained the central orchestrator of her own sound, the essential contributor and final arbiter of what fit or did not fit her musical persona.

Writing at the start of the nineties, it's easy to forget that a quarter-century ago there was no one else like Aretha Franklin. Pop music today is rich with glorious gospel voices and women singers in the mold cast by Aretha. As Bird gave birth to decades of altoists, Aretha became a model for people like Chaka Khan, Natalie Cole, Donna Summer, Martha Wash, Whitney Houston, Miki Howard, Marva Hicks, Vesta, Sharon Bryant. The list of her disciples is long. From the start—at least after our first experience in the studio—I saw she had raised the ante and upgraded the art form.

After Jim Stewart declined the opportunity, my instinct was to take her south anyway and bring her to Muscle Shoals, where I was still in the first flush of exhilaration with that wonderful rhythm section of Alabama white boys who took a left turn at the blues.

Before the trip we naturally mapped out a strategy. I had no lofty notions of correcting Columbia's mistakes or making her into a Mount Rushmore monument. My idea was to make good tracks, use the best players, put Aretha back on piano, and let the lady wail. Aretha, like Ray, was an inner-directed singer—as opposed, let's say, to Mary Wells, who came to us after her Motown successes. We soon realized that we could do nothing with Mary. The fault wasn't hers, nor was it ours; she was an artist who required the idiosyncratic Motown production, which was simply out of our ken. There was something unique about that little Detroit studio—the attitude, the vibes, the energy—that couldn't be duplicated elsewhere. The same is true of Memphis and Muscle Shoals.

It's interesting to consider why Aretha, a Detroiter, never signed with Motown herself, especially given that she was of the same generation as such Motown friends as Smokey Robinson, Diana Ross, and Martha Reeves—you'd think the connection inevitable. It's important to remember, though, that Berry Gordy's empire was built on a new phenomenon. In the early sixties, when his records started hitting, he had expanded the market. Like Phil Spector before him, Gordy was selling to white teenagers. This was a new formula—black music, produced by a black man and sold to white youth—and it became the backbone of Gordy's fortune.

Even though Atlantic and Motown were the only labels where the owners made the records, our approach was entirely different. I've never been interested in confecting teenage music. Ever since Ahmet began recording Stick McGhee in 1949, the gut of the Atlantic R&B catalogue was pointed at black adults. If white people went for it, fine; if not, we'd survive. But I've always been amazed by Berry Gordy. His music was incredible—the ethereal Smokey Robinson songs, the Temps, the Tops, Marvin Gaye, the Marvelettes, the Supremes, Stevie

Wonder. And he pulled off a miracle of marketing that never even occurred to me: he made his music acceptable, carefully covering it with a
gloss and glamour that enabled his artists to become fixtures on "The Ed
Sullivan Show." The sons and daughters of white-bread America became
the children of Motown, and even today that generation, now middle-
aged, remains loyal to the sound of Gordy's energetic sexuality, a mixture
of charm and innocence.

When Aretha arrived at Atlantic, she was not innocent. She was a
twenty-five-year-old woman with the sound, feelings, and experience of
someone much older. She fit into the matrix of music I had always
worked with—songs expressing adult emotions. Aretha didn't come to
us to be made over or refashioned; she was searching for herself, not for
gimmicks, and in that regard I might have helped. I urged Aretha to be
Aretha.

I was happy with the songs for the first album, most of which she
either selected or wrote herself. Preproduction went smoothly. Aretha
worked on her Fender Rhodes at home, doing a rough outline of the
songs. I would never dream of starting tracks without Aretha at the
piano; that's what made her material organic. She'd find the key, devise
the rhythm pattern, and work out the background vocals with either her
sisters, Carolyn and Erma, or the Sweet Inspirations.

The Sweet Inspirations became one of the pillars of the Atlantic
Church of Sixties Soul. Led by Cissy Houston (Whitney's mom), Estelle
Brown, Sylvia Shemwell, and Myrna Smith were fabulous background
singers who, like Aretha, instinctively understood harmonies; they could
match vibratos, switch parts, and turn on a dime. And like the great King
Curtis—our sax man, arranger, and in-house bandleader—they were
always relaxed, fun, and ready to offer a suggestion or innovative passage. Ultimately, it was only a matter of common decency to put them
under contract as a featured group. I suggested the name Inspirations,
which unfortunately turned out to be already registered (to a group of
acrobats!), so I added the "Sweet." In 1968, they had a top twenty hit,
the eponymous "Sweet Inspirations," produced by Tom Dowd and
Chips Moman in Memphis. In 1969 they sang background on Elvis's
"Suspicious Minds," also in Memphis. They spread soul all over the album *From Elvis in Memphis.*

Aretha was a natural for the Southern style of recording. Once she
had the basics—rhythm groove and vocal patterns—I knew she'd get
off on the spontaneity of the studio. I took her to Muscle Shoals with

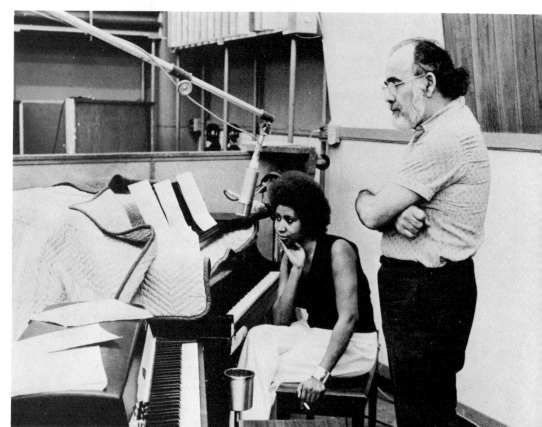

only a modicum of doubt. I was a little anxious about presenting Aretha and Ted with a wall-to-wall white band, and consequently I asked Rick Hall to hire a basic black horn section—either the Memphis Horns or a section led by Bowlegs Miller. In addition to the racial mix, I also wanted a certain sonority that the brothers would bring to the horn section. Hall goofed and hired an all-white section. Aretha's response was no response. I never should have worried—about her. She just sat down at the piano and played the music.

Tension between Rick and myself had been slowly but surely building. When deejay Daddy Sears handed me the duo Clarence and Calvin, for example, I turned them over to Rick for production. Calvin got into an auto accident, and Clarence went solo as Clarence Carter. Tremendous hits ensued on Hall's Fame label—"Slip Away," "Too Weak to Fight," "Patches," and "Thread the Needle," with its irresistible groove-grind. I adored Clarence, but at renewal time Rick conveniently forgot our agreement and brazenly cut us out.

Hall could be belligerent. So could Ted White. And so, as it turned out, could one of the trumpeters. The session began smoothly enough. The rhythms Aretha had worked out on "I Never Loved a Man (the Way I Love You)" were super-smooth, salty enough to bring out her soul, loose enough to let the head arrangement fall into place. Aretha was on acoustic piano, Spooner Oldham on electric. In the corner, saxist Charlie Chalmers unobtrusively worked out the horn parts. This was the first of eleven tunes. All Aretha's vocals were scheduled to be completed in a week; the second week would be for sweetening. For this initial session, though, I decided to record everything live—which turned out to be both a blessing and a curse.

The minute Aretha touched the piano and sang one note, the musicians were captivated. They caught the fever and raced for their instruments. "I've never experienced so much feeling coming out of one human being," says drummer Roger Hawkins. "When she hit that first chord," adds Dan Penn, "we knew everything was gonna be all right."

But everything wasn't. The trumpeter was getting obnoxious and drawing Ted White into a "dozens" duel; they were ranking each other out while drinking out of the same bottle. A redneck patronizing a black man is a dangerous camaraderie. I dreaded a flash point, but somehow we completed the song. Listening to the playback, I couldn't believe how good it sounded.

"It took two hours," Penn recalls, "and it was in the can. It was a killer, no doubt about it. The musicians started singing and dancing with each other, giddy on the pure joy of having something to do with this amazing record. That morning we knew a star had been born."

That evening euphoria turned to horror. It was Walpurgisnacht, a Wagnerian shitstorm, things flying to pieces, everyone going nuts. Back at the motel it was footsteps up and down the hall, doors slamming, and wild cries in the night. I don't know what touched it off.

"I was drinking pretty heavy," Rick Hall recalls. "And so was Ted. I was in his motel room trying to straighten things out while things were only getting worse. 'I should have never brought Aretha to Alabama,' he kept shouting, and I kept shouting back, and finally we did get into a full-blown fistfight."

At six that morning I was in Ted and Aretha's room, with Ted screaming at me for getting them mixed up with "these fuckin' honkies." There was no way to reason. By noon, Ted had taken Aretha and split for New York. I was left with one completed song and a piece of another, Chips Moman and Dan Penn's "Do Right Woman—Do Right Man," for which we had only drums, bass, and rhythm guitar, no Aretha keyboards, no Aretha vocals. (While we were recording "I Never Loved a Man," Chips and Dan had been in Rick's office struggling with "Do Right Woman," and I helped them break up a lyric logjam. They were stuck on the first part of the bridge—"They say it's a man's world"— when I came up with the quasi-Jewish line "But you can't prove that by me.")

I got back to New York and ran off two dozen acetates of "I Never Loved a Man" for my key deejays. Before long it was prime time. It was burning up the radio, phone lines were jumping, the thing was a smash, and there I was with my adenoids showing: we had a stone hit, but only *half* a single. An auspicious way to kick off the Aretha epoch!

I needed Aretha to finish "Do Right"—in a hurry. And I couldn't find her. Not in New York. Not in Detroit. She's having love problems, I heard; she and Ted had split up. This separation turned out to be temporary (later, permanent), but for a couple of weeks Aretha might as well have fallen off the face of the earth. Meanwhile, the pressure was building; with the deejays wailing on "I Never Loved a Man," the distributors were screaming for the record.

Finally Aretha materialized. In fact, she came to the studio at 1841

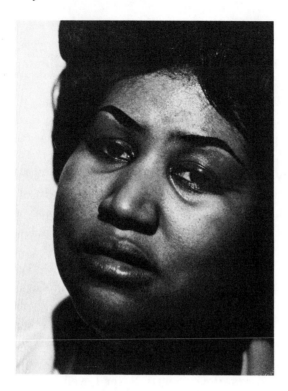

*Our Lady of
Mysterious Sorrows*

Broadway and made a miracle. She overdubbed two discrete keyboard parts, first playing piano, then organ; she and her sisters hemstitched the seamless background harmonies; and when she added her glorious lead vocal, the result was perfection. Moman and Penn like to shit a brick when they heard the final rendition.

I think of Aretha as Our Lady of Mysterious Sorrows. Her eyes are incredible, luminous eyes covering inexplicable pain. Her depressions could be as deep as the dark sea. I don't pretend to know the sources of her anguish, but anguish surrounds Aretha as surely as the glory of her musical aura. As we worked together—over the next eight years we would do fourteen albums—there were times when she would call me late at night and express some of the sorrow in her soul, intimating problems at home. Sometimes the calls would even have tender undertones. On the whole, though, our relationship was restricted to the studio. There she never hit a wrong note, never showed a second of self-doubt.

There I never pretended to critique her vocals, her judgment was impeccable, her execution miraculous, and all I could do was provide the right setting or offer the occasional suggestion. On a personal level, she remained private, apart, inscrutable, a woman of impenetrable solitude—yet she often displayed a great comedic talent.

If the first release, "I Never Loved a Man," was a success—Aretha's first million-selling record—the second single was a rocket to the moon. She took Otis Redding's "Respect" and turned it inside out, making it deeper, stronger, loading it with double entendres. She and her sister Carolyn (who, along with Erma, sang background vocals) came up with the famous "sock it to me" line. For Otis, "respect" had the traditional connotation, the more abstract meaning of esteem. The fervor in Aretha's magnificent voice demanded that respect and more: respect also involved sexual attention of the highest order. What else could "sock it to me" mean? Given the political climate, respect became a touchstone of an era of emerging ethnic and feminist pride. Aretha's "Respect" resonates on a number of levels and lives on.

For the rest of her debut Atlantic album, *I Never Loved a Man (the Way I Love You)*, Aretha rode the same track. When she arrived at the studio, she had already worked out her piano part, the lead and background vocal arrangements, set the keys, and hand-crafted the grooves. The songs were close to Aretha's heart. This was true not only of her own compositions ("Don't Let Me Lose This Dream," "Baby, Baby, Baby," and "Dr. Feelgood," which is straight from the Bessie Smith–Dinah Washington lineage of lay-it-on-the-line sexual celebrations) but also of tunes linked with artists who had moved her most—Sam Cooke's "A Change Is Gonna Come" and the Ray Charles–associated "Drown in My Own Tears." King Curtis contributed "Soul Serenade" and wrote "Save Me" along with Aretha and Carolyn. (Rick Hall was such a fan of "Save Me" that he used it to shape Etta James's "Tell Mama.")

This formula served for the majority of Aretha's albums, which tumbled out at the rate of two a year. The follow-up *Aretha Arrives* included "Baby I Love You" by Ronnie Shannon, writer of "I Never Loved a Man."

Next came *Lady Soul*, which yielded four hits. The first was the biggest. Songwriter Ellie Greenwich dropped by my office while I was listening to an acetate of Aretha busting up Don Covay's combustible "Chain of Fools." I'd brought Joe South up from Atlanta to play a special guitar part; we went for the Pops Staples sound by tuning the guitar down four or five steps and turning up the vibrato to the max, creating a deep, mysterious tremolo. For me the record couldn't be improved. But Ellie knew better; she loved the song, but insisted she heard another background part. "Sing it for me," I urged. She did, and it was perfect, so right then and there I whisked her into the studio and had her overdub the part on the final master, thickening the already extra-thick harmony.

"(You Make Me Feel Like) A Natural Woman" was a title I suggested to Carole King and Gerry Goffin, who brilliantly wrote it to order, a prime example of custom-made composition. The song has become part of Aretha's own persona, a product of her own soul. Aretha (along with Ted White) wrote "Since You Been Gone." Two other guitarists made significant contributions to the album—Bobby Womack and Eric Clapton. Ahmet brought Eric into the control room one day while we were doing a vocal with Aretha on "Good to Me As I Am to You." There was a spot for guitar obbligato. Eric didn't quite hear it that day, but he came back the next afternoon and killed it.

The centerpiece of *Aretha Now*, the fourth album, was "Think," another Aretha/Ted White composition with strong personal and political implications, a hit when it came out and a hit a decade later when Aretha sang it in the movie *The Blues Brothers*. (Listen closely and you'll hear how Tommy Cogbill's acoustic guitar obbligato in the background suggests "Dixie," throwing another ironic log on the fire.) Steve Cropper and Don Covay's "See-Saw" and Aretha's stirring cover of "I Say a Little Prayer" (by Burt Bacharach and Hal David) were also best-sellers. "Prayer" was a magic bit of luck: During a break, Aretha and the Sweets were goofing in the control room. For their own amusement, they started singing the Dionne Warwick hit. All the parts fell together, just like that, and I realized we could have a marvelous free record without even trying. Their ad-lib key worked out fine. With an unsweetened rhythm section, they knocked off "I Say a Little Prayer" in one take.

"The House That Jack Built," released as the B side of "Prayer," killed me. The groove still chills my blood; I can still hear Aretha crying "I got the house, I got the car, I got the rug, I got the rack, but I ain't got Jack!" as she wailed away in our Broadway studio twenty-five years ago.

This first quartet of albums resulted in nine top-ten pop hits and seven #1 R&B hits. The albums did around half a million per, and each single was a million-seller. Beyond the hits, the records demonstrated both the cutting edge of contemporary soul and its strong continuity with the past. For example, Aretha embraced my suggestion that she sing Private Cecil Gant's mid-forties "I Wonder," just as Ray Charles had sung it before her. She sang Ray's "Come Back Baby" and Sam Cooke's "You Send Me," honoring her history and predecessors.

Like Ray's, Aretha's crossover was spectacular. While it may surprise many to learn that neither had a platinum album, Aretha made a fantastic impact on American culture. She had absolute integrity, stayed true to her roots, and her raw vitality and honesty won her universal acceptance. Musicians, critics, kids, adults—everyone was wild for Aretha. She was the hottest thing going.

When she went to Paris in 1968, she sold out the Olympia Theater. I didn't make the trip and didn't like the live album recorded there. The band was put together by Ted White, and the leader was a trumpet-playing crony of Ted's from Detroit. On the whole, though, White stayed out of our way. After the Muscle Shoals debacle, he was a quiet nonparticipant at our New York sessions, no matter how stormy his relationship with Aretha. *Time* magazine's cover story on Aretha that same year reported Ted "roughed her up in public in Atlanta's Hyatt Regency Hotel"—an account that made her permanently press-shy.

In this initial period, she wasn't always easy. On certain days she'd sulk, on others she'd disappear. She'd arrive hours late or not at all. Heartache and drinking both took a toll. But when she did show, she more than made up for her absence. The songs she chose or wrote were loosely but significantly autobiographical. If she couldn't feel it, forget it; if she didn't live it, she couldn't give it. And although I'm sure five-and-dime psychologists could write volumes on her reliance on unreliable men, she actually broke the chain of songs of self-pity, those poignant but somewhat masochistic lyrics sung by her mythic soul sisters like Bessie, Dinah, and Billie. Aretha would never play the part of the scorned woman: she wouldn't beg her man to come back no matter what. Her middle name was Respect.

She devoted an enormous piece of her life to Martin Luther King, yet she never became merely a sloganeer or polemicist. She acted out of the purest wellsprings of faith and belief. To hear her sing "Precious Lord," the hymn she recorded as a teenager, at King's funeral service in 1968 was to witness what Yeats called "a terrible beauty," a holy blend of truth and unspeakable tragedy.

In the years we recorded together—and many triumphs were still ahead of us—I never heard Aretha utter a racist remark. She could enjoy and identify with modern rock, show tunes, and pop ballads. She was always culling albums for songs that might suit her. She didn't think in terms of white or black tunes, or white or black rhythms. Her taste, like her genius, transcended categories.

Not so incidentally, I heard last fall that Aretha's live gospel album *Amazing Grace,* which we did together more than twenty years ago, had just been certified double-platinum.

BOATS
IN THE
BACK-
YARDS

*B*y *1970,* I had three boats in two backyards. The first backyard was in East Marion, on the North Fork of Long Island, a part of the country I'd fallen in love with when I took Paul on that fishing trip; the second was in Miami Beach.

I'd sold the house in Great Neck and bought these two instead—not mansions, mind you, but simple roomy affairs, open to sky and sea and sun. In each backyard I had a twenty-four-foot skiff, and each skiff had two Merc 135-horsepower engines so I could zip out to the fishing grounds ten or twenty miles away and zip back to beat the weather. In Miami I also had the *Big A*—for Atlantic, of course—a forty-six-footer with a full-time captain who took me out into the Atlantic Gulf Stream, where we'd drag bait for the big ones—tuna, sailfish, white marlin and the occasional blue. Further, I had Tommy Aprea, my utility man and indispensable factotum, a great guy from the streets of New York who knew everything about boats and cars, cooking and fishing.

"Jerry became a hell of a fisherman," Tommy Dowd remembers. "He was always dragging friends and musicians out on the boat. One time in Miami we were on the *Big A* in the middle of the ocean when the engine crapped out. 'What's wrong?' Wex asked the captain.

"'Distributor cap,' the captain replied. 'We're going to have to be towed in. Hope we beat the storm.'

"'You mean you don't have another distributor cap?' asked Wex.

"'No.'

"'How much do the fuckers cost?'

"'Seventy-nine cents.'

"Now Jerry was beside himself. 'You mean to say,' he was screaming, livid, 'that for seventy-nine fuckin' cents my life is on the line?! You should have a gross of those things on board—two grosses, for chrissake!'

"We got towed and barely beat the storm, with Jerry yelling all the way back about his life being worth more than seventy-nine fuckin' cents."

How much was Atlantic Records worth? That was the question. The houses and boats came as a result of our sale to Warner Bros.–Seven Arts in 1967; Ahmet had finally agreed to go for the capital gains. Somehow a Wall Street society drone came into the picture to represent us; his main qualification seemed to be his family name and a wife who lunched at Mortimer's. His "negotiations" with Warner yielded us $17.5 million, which has gone down in the annals of the music history as something of a joke. The Wall Street perception was that we had undersold by at least half. I had mistakenly figured we were at our zenith—after all, *Time* magazine had run a feature article on our success—but this wasn't the first time I was wrong.

It's been said that my nagging insecurities led to this misfortune, and that's probably right. At the time, though, the misfortune seemed more like a fortune—at least to the son of a window washer. When I pocketed my share of the proceeds, the first person I called was Cy Ampole, my childhood pal. "Bennett Avenue," I said, "has its first millionaire." I was buzzed, not at all concerned that our negotiator had underpriced us— or that had we waited a year and factored in Aretha's chart-topping sales, we could have demanded twice that figure. Mo Ostin, a friend who now heads Warner Records, calls Ahmet and myself "the Babe Ruth and Lou Gehrig of the music business," sluggers from the era before the big bucks. These days, when I read about David Geffen (an Ertegun protégé) getting over half a billion from MCA for his lucrative label, it really makes me wonder . . . but it passes. I have no regrets. The sale meant comfort and security for the rest of my life.

While the negotiations were still under way, we got a strange call. Frank Sinatra wanted to meet us. He had a vested interest in all the Warner record operations; as a part owner, he had to approve any merger or acquisition. Fine; I'd always been a great fan. A bevy of lawyers and bean counters picked up Ahmet, Nesuhi, and me and limoed us over to Sinatra's place on East 72nd Street, where they nervously advised us not to be too assertive with him, to be careful not to ruffle the Chairman of the Board.

Up in the penthouse, Frank was waiting, and within minutes he sent the suits packing, because we were talking Harry James and the Music Makers, the Dorsey brothers and Buddy Rich; we were talking Hoboken and the Rustic Cabin, Alex Wilder and Mabel Mercer and Lady Day at Café Society. We were pushing all the right buttons, dishing the dirt for hours on end. The sale was approved.

Somewhere in the seventies we had our only other encounter. Mo Ostin thought Sinatra and I might be a productive combination in the studio. I visualized him singing standards with a small group, an octet of superb jazz musicians with, say, Al Cohn playing and writing sparse, swinging jazz charts. Enough already with Nelson Riddle's big sound— let Sinatra get intimate. I sent Frank's office dozens upon dozens of songs he hadn't sung (once I get started, I'm hard to stop on song selection), and the project was percolating nicely when the phone rang in my bungalow at the Beverly Hills Hotel. "Wex," said the caller, "Francis Albert here." Hearing his voice was a hoot, and we discussed the enterprise. He seemed jazzed enough, but somehow, like so many Hollywood dreams, it got lost in lawyers' offices.

The fact that we underpriced Atlantic was not lost on us for long. For the first year or so after the sale, during the honeymoon when the new owners were anxious to mollify us and keep our management team intact, we kept going back to the well. We went after the perks with a vengeance. For me the biggest perk was the *Big A*, but there were other goodies, like stock options. Ahmet and I would sit around and plot how to get more out of the corporate coffers. Our target during this initial period was Elliot Hyman, a tall, gaunt guy whom we drove crazy. One day, exasperated by our continuing demands, he removed the jacket of his pin-striped suit, turned around, and bent over to present his rear to Ahmet. "You wanna stick it in here?" he asked. "Will that be enough for you?" Ahmet laughed and said, "Who can tell?"

Other accounts imply Ahmet was irked with me for advocating the sale. There were intense discussions, yes, but no acrimony. A free thinker and cool master of his own mind, Ahmet's never expressed anger at me for moving too fast. He accepted full responsibility for his own action.

He and Nesuhi also embraced the corporate world with far more aplomb than I. This was especially true two years later when Steve Ross bought Warner–Seven Arts and turned it into Warner Communications (and, two decades later, into Time Warner). Ross had started out with his father-in-law's funeral parlors, then parking lots, then the Kinney Corporation, ultimately creating one of the major enterprises in American entertainment and communications. Ross promised Atlantic autonomy and never wavered from it. He and the Erteguns, the sons of a diplomat, got along famously, though as George Trow astutely observed, "Ahmet's blue blazer and yellow shirt implied a different style from the style implied by Ross's blue blazer and light-blue turtleneck. . . . Ross seemed uncertain in the face of Ahmet's sophistication and glibness."

In the seventies, Ahmet's corporate fortunes rose while mine declined. Beyond the fact that his view of the market proved more cutting-edge and commercial than my own, his style proved not only acceptable but actually superior to the style of the guys running international corporations. As for me, I assumed the attitude of a dropout and something of a sore winner. I sold my Warner stock early on—not exactly a vote of confidence on my part and, even worse, another hasty financial move. The stock zoomed, but I didn't care. I had the mindset of a small-label owner. Like a grocer or baker bought out by a big chain, I had little in common with the new team. Didn't cultivate them, didn't care.

I did, however, urge the brothers Ertegun to make an investment in René Magritte, the Belgian surrealist. Through Daniel Filippachi, bosom buddy of Nesuhi's, we obtained eleven major Magritte oils. Nesuhi brought them back from Paris and we gathered at Ahmet's East Side townhouse, flipped a coin to determine first choice, and whacked them up. That was only the start. By the time of his death in 1989, Nesuhi had built up one of the important surrealist collections in private hands. At one time I owned as many as fourteen Magrittes, but I sold nearly all of them (again, too soon and too low). As much as I adored the paintings, it bothered me to see that much money hanging on the wall.

In the office, even as I planned to fulfill my fantasy of living by the sea, I was also determined to build an A&R department—something, amazingly enough, Atlantic had never developed. That's another reason Warner was so anxious to placate us. We were profitable but enigmatic. We did business like we made records—through improvisation rather than budgets and projections. Early on, Warner realized Atlantic was nothing more or less than the collective instincts of three partners.

I was fully prepared to reward myself for a lifetime of backbreaking work. But I also knew if I continued to make records, which I had every intention of doing, I'd need backup. So I hired a staff of assistants.

"When I got to Atlantic in the late sixties," says Mark Myerson, my

first assistant, and son of old friend and longtime music exec Harry
Myerson, "I was told to take the limo out and meet Wexler at his home.
Allen Toussaint, the New Orleans writer and arranger, was with me.
When we arrived, the action was fast and furious—Jerry in his shortie
pajamas on the phone, Shirley attending to his every whim, Wex and his
kids listening to test pressing and mixes, everyone critiquing everything—music, music, music, phone calls, phone calls, phone calls. Jerry
was born with a phone in his ear. It made no difference where he was.
He was convinced he could run the company from anywhere."

In truth, I wasn't convinced that I *wanted* to continue running the
company in my crazed/obsessive manner. What I wanted was freedom
from the fatigue of daily management. For the past fifteen years, Ahmet
had grown accustomed to having me mind the store, and my move to
Florida meant that more in-the-office supervision fell to him. But if he
disliked it, he never let on.

"There was definitely factionalism in the company," Mark remembers, "the Wexler camp and the Ahmet camp. Nesuhi floated above it
all, elevated on his jazz cloud."

"Wexler," says Jerry Greenberg, an assistant who ultimately rose to
replace me, "was a maniac, but a great maniac. Learning the business
from him was like going to boot camp in Parris Island—you came out
either a man or a corpse. Moving to Florida made no difference. He
never stopped working deals. Once he called my house on Yom Kippur
wanting to discuss an urgent business matter. My wife said I was in syn-
agogue. 'What's the number there?' he wanted to know. 'I'll have him
paged.'"

WBAI is the voice of the "radical" underground culture of New York
City, hardly the most propitious breeding ground for a pop hit. It was on
this station that I heard Jerry Jeff Walker's "Mr. Bojangles" being played
to death. I jumped on it—acquired the master rights for Atlantic and
half the publishing. I also signed Jerry Jeff, commending him to the tender ministrations of Pasha Arif Mardin. They made some great albums
together.

Perhaps the best deal I made in this period involved Jimmy Page
and Led Zeppelin. I knew they were forming in England and had already spoken to other labels. But it was a tip from the British singer
Dusty Springfield that really encouraged me to go after the group.

I was familiar with Page's work through Bert Berns, who'd brought him over from London to do session work for us back when he was known as Little Jimmy Page. I remembered he played his ass off. I also knew John Bonham was a hell of a drummer, but I'd never heard Robert Plant sing. It didn't matter. Dusty's endorsement was so enthusiastic and her taste in music so impeccable I went on the hunch.

Clive Davis and Mo Ostin were also in the horse race, but I prevailed by offering Zep a five-year contract with a $75,000 advance for the first year and four one-year options. Their lawyer, my friend Steve Weiss, said that for another $35,000 we could have world rights. I called Polydor, our English distributors, and suggested they chip in $20,000, but they passed. That meant it would cost Atlantic the full $110,000. We paid up—and even if the advance had been $11 million it wouldn't have made any difference; any up-front money would have been recouped, since Zep was the biggest seller of the seventies.

I was proud of the signing but, as it turned out, didn't really hang out with the group. Ahmet got along famously with them and their manager, Peter Grant, and soon took over their care and nurturing. "Come out to the Zep concert," Ahmet was always urging. "Come catch Yes at Madison Square Garden." "Let's go hear Iron Butterfly."

"Sorry, Ahmet," I'd say. "No eyes." I was more interested in what was happening down South.

It was during this same period that I co-produced, along with Tommy Dowd and Arif Mardin, what turned out to be the semilegendary *Dusty in Memphis*. I still love the album, although the sessions themselves were grueling. Dusty has to be the most insecure singer in the world. When I signed her, she was coming off hits—"The Look of Love" (the theme song from the James Bond spoof *Casino Royale*) and "You Don't Have to Say You Love Me." I was criticized for taking Dusty down South—everyone said the South was for R&B, not pop—but I had a hunch. You won't hear much of a black influence in her voice, yet she's deeply soulful, her intonation pure. As with Aretha, I never heard her sing a bad note.

"All Jerry did was talk about Aretha," remembers Dusty, "and I was frankly intimidated. If there's one thing that inhibits good singing, it's fear. I covered the fear by being in pain. I drove Jerry crazy."

The craziness actually began before we went south. In searching for songs, I came up with over a hundred. Dusty came out to the house, where we sat for hours, ass-deep in albums and acetates. Out of the

*With Dusty
Springfield*

hundred-plus songs, she approved exactly zero. I'd struck out, but I persevered. An artist of her fragile sensitivity had to be selective; to say yes to one song was seen as a lifetime commitment. After months of agonizing evaluations, we settled on eleven tunes: four by Gerry Goffin and Carole King; two by Randy Newman; Barry Mann and Cynthia Weil's "Just a Little Lovin'"; a song by Bacharach and David; and "Breakfast in Bed," a sly piece of seduction by a couple of the better Alabama writers, Eddie Hinton and Donnie Fritts.

My original plan was to record in Muscle Shoals, but selecting the songs took so long that we had to cancel and move the sessions to Memphis, where Chips Moman and crew were more than up for the job. Dusty, though, was all raw nerve ends and neuroses. She wouldn't put her voice on a practice track, making it tough for us to work up the arrangements. She wouldn't sing at all.

We finally cut her vocals back in New York, but in spite of the sturdy anchors provided by the Sweet Inspirations, the sessions were hell. The emotional push and pull between me and Dusty was tricky. Singers always cry for more track in their headsets; my method is to give them less, forcing them to sing harder. In Dusty's case, she pushed me to boost the track so high she couldn't even hear herself singing. At one point she hurled an ashtray at me. She also called Tom Dowd, a noticeably easygoing man, a "prima donna." "The only prima donna here, Mademoiselle Springfield," said I, "is you."

Yet, despite everything, I finally got the performances I was after, and I still marvel at her vocals. Her first single, "Son of a Preacher Man," went top ten. The song was marked for Aretha, but she passed, perhaps because it hit too close to home. The idea that Dusty—the Great White Lady, the Ice Queen—could turn the tune into a smash is proof that a powerful song is a powerful song and can be a hit sung by practically anyone. (Aretha finally did cut "Preacher Man," just as she ultimately did "Let It Be," the hymn written for her by John Lennon and Paul McCartney. She held off for over a year, until the Beatles tired of waiting and sang it themselves; Aretha's version, needless to say, was too late.)

Another song on the *Memphis* album was helped along by some promotional zeal. Though Atlantic was sold, I was pushing my records just as hard. I had flourished in a smaller context in a smaller time, before the advent of the mighty rack jobbers. So when it came to moving merchandise I believed in, I resorted to the old tricks—sending out white-label acetates to deejays and program directors, hyping the market with advanced copies of singles. In Dusty's case, we had recorded a marvelous, ranging melody by Alan and Marilyn Bergman and Michel Legrand, "The Windmills of Your Mind," nominated for an Oscar as theme song for *The Thomas Crown Affair*. To prepare for a possible win, I doped out a plan: I pressed up three thousand 45-rpm singles, had them packed special delivery and stamped ACADEMY AWARD WINNER! OPEN IMMEDIATELY! The minute the song won, Henry Allen—then head of the stockroom, later head of our R&B department—ran to the central post office, and the next morning deejays all over America got the good news.

More good news came in over the phone one day: Rick Hall was calling from Muscle Shoals, so excited about the new Wilson Pickett single that he insisted on playing it for me long-distance. The vocal was fabulous, but it was the guitar solo, a running obbligato over and under Wilson's impassioned cries, that held the whole thing together. I knew all the session guitarists, but not this guy. So who was he?

"Wilson calls him Sky Man," said Rick, "'cause he likes to get high. He's got hair down below his butt. He's a hippie from Macon, but I'll be damned if he didn't talk Pickett into singing the song. Wilson said a Beatles tune didn't fit him. The hippie said, 'What's wrong, you don't got the balls to sing it?' That's all Pickett needed to hear."

"But who the hell is the hippie?"

"Name's Duane Allman."

Wilson's "Hey Jude" became a million-seller—but, more importantly, Duane Allman became my friend. I loved his playing so much I bought his contract from Hall for $15,000. At the time, since Duane wasn't a singer, writer, or bandleader, that was a lot of money. Rick thought the heavens had opened. Phil Walden, Otis Redding's manager and the man who ultimately built the Allman Brothers Band, put the group on Capricorn, the label we'd formed together. Before then, though, I used Duane as a session player with Aretha, King Curtis, Ronnie Hawkins—with virtually everyone. He was always more than a sideman or soloist; he had the mind of a producer and would come up with scores of righteous suggestions.

Duane was so pale-faced he looked like a photographic negative; he was a kick-ass good ol' boy with a beautiful personality and great feel on his ax. He played no-bullshit blues, and he phrased like the authentic black guitarists, weaving melodic segments like elaborate tapestries. His chops were huge. He was a fine, light-fingered acoustic guitarist and Dobro player. Whenever he felt the need, he could even produce a manual slide effect. Many slide players sound sour, but Duane effected clear intonation with perfect overtones. He could blow excellent bossa nova and jazz; when he jammed, he showed a solid grounding in bop. And he plucked excellent country guitar, à la Hank Garland or Chet Atkins. His heroes were B.B., Albert, T-Bone, Slim Harpo, Eric Clapton, and Robbie Robertson. He also adored Robert Johnson and Blind Willie Johnson.

"I introduced Duane to Eric Clapton," says Tommy Dowd. "Duane was basically Jerry's discovery and Eric was Ahmet's."

"I was at the Scotch Club in London, where Wilson Pickett's band was playing after hours," Ahmet remembers. "My back was to the stage when I heard this amazing musician. 'Wilson,' I said, 'your guitarist is fantastic.' 'My guitarist,' said Wilson, 'is having a drink at the bar.' I turned and saw this young man with an angelic face, a beautiful young man playing like one of the great Delta blues masters. That was Eric

Clapton. Cream became one of our most popular groups of the late six-ties, and Eric became one of the century's great musicians."

Tommy picks up the story. "I took Eric to hear Duane. We sat in the first row, and when Duane saw who was there he froze, as though God were in the house. Eric studied his every move. Later, back in the studio, they jammed all night—long-lost brothers miraculously reunited—till seven the next morning, trading licks, trading lessons. It was a four-way conversation. The guitars were talking to each other while their heads were saying something else. By then the Allman Brothers were formed and Eric had Derek and the Dominoes. That night was the beginning of the union that led to the historic 'Layla' session at Criteria in Miami."

Criteria was Atlantic South, my recording headquarters in Miami, which, despite a number of memorable dates and a cast of crazy char-acters, never turned into the permanent home—a Muscle Shoals, say—that I had envisioned. Before I tell that story, though, I need to insert an unhappy chapter. I'd like to skip over it, and wish it hadn't happened, but it did—and it scared the holy shit out of me.

MIAMI

VICE

In 1968, there was something sick in the air—an anger, a frustration, a tension that had already reached the boiling points in the inner cities of Newark and Detroit. It might have been triggered by the murder of Martin Luther King some four months earlier, but that obviously wasn't the only reason.

I understood prejudice, had seen it my whole life, and always thought I was on the right side of the issue. As a Jew, I didn't think I identified with the underclass; I *was* the underclass. Additionally, the music I was helping produce reflected my own view of the politics of the time. It was a proud music, defiant, hopeful, demanding. It was Aretha Franklin's music.

And it was on Aretha's behalf that I was supposed to accept an award from the National Association of Television and Radio Announcers (NATRA) at their 1968 convention at the Sheraton Four Ambassadors Hotel in Miami. In attendance were Jesse Jackson and Coretta Scott King.

I arrived at the Bayfront Auditorium tuxed up and feeling fine. I was at a table with our promo men, Dickie Kline, Joe Galkin, and Juggie Gayles. The speakers were calling for black takeover of the record companies and R&B radio stations. Emcee Bill Cosby was a vociferous advocate, whipping it up. Black power was on the agenda, and I'm all for it—black political power, black economic power, black management jobs, black ownership, black-run labels.

But these shakedown artists had no program; it was just old-fashioned, take-what-you-can-get blackmail. Suspicious characters had been running around the hotels hitting on label and station owners.

Under the guise of concerned citizens, hoodlums were camouflaging extortion with the rhetoric of the movement.

It might seem ironic that the moment of terror arrived when my cohort, soul brother, and longtime collaborator King Curtis leaned over and whispered in my ear, "We're getting the fuck out of here."

"Why?" I wanted to know.

"Someone's after you with a gun. You're marked."

Marked! Me? What the fuck!

Another brother materialized by my side—blues singer Titus Turner (who wrote the ingenious "Around the World" for Little Willie John with the classic line "If I don't love you, baby, grits ain't groceries, eggs ain't poultry and Mona Lisa was a man"). To have two black men in the business volunteering as my bodyguards was comforting, but no less scary. They obviously knew what's happening: my life was on the line. With Titus showing his piece, they whisked me out of the auditorium in nothing flat.

Things got worse. I was hanged in effigy, the rumor went. Marshall Sehorn, a white New Orleans record man, was pistol-whipped in his hotel room. Phil Walden received death threats. And all the while I was laying up in my house in Miami Beach, trying to come to terms with the confusion and fear. I was never given specific charges. I heard vague mumblings about ripping off Aretha. Neither Aretha nor her manager and brother, Cecil, had any complaints—ever. After this nightmare, in fact, Aretha and I went on working together for seven more years, nine more albums, and a dozen more hits. Even when we separated, there wasn't a moment of rancor or mistrust. By the mid-seventies Aretha simply required fresh production input, which she found in the marvelous work of Curtis Mayfield.

No matter; the threats bothered me. I felt angry, undervalued, scared, unsure of what to do or say. I wanted to trot out my long list of liberal credentials, wanted my sincere love of the music and its practitioners to be acknowledged. Look how I helped Ray or Wilson or Otis. But who gave a shit about my self-justifications? I lay low. I shut the fuck up. In the heat of overpoliticized times, reasonable dialogue was an unreasonable expectation. All I could do, all I knew how to do, was go back to work. Keep making records.

After this incident, I was accused of dumping black musicians for white, but that's bullshit. In addition to Aretha, I kept working with Wilson, Sam and Dave, King Curtis, and in the seventies there were Roberta Flack, Donny Hathaway, Allen Toussaint, Harold Battiste, Bernard Purdie, Cornell Dupree, Chuck Rainey, Eric Gale, Al Jackson, Billy Preston, Hubert Laws, the Staple Singers, Mavis Staples, the Sweet Inspirations, Etta James—to name a few. I did put together a rhythm section in 1969 that happened to be white. "Happened to be" is the key phrase, because these boys could burn. They played as funky as you please and just happened to be available, just happened to be open to my idea—which turned out to be both lovely and lousy—about moving to Miami.

HIGH

TIMES

The hot sun, the warm winter, the fresh fish, the boat in the backyard . . . I bought the whole bit. I'd loved Miami Beach since I was stationed at the White House Hotel during the war. If ever I were to relax—and I never would—it would have to be in a subtropical climate. Moreover, I was convinced I could create a musical climate of my own. Not only did I want a boat in the backyard, I wanted a band as well—at least a band at my disposal—in a studio down the street.

My first choice was the Muscle Shoals group. By then the rhythm section was fixed at Barry Beckett, David Hood, Roger Hawkins, and Jimmy Johnson. I loved these guys and wanted them on a permanent basis. They had long since left Rick Hall and opened a studio of their own with my backing, a little down-home ex–funeral parlor immortalized by the title of Cher's 1969 solo album, *3614 Jackson Highway.* In fact, I went down to produce that record; I love Cher's voice and was excited about the project.

"In case of a tie," I told Sonny before the sessions began, a little worried about who would be the boss, "I win." I picked the songs—three by Dylan, an Aretha cover, a Stephen Stills, an Eddie Hinton (lead guitarist on the date)—but I also picked up pneumonia and went to the hospital before the actual singing started, so Dowd and Mardin took over. I never made it to the control room.

The next Muscle Shoals sessions, during that summer, were with Lulu, whose "To Sir with Love" had been huge; but they yielded only a mini-hit in "Oh Me Oh My (I'm a Fool for You Baby)," which later was covered by Aretha. Since Cher's record had produced no hits, for the most part I was striking out.

Cher and others at 3614 Jackson Highway

"We'd been toiling away," David Hood remembers, "in the new studio Jerry had helped set up, and all of a sudden we're cold as ice. We're dying for a smash, dying to prove ourselves, but nothing's happening. We're frustrated, Wexler's frustrated—and then out of nowhere Ahmet Ertegun slides into town. Naturally we'd heard of him—he was our pal Jerry's legendary partner—but we'd never worked with him before. He shows up with a singer, R.B. Greaves, and a song, 'Take a Letter, Maria.' While the band puts the arrangement together, Ahmet's riding around town in his big rent-a-car buying cowboy boots. He gets back to the studio, sits behind the board, noodles pictures on a yellow pad, and gabs on the phone. Unlike Jerry, there's nothing scary about Ahmet. He's relaxed. He casually nods his head after the second take. A few weeks later the record rockets to number one. The whole thing was so easy I think it kind of bugged Jerry."

In his sardonic style, Ahmet took pains to give me the inside scoop on how Muscle Shoals really functioned, although he'd never been there before and would return only once again—a memorable trip involving the Rolling Stones, whom Ahmet signed in 1969. Atlantic would distribute the group for the next fourteen years, from *Sticky Fingers* through *Undercover.*

"I arrived in L.A. early one morning, attended many meetings," Ahmet explains, "and, late in the day, was informed that Mick Jagger wanted to talk to me. We arranged to rendezvous that night at the Whiskey, where Chuck Berry was playing. After several drinks, jet lag was taking its toll, and by the time Mick showed up I was slowing down. Chuck was blaring away and Mick was sitting next to me, saying, 'The reason I wanted to see you, Ahmet, is because our contract is up, and . . .'—but by then I had dozed off. Someone kept shaking me—'This is important, Ahmet, wake up, wake up'—but I'm afraid I kept nodding out while Mick was saying how interested the Stones were in Atlantic, a label they had long admired. My insouciance served me well, you see, because Mick loathes pushy people. He loved the fact I fell asleep in his face. He finds indifference intoxicating. The next day he came to my hotel and put it simply. 'We don't want to shop around. We want to be on Atlantic.'"

Late in 1969, the Stones came to Muscle Shoals and I was there, ostensibly to expedite matters. I was little more than an onlooker. The Stones were touring the U.S. and came in on a bootleg session. Because of union complications, they weren't supposed to record in the States.

"It was freezing winter," Keith Richards recalls. "In the midst of this hysterical, whirlwind nonstop tour, we fly in from Texas. We're in that ice-cold studio, drinking brandy and wrapped in blankets, isolated in this little hick town with absolutely nothing going on."

"We jammed for one day," says Jim Dickinson, a monster keyboardist who wound up in my house band in Miami, the Dixie Flyers, "and then the Stones got to where they worked at night. They cut 'You Gotta Move' the first night, 'Brown Sugar' the second, and 'Wild Horses' the third. I got on 'Wild Horses' because Ian Stewart, their regular piano player, wouldn't play minor chords. They offended him aesthetically. He was a boogie-woogie man."

Dickinson, an unstoppable self-promoter, cut the tracks only be-

With Mick Jagger

cause Barry Beckett was home sick that day. Like Barry, though, Jim did the South proud. I still believe Jim is the baddest key-of-C piano player extant.

The Stones' stay was brief but memorable. "No one knew who they were," says Jim. "We were having breakfast in the Holiday Inn, for instance, and there's Bill Wyman's wife dressed from head to toe in white fur. The waitress asks, 'Are y'all in a group?' 'Yes,' says Wyman. 'We're Martha and the Vandellas.'

"The Holiday Inn has a grassy knoll," remembers Muscle Shoals music historian Dick Cooper, "where the Stones sat and watched the traffic go by. This is the main drag of downtown Tuscumbia, Alabama. They were amused and delighted not to be recognized by a single soul."

My own most vivid memory, though, is of the sessions themselves. I was knocked out by Keith's and Mick's consummate professionalism. As producers, they knew exactly what they wanted and how to get it. Their musicianship really came into play in the studio process. They controlled their craft and ran the whole show with dead-on direction. I was confabulated.

I was about to try for the same thing in Miami—a smooth-running drill for producing great phonograph records—but the boys in Muscle Shoals were reluctant to follow me. They finally had their own shop and weren't about to leave Alabama. I couldn't blame them and decided instead to get a little help from my friends in Memphis.

Memphis had always been good to me. I considered it home territory. Chips Moman had a wonderful house band in his American studio, scene of dozens of Atlantic sessions. I'd loaned Chips five thousand dollars on a handshake to start up his operation. When he discovered the Box Tops—who hit big with "The Letter" and "Cry Like a Baby"—and gave them to my competitor Larry Uttal at Bell Records, I was miffed. No matter; Chips and I remained tight.

Jim Stewart was another story. When money started getting funny at Stax and business slackened after the death of Otis, when they were having management problems and we couldn't come to terms on renewing a distribution arrangement, Jim took it to Gulf & Western. Then came the shocker—to him as well as to me: Atlantic owned every one of his masters. In no uncertain terms, the ownership was in the original contract drawn up by Atlantic's lawyer Paul Marshall. I hadn't known, hadn't read the fine print, and neither had Jim. I felt lousy, certain that Stax was entitled to retain those enduring records produced in their own studio; but the contract specified otherwise. I couldn't act unilaterally because by then I was an employee, no longer a partner. I argued with the corporate bosses on Jim's behalf; the new owners, however, had absolutely no reason to return valuable property which was incontestably a key part of the overall Atlantic assets. There was no righting this wrong; Jim was screwed, and I feel bad about it to this day.

In Miami, I sought to build my own little Stax, a clean soul machine that would turn out great music and hit records. My good buddies Stanley Booth, the writer, and Jim Dickinson put together the Dixie Flyers— a name out of Flannery O'Connor, who wrote, referring to William Faulkner, that when the Dixie Flyer comes down the track you better get out of the way. Thus was born the only rock band named after Mr. Bill, a fact that made Shirley, a Faulkner freak, extremely happy.

Aside from Jim, the Flyers were Tommy McClure on bass, Sammy (Beaver) Creason on drums, Mike Utley on keyboards, and, on guitar, the legendary Charlie Freeman, Steve Cropper's mentor in Memphis and a full-blooded Indian, who once referred to me as a "full-blooded New York Jew." According to Tom Dowd, "Essentially the Dixie Flyers would go on to become Kris Kristofferson's band. But while they were in Miami they were a red-hot funk outfit."

The Dixie Flyers: (from left) Tommy McClure, Mike Utley, Tom Dowd,
Wex, Sammy Creason, Charlie Freeman, Jim Dickinson

In this same period, I also tried it with a Louisiana band, Cold Grits.
They backed Pickett on "You Keep Me Hangin' On" and were supervised by black deejay Dave Crawford, whom I put together with Brad
Shapiro to form an efficient salt-and-pepper production team. (A couple
years later, I signed the J. Geils Band out of Boston for $30,000 on Jon
Landau's recommendation. I wanted Jon to produce them, but when he
backed off I was in a jam. I brought Dave and Brad to complete the job,
which they did in exemplary fashion.)

Tom Dowd moved to Miami, ensuring that our sound would be
state-of-the-art. With my house band down the street and the *Big A* in
the backyard, I was in high cotton. But it didn't last. I should've known
there never were enough projects to keep a house rhythm section working steadily. Booker T. and the MG's lasted by becoming recording artists in their own right. The Muscle Shoals boys found longevity by never
leaving home and by owning the studio. My conception—to import and
keep a cohesive group—was naive.

For a while, though, the Dixie Flyers were flying high. I didn't know
that they were doing everything in the drugstore, but I did know they
were some wild motherfuckers. It was wild times, and into this wild mix
came the wildest man of them all.

D*r. John* is Mac Rebennack, and Mac Rebennack is the blackest white man in the world.

Unlike Monte Kay, Johnny Otis, Symphony Syd, or Mezz Mezzrow, all of whom moved into the black nation on green cards, Mac has no temporary visa. His talk is black, his soul is black, and God knows his music is black. Growing up in New Orleans, he was the only white member of the black musicians local. He was raised in the bayous and back alleys of the Crescent City, absorbing every nuance and delicacy of that musical menu, absorbing its exotic rhythms and special syncopations in ways that astound me to this day. No one has taught me more about music than Dr. John, whether it's rock, R&B, soul, or funk. Not only is he one of the two or three great pianists of the era, but his singing voice demands comparison with his masters—Ray Charles, Charles Brown, Fats Domino, Percy Mayfield—and his songwriting is brilliant. He himself is brilliant: scholarly, strange, street, a walking textbook, a living history of the piano-playing legends who preceded him. Our relationship has been complex, deep, fruitful, marred by estrangements of painful proportions; yet, in the end, Mac's my man.

To backtrack a bit: Sonny Bono, while working for Art Rupe of Specialty Records in the late fifties, spent a lot of time as a promo man in New Orleans. Later Sonny got Harold Battiste, a talented local arranger, to do Sonny and Cher sessions. Harold used Mac—everybody in New Orleans did—and thus the connection was made; Mac played and toured with Sonny and Cher. Sonny then hipped Ahmet to certain bootleg sessions in which Mac was eventually turned into Dr. John, the Night Tripper. Atlantic released four records in the mid-sixties—*Gris-Gris, Babylon, Remedies, The Sun, Moon & Herbs*—without any input whatsoever. They were Mac's pure products, just like the creation of his mythical Dr. John persona, a twist on the New Orleans voodoo archetype, a riff from Prince La La. The Mardi Gras culture and high-flying hippiedom made for a potent mix—Dr. John in bandanas, headdresses, and hats of fabulous feathers, his face painted in every color of the psychedelic rainbow.

I was moved by the music's mysteries and beautiful cloudy sound. But I didn't know Mac and hadn't spent any time with him until December 1969, when we bumped into each other at a Los Angeles studio.

Dr. John

There's a tape of that meeting. The encounter turned out to be unforgettable, at least for me. We both might have been a little high, and we were certainly excited to finally see each other. We knew our musical passions ran along the same lines, but we had no idea that the rapport would be so right.

Actually, I had *seen* Mac in 1955 at Cosmo Matassa's studio on Governor Nichols Street. When we weren't happy with a piano player, Cosmo would hold up his hand and tell us to give him thirty seconds, then run to the corner and come back with a clutch of new players. That's how much talent was running around the neighborhood. One of those musicians was a cherubic choirboy with hands that danced over the keyboard like a funky Horowitz. He was a prodigy, absorbing the guitar licks of Walter "Papoose" Nelson, the second-line drumming of Earl Palmer and John Boudreaux, the sax licks of Alvin "Red" Tyler, the piano playing of James Booker, Fats Domino, Al Johnson, Huey Smith, and, naturally, Professor Longhair. His father was an appliance dealer who sold R&B records over the counter. His mother was a onetime model, blondined and corseted, who later on told me, "Don't let Malcolm fool you. He's a high-school graduate and he can talk as good as you or me."

His history was all tied up with Shirley and Lee ("Let the Good Times Roll"), Roy Brown, Archibald (the first to record "Stagger Lee"),

Albert Grossman, Mac, and Wex

Lloyd Price ("Lawdy Miss Clawdy"), Shooks Eaglin, Guitar Slim, Smiley Lewis, Earl King, and the great producer/promoter Huey Meaux. He'd been an A&R man for Johnny Vincent at Ace Records and had his first hit as Morgus and the Ghouls ("Morgus the Magnificent") back in 1959. In short, Mac was all over everything that had anything to do with the funk and folklore of New Orleans.

New Orleans had stayed in my mind from the time I first heard Jelly Roll's records back in Washington Heights to when we went there to record Joe Turner and Professor Longhair. And the more Mac and I talked that day in L.A., the more amazed I was at the scope of his knowledge and the way he could demonstrate, on piano or guitar, specific and complex changes in the city's rhythmic evolution. He was a large physical and spiritual presence with a trademark coon-ass accent. At any rate, from that moment on, after our chance-meeting nonstop bullshit session in the studio, our friendship was forged. If it was a father-son thing, it was also a chronologically inverted student-teacher relationship, with me as student, Mac as teacher.

Months passed. Back in Miami I was working on instrumental tracks

with King Curtis, one of my constant sources of inspiration and information. (I had produced Curtis's *Great Memphis Hits* a couple of years
earlier, but always felt that King, like Mac, gave more than he got, his
musical mind advanced far beyond mine.) One day the phone rings and
it's the nut ward at UCLA. The head shrink's talking about a certain
Malcolm Rebennack who, after a horrendous European tour, suffered a
nervous breakdown, is about to check out, and is in need of care—spe-
cifically, a methadone program available in Florida but not California.
Am I willing to take charge? Yes, of course.

Mac, his wife, Lorraine, and their baby girl fly to Miami, where I
find them lodging. I hook Mac up with the Dixie Flyers. Musically, it's a
match made in heaven. Lorraine, a bagel baby from Brooklyn and a
wonderful person, becomes a close friend of our family. I call her Mama
Roux the Shmata Queen because she's the one who concocts Mac's
spaced-out, swamp-rat stage costumes; she creates Dr. John.

"Jerry became our caretaker," Lorraine remembers. "He became
our big daddy. Whenever we were in trouble, we called Jerry. He never
acted like a record exec; he was one of the cats, one of us. He'd be
producing Aretha in the studio and baby-sitting our little girl at the same
time. That's how much I trusted him.

"We were all hippies, and Jerry and Shirley lived this cool middle-
class life we found attractive. Not that they had a mansion, but compared to our hovels it seemed that way. They had the best chocolates
and wines and were the most wonderful hosts you can imagine. They'd
tell us stories of the old days while we sat around like their children. In
truth, Jerry was more attentive to us—the musicians and the musicians'
old ladies—than he was to his own kids. Jerry was so caught up in the
enthusiasm of his work he overlooked his children. Tommy Aprea, Shirley and Jerry's helper, had become a big-brother figure to the kids. Anita
said to me, 'You can get more out of my father than I can.'

"While Jerry was a pal, he was also something of a rogue. He cracked
us up because when we got him pot, the joints had to be rolled. He never
learned to roll a J. But he had learned business, and I also felt that for
all his friendship, we also got screwed. Unlike other record guys, though,
when Jerry screws you, he's kissing you at the same time. He brought
Mac from L.A., for instance, put him in the methadone program, and
paid him three hundred dollars a week as a member of the house band.
But when Mac started playing extra sessions—and there were dozens of
those—we never saw extra money. On the other hand, when Mac got

busted in Hazelwood, Missouri, it was Jerry who found a Chicago lawyer to get him off. It was Jerry who had Mac hook up first with Albert Grossman and then Phil Walden as managers; and when both deals soured, it was Jerry who came to our rescue.

"My main memories of that period in Miami, though, are of the music. You can't believe how exciting it was. Every week, every day something wonderful was happening at Criteria, with Jerry in the middle of it. The Allman Brothers; Delaney and Bonnie; Crosby, Stills, and Nash—we were all living a dream."

Hold the dream, though, while we take a quick trip back to New York—as I often did in that period—for a taste of record-business realism.

MASTER-
PIECES
AND
MISTAKES

I didn't like David Geffen and David Geffen didn't like me. Thinking back, I can hardly blame him. Maybe I'm unreasonably prejudiced against agents in general, and Geffen was the agent to end all agents. I felt his aggression went beyond the bounds of civilized behavior; and when David came to see me about releasing one of our solo artists, Stephen Stills, so that Crosby, Stills, and Nash might be formed over at Columbia Records, I lost my temper and threw him out of my office.

His version of the story, though, is an interesting indication of my shortsightedness. "I thought Atlantic Records *was* Jerry Wexler," he says. "I knew his accomplishments and went to him with great respect. I'm not saying I was completely in control of my emotions, because I wasn't. I was a twenty-six-year-old kid, all raw ambition. I knew what I wanted and was determined to get it. But Wexler wouldn't even listen to me. He was incensed and unreasonable. He treated me like dirt. He screamed and yelled and acted like I was looking to rob him.

"The next day, though, I spoke with Ahmet Ertegun, who could not have been more charming. He invited me to his office, where we sat and calmly discussed the matter. Ahmet was the most sophisticated, amusing, and engaging man I had ever met in my life. He did what hotheaded Wexler should have done: rather than me talk him into releasing Stephen, he talked *me* into putting Crosby, Stills, and Nash on Atlantic. Now that's a smooth executive! Crosby, Stills, and Nash became a multi-million-selling group, and I became Ahmet's protégé.

"Later I saw how the intramurals were played out at Atlantic, the political divisions between Wexler and Ertegun. I became an Ertegun person. Ahmet owned me. It was Ahmet's financing which enabled me to begin my Asylum Records and sign Joni Mitchell, Jackson Browne, the Eagles, and Linda Ronstadt. I had a feeling Jerry resented my successes. Because I didn't fail, he became even angrier at me."

I was blind to Geffen's business genius. Later I saw his devotion to his artists. His group of California rock poets worked for him without a contract—that's how deep their trust ran. And they were right; David worked their careers twenty-four hours a day, his sole focus the promotion of his artists. Yet unfortunately, as he grew into an industry force, he and I would clash again—this time with even more venom.

At the start of the seventies, my clashes were increasing. My home life was turbulent. Shirley and I were fighting all the time, contending in an unnamed arena for an unspecified prize. The kids were distraught, a situation I saw but was helpless to change.

I was also clashing with the corporate world. I had no patience for their committees and endless meetings. I gave the Warner bosses little if no mind because my own preoccupation was exclusively musical. They left me alone because I was still making them money. I was still Aretha Franklin's producer, with any number of records coming down the chute. I lost myself in the music. With music surrounding me—especially Aretha's glorious music—nothing else seemed to matter.

In Miami, there were the sanctified sessions that produced *Spirit in the Dark*. The title song, Aretha's own, is a haunting miracle. "The thrill is gone," sang Aretha, the Dixie Flyers underlining her pain with blues-biting support, her vocal a model of heart-stopping highs and lows. Mac Rebennack was on my mind, and when Aretha sang Mac's soaring "When This Battle Is Over," Duane Allman was all over his guitar. It was also in Miami that, on a humid night that has stayed with me forever, Aretha set down a "Rock Steady" that will keep rocking as long as electricity wires sound. Not only was Dr. John a percussionist on the cut, but a new talent with potential as large as Lady Soul played electric piano over Aretha's own acoustic gems. That was Donny Hathaway, whose own chapter in my life and the life of my label was already being written.

Writers inundated me with material for Aretha, who was open to it all, especially and surprisingly to rock tunes. I was inclined to push Aretha towards the Southern soul material—Chips Moman and Dan Penn's eternal "Dark End of the Street" (the classic version being James Carr's), Al Bragg's "Share Your Love with Me," Jimmy Reed's "Honest I Do"—

and also towards pop fare like the Bacharach/David "This Girl's in Love with You." Aretha's own writing continued to flourish: "Call Me" was a huge hit in 1970 (and again in 1991, when, reinterpreted by Phil Perry, the song climbed back to top of the R&B charts).

I was wrong, however, to give Aretha songs that emerged from the counterculture but lacked meaning for her hardcore black constituency. For example, when she recorded "The Weight," a hit for the Band, a group I much admired, Robbie Robertson, Stephen Stills, and David Crosby greeted me with accolades and hugs; they thought it was wonderful. Yet Aretha's version was a resounding flop. Who the hell could decipher the esoteric lyrics? I take it as an article of faith that Aretha Franklin can go pop, but not without a black base. Her first fans, her home support, must be directly addressed.

You'd think I'd have been smart enough to learn from my first mistake, but I wasn't. A couple of years later Aretha released Elton John and Bernie Taupin's "Border Song." Great songwriters, great song, gutsy gospel changes—but who knew what the lyrics were saying? Rock lyrics are often fretted with ambiguities and abstractions. R&B lyrics, on the other hand, have to tell it like it is.

In 1971, when I arranged with Bill Graham for Aretha to appear at the Fillmore West in San Francisco and cut a live album, I had doubts. How would she be received? I considered the musical tastes of the Flower Children infantile and retarded, but I was dead wrong: they were swinging from the rafters, swarming the stage, packed beyond capacity. It was thrilling to see the King Curtis band backing her. The rhythm section was cooking on high flame—Billy Preston on organ, Cornell Dupree on guitar, Bernard Purdie on drums, bassist Jerry Jemmott, and Aretha herself on funky Fender Rhodes.

I positioned myself in the balcony next to the PA man. If the PA mix was good, it meant the audience would be happy—and responsive. It also meant the feed to Arif in the sound truck would be clean and the music well recorded. (In this instance, the rhythm section was right but I had to overdub background vocals and horn parts back in New York. Using the exact same singers and musicians, I was able to replicate the original sound.)

Later, Aretha would call the Fillmore concert a highlight of her career. What overwhelmed her—and surprised me—was the musical intelligence of the hippies. They picked up on her every shading and nuance; they were attentive, appreciative, and hip to exactly what was happening, technically and emotionally, as she went through "Respect" and "Love the One You're With," "Bridge over Troubled Water" and "Eleanor Rigby," "Make It with You" and "Dr. Feelgood," until she left the stage, walked through the screaming crowd, and came back with— no one could believe it—Ray Charles in tow! "The Right Reverend Ray Charles!" Aretha announced.

"I happened to be in San Francisco," Ray remembers, "and someone said Aretha was performing. Well, far as I'm concerned, she's the right one, baby. I'm not much for hanging out, but I *will* go see Aretha. She's my one and only sister. So I get to the Fillmore and I sit way in the back, trying to be inconspicuous and not bother no one, when all of sudden someone spots me and next thing I know Aretha's come to get me, talkin' 'bout 'I discovered Ray Charles!'"

On stage, they sang and played "Spirit in the Dark"—a meeting of two souls, two geniuses from two distinct periods of my life, merging so easily, so naturally, so inevitably that all I could do was sit there and weep.

A year later I was in a front pew at the New Temple Missionary Baptist Church in Los Angeles, listening to Aretha sing "Precious Lord," my cup running over. We had gone from the Flower Children to the Saints, and the transition could not have been more successful. This, after all, was Aretha's spiritual house. It was also a long time coming. "It had been eight years since I'd recorded in church," said Aretha. "It's a feeling you get there you just don't get anywhere else."

Amen. My persistence had paid off. I'd been after Aretha from the beginning to return to church and sing the Christian songs closest to her heart. The double-LP live album, *Amazing Grace*, was a startling reality. None of us—not my co-producer, Arif Mardin, not even Aretha her-self—was quite ready for the quality of the performances. Aretha was on fire. The backing of her old friend Reverend James Cleveland and his mighty Southern California Community Choir, plus the presence of her father and his evocation of her childhood ("I was moved not only be-cause Aretha is my daughter but because Aretha is a stone singer!"), inspired her beyond human limits. This was the stuff of myth. She sang Clara Ward ("How I Got Over"); a medley of Thomas A. Dorsey ("Pre-cious Lord, Take My Hand") and Carole King ("You've Got a Friend");

"Amazing Grace"; Marvin Gaye ("Wholly Holy" from *What's Going On*); and Rodgers and Hammerstein ("You'll Never Walk Alone"). Aretha shedded the arrangements and we snuck in the devil's rhythm section, the secular grooves of Cornell Dupree, Richard Tee, Chuck Rainey, Bernard Purdie, and Latin percussionist Pancho Morales. (Ken Lupper, Reverend Cleveland's protégé keyboardist, was an astonishing extra added attraction.)

On "Precious Memories" Aretha and Reverend James sang a remarkable duet, the choir's mournful chant in marked contrast to the lead singers' cries of "sacred secrets . . . sacred secrets . . . sacred secrets" . . . until the sanctity of the moment was frozen and fixed in memory and time.

There's the metaphysical Aretha and there's also the down-home, pots-and-pans, cooking-up-a-storm Aretha, arriving in the studio with baskets of homemade chicken, ribs, and hamhocks. Or Aretha leaving the presidential suite of the Fontainebleau in Miami to hang out in the neighborhood with my R&B deejay pal Fat Daddy, who hipped her to the best pig's-feet joint back of town. Back at the hotel, walking through the opulent lobby, the damp pig's feet went through the take-out bag and spilled all over the carpet. Aretha didn't miss a beat. She kept on walking, straight into the elevator and up to her room.

She was regal and she was also Mother Earth. I'd be waiting for her at the studio, and she'd keep a group of musicians waiting an entire day; but the moment she walked through the door with a mountain of food for the boys, all was well. Joy was everywhere. Magic was about to be made. Aretha was about to sing.

I also remember sad moments with Aretha, when she seemed absolutely alone: once in Miami Beach when she came down with pancreatitis and no one in her entourage was around, no one was there to care for her, and I drove her to the hospital and wheeled her down the halls until I found a doctor to treat her.

To my way of thinking there are three qualities that make a great singer—head, heart, and throat. The head is the intelligence, the phrasing. The heart is the emotionality that feeds the flames. The throat is the chops, the voice. Ray Charles certainly has the first two. His voice is wonderful, but you wouldn't consider it bel canto. Aretha, though, like Sam Cooke, has all three qualities. Her gift seems to have sprung, like Minerva, full-fledged from Jupiter's head.

King Curtis and Delaney Bramlett

On August 15, 1971, one of my closest friends and colleagues was murdered. It happened only months after Aretha's Fillmore West concert, at the very peak of King Curtis's solo career. Some felon, a vagrant who wouldn't move from the stoop, stabbed him to death in front of the building that Curtis owned on West 96th Street. Just like that.

Sitting in St. Peter's Lutheran church, tears streaming down our cheeks, none of who worked and lived with Curtis could believe he was gone. Aretha sang "Never Grow Old," but I had never felt such rage, such fury at fate. I thought about how much I admired Curtis Ousley (his real name) and how pointless this death was, a chance occurrence. He was a great saxist—not voguish, mind you, just great. His was a towering presence. Six foot one, powerful, cool, and radiant, he always was in charge. He loved to eat, shoot dice, record, ride his bike, and make shrewd record deals.

I remembered how he became great friends, through our office, with Delaney Bramlett and Duane Allman, and that period when these three lived and played together in an incredible free-style mode. So

many memories: shooting pool at my house in Long Island with Curtis
and Tony Joe White; fishing for sail off the *Big A* in the Gulf Stream; his
woman Modeen grilling steaks at four a.m. in their apartment on Central
Park West after a session; hanging out in Harlem after the gig at Small's;
parties at Ahmet's with King blowing behind Esther Phillips and Ahmet
singing duets on the blues—I love the way Ahmet sings the blues. Curtis
and Arif were recording an album in Memphis the night Martin Luther
King was murdered, and I urged them to come home, but they hung in
the terror-racked city long enough to complete the project.

Curtis was noble, ballsy and streetwise like nobody I ever knew, and
it was a rancid irony that he was killed on his own front steps by a passing
junkie. I loved the man, and even though *Down Beat* won't give him
house room, he belongs forever with Prez and Rollins and Trane, with
Lockjaw, Jug, and Gator Tail.

SWAMPED

*A*round *the start* of the seventies, the music that caught me was Swamp. Everywhere I looked, everywhere I traveled, I saw evidence of this new and old amalgamation of sounds.

At drummer Sammy Carson's Halloween party in Memphis, his new boss, singer Tony Joe White, held his breath to close his pores, removed a black widow from his personal Mason jar of spiders, and put it on the back of his hand. The spider bit, and the assemblage murmured an orison of "far out"s; then somebody put Tony Joe's "Roosevelt and Ira Lee" on the box. Tony Joe offered a spider to Don Nix, who'd been wearing a Dennis Hopper *Easy Rider* getup for the last five years, roaming the savannahs in pursuit of some private musical vision (a keeper of the flame, he was songwriter and musician and producer). Nix passed the spider in favor of a roach.

At 3614 Jackson Highway in Muscle Shoals, embryonic guru Eddie Hinton was working out a Taj Mahal lick. The session was Ronnie Hawkins's first for Atlantic—a Wexler/Dowd co-production—and the tune was Bo Diddley's "Who Do You Love." Ronnie owned a couple of farms and nightclubs outside Toronto, but he was still stone Arkansas Swamp. You never heard a bitter breath or bad vibe from the guy who lost Rick, Levon, Garth, and Robbie to Dylan and John Till to Janis Joplin.

At the Ash Grove in L.A., the Monday-night jam featured Taj on harp. Leon Russell was sitting in on piano when suddenly Big Boy Crudup came on to sing, creating some kind of blues band. More Swamp.

At Ungaro's, 70th near Broadway, Dr. John extinguished his flambé headgear, waited for the goofer dust to settle and the gris-gris to dry before applying ass to piano stool. Delaney Bramlett, Eric Clapton, and Ginger Baker sat in, and the clouds exploded.

At another studio in Muscle Shoals, Rick Hall's Fame, Bobbie Gentry cut her fantastic "Fancy." Two weeks later, at Criteria in Miami, Brook Benton did Tony Joe's "Rainy Night in Georgia," a song I'd slipped to his producer, His Soulful Turkish Eminence Arif Mardin.

In Memphis the MG's were still racing and Chips Moman's guys at American were running with Elvis, Dusty, and Herbie Mann. Father Mose Allison was carrying on his spare, flame-under-a-bushel style. John Fogerty gave credence to the movement; nervous Doug Kershaw was making small seismic waves; and Clifton Chenier was reviewed by Greil Marcus.

It was all the Southern sound, R&B played by Southern whites. It was up from Corpus Christi, Helena, Florence, Thibodaux, Tupelo, Tuscaloosa, and Tuscumbia. It was Joe South with his low-tuned guitar; it was Willie Morris, born in the Delta, schooled in Texas, and newly arrived in New York as editor of *Harper's* at thirty-two, who called Mississippi blacks his kin.

It was country funk. The Byrds put something into it that somehow fit with Cow Cow Davenport's buck-dance thing, Otis Redding's horn ideas, and Tommy Cogbill's structured variations on James Jamerson's free-ranging Motown bass lines. It wasn't rockabilly, although echoes of early Sun are there, ghosts of Elvis and Cash and Vincent. Listen to "Suspicious Minds" with the Sweet Inspirations backing the King and you'll hear it. These sounds weren't super-overdubbed; there was no use of feedback, ten-foot amplifiers, excessive reverb, or souped-up treble.

More? Well, the Sir Douglas Quintet (a.k.a. Doug Sahm) and Johnny Cash and Merle Haggard; they surely added to the mix, along with Jerry Lee Lewis and the great, underrated Charlie Rich.

It was in the soil, the grits, the field lore, the drinking water, the sure-footed rhythm, the plain earthy talk. Out of all these ingredients issued the clarity, the mess, and the majesty of the deep-down Southern Swamp.

Soon came a duo who lured me even farther into the Swamp: Delaney and Bonnie.

Don Nix had discovered them, Stax had signed them, and their first album excited everyone at Muscle Shoals, which is where I was when

Ahmet called me to say that they were available. "Grab 'em!" I yelled. "Grab 'em quick!"

Ahmet roped them in, and the next thing I knew I was at the Ertegun townhouse on the Upper East Side, listening to Mississippi-born Delaney slurping champagne and saying I'm his man. Bonnie tells me I'm her Gurdjieff and, man, I'm lapping it all up.

Ahmet and Mica had put on the ritz in their grand high-society, lowdown-musician manner. Jerry Zipkin—whom Ahmet calls "the social moth"—was whispering into the ear of a bejeweled socialite, and Babe and Bill Paley were there along with playwright Jack Richardson. And Wilson Pickett, who'd just come up with me from Miami, where we cut "Sugar Sugar," the unlikely Archies song that would break Wicked's cold spell and put him back on the charts. Watching Pickett rap with another Atlantic artist—Carlyle Hotel cabaret singer Bobby Short, on the arm of restaurateur Elaine Kaufman—was no small entertainment.

Delaney and Bonnie and I hung tight. They wanted me to produce them, and I was ready—ready to get back to Miami. Delaney needed a slide guitarist and suggested Ry Cooder. Ry was booked, so I recommended Duane Allman. Delaney was suspicious—hadn't heard of him—but when Duane came down they formed an instant and intense musical bond. Later they hung out at my place on Long Island with me and Shirley and the kids, and we'd sit at water's edge listening to their acoustic guitars, sweet notes floating over the Sound, the songs of Blind Willie Johnson and Jimmie Rodgers, soft country melodies and sad Delta blues. I'm still kicking myself for not turning on the tape recorder.

*B*onnie was blazing hot. She came from Ike and Tina Turner territory, southern Illinois across from St. Louis.

"When Bonnie first saw the Turners," says Lorraine Rebennack, her best friend, "she pointed to Tina, whipping her head around and shaking her ass on stage, and said, 'Baby, that's what I want to be!'"

She got her wish—in a way. Bonnie became the first white Ikette in the Ike and Tina Revue. By the time she married Delaney she was the star of his show, with green snakeskin boots running from her toes to her crotch.

The album I produced, *To Bonnie from Delaney*, didn't quite catch the fire of their live performances. They were so hot by then that George Harrison, Dave Mason, Leon Russell, and Eric Clapton traveled with

Bonnie, Delaney, and Duane Allman

them as sidemen. (Years later, in Willie Nelson's bus, Eric would say, "Delaney taught me everything I know about singing.") The highlight of the record was Little Richard's piano cameo on "Miss Ann." I had actually signed Richard, who was deep into a gospel-only bag. I figured I could con him into doing the devil's music, but no such luck. We wound up with a compromised mess—nowhere songs like "Shake a Hand" and "Take Me to the Rock." I wanted the rock to roll; but only during the breaks, with the tape machine off, would Richard roll out those incredible blues runs, blowing everyone away, me praying that he'd bless us with secular stuff. Didn't happen.

The closest I myself came to a spiritual experience involved Delaney and Bonnie, my wife Shirley, and our friend and employee Tommy Aprea. At the height of the Age of Aquarius, I took a trip to the Empyrean Isles without leaving East Marion, courtesy of some jet-fueled acid someone slipped me. I didn't know I was taking it—hadn't been warned—but wound up a joyful Jew nevertheless. I was up all night. The next morning I was still going at it, explaining everything to everyone, dispensing cosmic information with the sagacity of an Old Testa-

Dinner with Delaney and Bonnie, Mac and Lorraine, Paul and Lydia

ment prophet. I saw into the center of the rose, into the mystery of all consciousness, explaining the origin of matter and the structure of Red Allen's trumpet solos. I wouldn't shut up, and my hunch is that, despite the logorrhea, I wasn't unentertaining. I say that because not long afterward my friends—Delaney, Bonnie, Mac, and Lorraine—did it again, this time fucking me up on some hallucinogen at the Palamino in the San Fernando Valley.

"Jerry could get paranoid behind drugs," Lorraine says, "but that night he was positively ecstatic. We loved listening to him, even though we did start worrying that his mouth muscles might collapse from overuse. We didn't think he'd ever come down or shut up."

We were all up in the seventies; the music kept us up, music coming at a phenomenal clip. Living in Miami, every time I turned around someone was coming through Criteria. Duane Allman, for example, had hooked up with his brother Gregg and guitarist Dickey Betts to form the Allman Brothers Band, managed by Phil Walden and recorded on our Capricorn label.

Unlike corporations such as CBS and RCA, preoccupied with a unified logo, I always pushed the idea of subsidiary labels. It didn't cost a zloty and was an easy way to pacify an artist or a heavyweight manager. (CBS's credo: *It's gotta come out on our label and we won't pay more than 5 percent.* Our credo: *We'll put your record out on any damn label you choose and we'll pay 10 percent.*) As a result we had a slew of successful sublabels—Dial, Fame, Dade, Alston, Stax, Volt, Capricorn, Rolling Stone, and so forth. While the majors were sleeping on this issue, we mopped up. Today, with Prince's Paisley Park and Michael Jackson's Nation Records, the practice is so standard it's practically meaningless. It always was.

*T*he Allman Brothers," says Phil Walden, "became the people's band. They were Southerners living in the South playing Southern music."

"We did everything we could against being commercial," Dickey Betts remembers. "We used our guitars like a brass section, playing all these harmony lines. Harmonies that sounded like they took a month to write were actually improvised. It was musical telepathy. We were into individual expression. We were also lucky that the times were right for free thinkers. It was a free period. Our models weren't big moneymakers, but the blues giants of the thirties and forties—Robert Johnson, Elmore James. If it hadn't been for FM radio, we would have never been heard."

"When I told Wexler," says Walden, "that our Fillmore East live album would have to be two LPs and contain at least one sixteen-minute song, he resisted. 'Not every note,' he argued, 'is vital to our heritage.' I said, 'Jerry, the boys are pure artists and that's the way it's got to be.' Jerry agreed. He understood."

What I understood was that I had never heard a guitarist I found as satisfying as Duane. That's why in October of 1971, I found myself ranting against the gods again, bewildered and shocked. At age twenty-four, Duane was gone. Home in Macon, swerving to avoid a truck, Duane had lost control of his motorcycle, fell under the bike, and died of injuries. There I was, back in Georgia, at another podium, in another church, delivering another eulogy for another soul man from Macon.

"Jerry called me and Mac with the news," says Lorraine Rebennack. "We were in Woodstock, visiting the Band. We flew down on the Warner corporate jet with Jerry and no one could speak. Mac played at the service—so did Delaney—and it was the first time I'd ever seen people

Duane Allman's funeral: Dr. John, left; Gregg Allman, right

wearing jeans to a funeral. It was simple and beautiful—the music was beautiful—and sad beyond anything I had ever experienced. Mac was devastated, and so was Jerry."

Mac and I found each other especially simpatico in those days. We'd become working partners in what I consider one of the gems of my career—Dr. John's *Gumbo* album. The concept was more grits and less gris-gris. Mac was ready to shed the voodoo garb. No night-tripping, "just basic good-time New Orleans stomp," said Mac, "with a sprinkling of Dixieland and Spanish rumba blues." My enthusiasm for the album was unbounded. Mac and I saw eye to eye, groove to groove. Authenticity was the key—real songs with real players playing with real feeling. Fuck chasing hits; just do the thing right. And when it comes to Crescent City sounds, no one's righter than the good Doctor.

We chose the songs together. I called in New Orleans arranger Harold Battiste to do the horn charts and gave him co-producing credit. Ironically, we cut the sides in L.A. That's where Mac and his homeboys were living—guys like saxist Lee Allen and drummer Freddie Staehle. Freddie was terrific, an Elvin Jones R&B–playing white man with tremendous chops. But once the session got started, he just wouldn't hit a definite backbeat on two and four. Instead he was weaving his second-

line patterns without ever accenting the downbeats. I kept after him to
no avail, and finally got mad. I went out in the studio and started hitting
the snare on two and four. Finally Mac came over. "I don't know what's
wrong with the motherfucker," he said about his friend. "He used to be
some kind of all right, but ever since he got into Scientology, he won't
play no two and four nohow." No matter; his timing was so right that
dubbing in the backbeat was a cinch.

The album was a shuffle down memory lane, back to the Chipaka
Shaweez from the Seventh to Ninth Wards, Mac's home turf. We did
"Iko Iko" (written by James Crawford, who operated under the name
Sugar Boy and the Cane Cutters, and cut by the Dixie Cups back in the
sixties on Leiber and Stoller's Red Bird); "Blow Wind Blow" (by Izzycoo
Gordon of the Spiders); "Big Chief" and "Those Lonely Lonely Nights"
by Earl King (whose encyclopedic knowledge of New Orleans R&B rivals Mac's); Ahmet's "Mess Around"; "Stack-O-Lee"; "Tipitina," a redo
of the classic that Ahmet and I produced on Professor Longhair twenty
years earlier; and a long Huey Smith medley.

All the time we were recording, I was learning, interacting with Mac
in a way I never had with Ray Charles. With Ray I got out of the way,
but with Mac I like to think I was part of the way. Those New Orleans
rhythms, coming out of the parades and marches and funerals, bands
playing heavily accented downbeats while the folks—waiters, waitresses, street vendors, little kids—danced on the sidelines with parasols
and tambourines, creating beats of their own, spontaneous second-line
syncopations, New Orleans with its mythology of cajun princes and
prison music . . . it all seemed encapsulated in the musical body of Mac.
I was such an apt student of Macology that I was able to spin out the
liner notes in his voice. I set it down as though Mac were dictating to me.

Ironic, then, that I would wind up alienated from Mac, more so than
with any musician I ever worked with. Today I know that I overreacted
and, in fairness, not justifiably. But it's part of the story.

"GIVING

UP"

My daughter Anita would play the song on the piano for hours on end. In her clear and lovely voice, she'd sing: "Giving up is hard to do . . . Giving up is so hard to do."

The song haunted her and started to haunt me. "It would be perfect for Donny Hathaway," she said.

King Curtis lucked up on Donny Hathaway in the late sixties. He'd come back from a deejay convention in Washington, D.C., raving about this guy who'd been working with Curtis Mayfield in Chicago. King was so excited he rushed straight from the airport to my house in Great Neck with a copy of Donny's self-produced, unreleased album. One listen and I was hooked. I signed him in a flash and we released *Everything Is Everything* in 1970, with Donny's songs, Donny's arrangements, Donny's piano, and, most significantly, Donny's gorgeous plush-velvet voice—a broad-stroked, big-bottomed, misty-blue pop-jazz-church voice, an important voice destined to influence a new generation of soul singers: George Benson, Peabo Bryson, Michael Henderson, Jeffrey Osborne, James Ingram, Luther Vandross.

I was certain that Donny was the next major artist after Aretha. And I was even more certain when Aretha herself, rapping with Ray Charles backstage at the Fillmore West, was saying the same thing: Watch out for Donny. Ray, 'Retha, and Donny. The tradition was intact. Soon the word was out. Carole King, Steve Stills, everyone was talking up Donny, especially "The Ghetto," his master tone poem from the first album. Analogies were being drawn to Marvin Gaye, whose *What's Going On* was released in the same time zone, deeply influencing Hathaway's aesthetic and social sensibilities.

I co-produced the second album, *Donny Hathaway*, with Arif, who contributed enormously to Donny's overall sound. That's the record with the definitive versions of Leon Russell's "A Song for You," Bobby Scott's "He Ain't Heavy, He's My Brother," and Billy Preston's "Little Girl." (I cherish a memory of playing Donny's interpretation for Billy: Billy sitting there speechless, his head moving with the music, his face streaked with tears.) It was "Giving Up," though, that highlighted the album and is a benchmark in the art of forthright emotional vocal communication. I consider this one of the two or three greatest productions in Atlantic's long history, worthy of placement alongside Ray's "What'd I Say" and Aretha's "Respect." Most songs are lucky to have a single climax, but "Giving Up" has at least four; Donny's arrangement builds to peak after peak, King Curtis's bone-chilling tenor break lifting the spirits to ever greater elevations. It's just a stone masterpiece.

Donny's musical mind was complex. He studied Les Six, the French modern masters: Louis Durey, Arthur Honegger, Darius Milhaud, Germaine Tailleferre, Georges Auric, and Francis Poulenc, all of whom adored Erik Satie. Donny could play Satie; he could play anything. He was different from many of his pop composer colleagues. His constructions were never simplistic but were based on complex jazz chords. Those songs that have become standards—"Someday We'll All Be Free," "This Christmas," "Take a Love Song," "The Ghetto"—are perfect vehicles for improvisation, the sure sign of jazz-rooted compositions. When he sang a standard—listen, for instance, to his magnificent interpretation of "For All We Know" with Roberta Flack at the piano and Arif's strings soaring behind him—his phrasing is informed not only by the sweetness of Sam Cooke but by the sophistication of Sinatra. Unlike Sinatra, though, Donny is sanctified. In that sense he joins hands with Aretha and Ray, church pianists all. Listen to how Donny and Aretha trade piano licks—Donny on electric, Aretha on acoustic—in her reading of "Bridge over Troubled Water." We turned the song so upside down that the next time I saw Paul Simon I was a little apprehensive. Paul loved it.

Donny was exceptionally bright. Saturated in music, he had all sorts of theories of time and harmony, many of them beyond me, some of them bordering on the eccentric. He could be funny and engaging; he could also be a space cadet. He was on the edge emotionally and would deliver endless monologues on the abstract mathematics of music which even musicians found incomprehensible—not to say intolerable. I remember Donny holding forth on some arcane rhythm matter at a session with drummer Grady Tate. Grady's a great guy, but in his presence you better walk right. "Look," he finally said, "we're musicians and can't pick up on what you're saying. Tell it right or we're walking." They went back to work—and got it right.

Another bad studio scene involved Al Jackson, the peerless Memphis drummer. I'd brought him to New York to back Donny on "Giving Up." Guitarist Eric Gale was on bass. Perversely, Donny got hung up on a delusion: he insisted that Al was off time with the second beat in every measure. If there ever was a drummer who had the backbeat exactly in the pocket it was Mr. Jackson. Time after time Donny stopped the take a few bars into the track.

"What's your problem with two?" I asked him.

"It's wavering, man. Can't you hear it?"

"Sorry, Donny. It's exactly on the money."

Al graciously asked Donny to show him his error. Donny went to the drums and played his notion of the time. It was precisely what Al had been playing, and everyone in the band knew it. But they went back and forth for hours, and nothing got done.

It was nearly three a.m. when Donny finally jumped up. "That's it!" he told Al. "That's the time I've been looking for!" But nothing had been changed; it was the same groove Al had been playing all night. Nonetheless, the session kicked into high gear and we were able to put some solid sides in the can.

Donny and I were close, and it didn't take me long to learn of the powerful, painful battles being waged within his heart and soul. He'd say, "Maybe I can sing, Jerry, but look at the way I look. I'm shaped like a pear." His sexual identity was rife with uncertainty; loneliness never left him for long.

At the same time, his career took interesting turns. Nesuhi and his assistant Joel Dorn had signed and been developing Roberta Flack, the marvelous pop/jazz singer (the antecedent, in my view, of Anita Baker). Calling from Miami, I suggested a Roberta/Donny duet on Carole King's "You've Got a Friend," which Arif and Joel produced into a hit.

Roberta's first solo album, however, was languishing. And it was my daughter Anita who got the ball rolling. By now she'd quit college at California Institute of the Arts to work as an assistant to my assistant

Mark Myerson. "We have this incredible new singer," she said, "and no one knows about her."

"Anita was always looking for Jerry's attention, approval, and affection," Mark says. "Those were not always attainable. Sometimes you got closer to Jerry with good business ideas, and Anita's idea about Roberta was right. Roberta was dying on the vine."

By then Anita was involved with a black man she had met back in Great Neck, Jimmy Douglass. Jimmy had been working at a supermarket crushing boxes, but Anita was convinced he had a good musical ear. I put him to work in the studio, where he quickly earned his stripes and eventually became a first-class engineer and remix man. Jimmy was as stoked as Anita about Roberta Flack.

I took action and set up live performances to showcase Roberta in five key markets. We hand-delivered invitations to distributors, record dealers, deejays, and press people. Before long, the orders started pouring in. That helped set up Roberta's trio of monster hits—"The First Time Ever I Saw Your Face" (1972), "Killing Me Softly with His Song" (1973), and "Feel Like Makin' Love" (1974).

Donny's career was helped by the series of stirring duets he'd sung with Roberta. ("Where Is the Love" was a million-seller.) Then he stopped singing with Roberta and experienced something of a slump. For a long while Donny couldn't break out of his holding pattern. He scored the film *Come Back Charleston Blue* for Quincy Jones and sang the theme to the TV show "Maude"; he freelanced around, but nothing big. Then, in 1978, he reunited with Roberta and cut "The Closer I Get to You," a huge hit.

Ironically, that was when despondency and self-doubt got the best of him. In 1979, Donny fell to his death from a room at the Essex House hotel on Central Park South in New York. His sad demise is shrouded in mystery. I have no inside information. All I know is that he was a kind and gentle man. Sometimes I think his artistic sensibilities were almost too exquisite. Was he made mad by the intrinsic limitations of art—the same madness, say, suffered by Bird or Bix? I don't know. But I loved Donny and continue to derive sustenance from his records. When he died he was only thirty-three, and already being called a giant; I often think of what he might have accomplished. His talent had no limits. The beauty of his voice and the sweetness of his soul remain a permanent part of the liturgy.

*M*eanwhile, in 1972 Delaney and Bonnie were in trouble. He had gone off to produce their new album in L.A., using Ike Turner's new studio. For my money, Ike's one of the great studio men, a marvelous musician, and I quickly approved the budget, issued purchase orders, and waited for the results. I waited months. I heard nothing, not a single note. After a year, I decided to get on a plane and see what the hell had gone wrong.

"I feel sorry for you, Wex," Delaney said when I arrived in the studio, "because you're going to have to figure out which of these eleven cuts to release first. Every one's a smash."

When I listened to the tapes, I didn't hear smashes. I heard dog meat. The rumors—that Delaney and Ike were coked out—seemed substantiated. Superb artists both, they'd blown it. The album was un-releasable. I was back in Miami before Bonnie caught up with me. She was not only drunk but terrified. Apparently Delaney had been beating her up.

"Jerry was sweet with Bonnie," says Lorraine Rebennack. "He was supportive. But he was also crafty. He said to her, 'Look, do me just one more favor. Let me sell your contract.'"

Both as a couple and as an act, Delaney and Bonnie were history, and I knew it. I got hold of Steve Weiss, the lawyer friend who had brought me Led Zeppelin, and asked him to try to sell Delaney and Bonnie. As far as the world knew, they were still hot. Clive Davis at Columbia paid Atlantic $600,000 and another $100,000 to Delaney and Bonnie. We threw in the dog-meat album. I had to do it; a business obligation, it had nothing to do with my attachment to the artists. I'd done the same with Solomon Burke and Wilson Pickett after their sales had peaked.

But when Atlantic rushed out *Delaney and Bonnie's Greatest Hits,* Clive took offense, and we traded jabs in a heated correspondence. I pointed out that it's traditional—and certainly legal—for the ex-label to repackage records by recently departed acts. Columbia, in fact, had done the very same thing by promoting old Aretha sides as her *Greatest Hits* after she had hit big on Atlantic.

Delaney and Bonnie's new album crashed resoundingly, and turned out to be their last. They never sang another note together.

In 1972 in L.A., I got a call from Big Nate McCalla in Morris Levy's office in New York, where Anita, having quit Atlantic, was now working. He hinted she was having problems. At first I didn't get it, so Big Nate came right to the point. "She's on scag," he said.

I flew back—out of my mind, desperate—to reclaim Anita, take care of her problem, and get her cleaned up. It wasn't easy, and I wasn't good at it. In today's psychological parlance, I suppose I became her enabler, perhaps her super-enabler. I bailed her out, over and over again. For the next fifteen years, I put her into programs, bought her excuses, believed her promises to quit. Half knowing the truth, half denying it, I allowed her to manipulate me. I embraced hopes—some real, some false—not quite realizing that an addict has only one job: to score junk, using anyone, any way. Anita was smart, and also a schemer; in her relationship with me this combination was lethal.

"Jerry had his eyes closed to Anita when she worked for Atlantic," says Mark Myerson. "He was away in Florida, and none of us had the heart or courage to tell him. She was a warm and wonderful person, but she really couldn't function. She was hooked. It was only when she worked outside of Atlantic that Jerry got the word."

Matters were further complicated when Anita told me it was Dr. John who had introduced her to heroin. I took her at her word, overlooking her inclination to create conflict and undermine relationships. I knew when she was in California she'd grown close to Mac and Lorraine, just as the Rebennacks were close to us when they lived in Miami. Anita had actually gone on the road to sing backup on the "Night Tripper" show. According to her, that's where it all began. I was bitter.

"Who knows where it began?" asks Lorraine. "Anita was shooting drugs for as long as I can remember." "Anita was looking to cop from anyone who had it," remembers Fathead Newman, who was also on the scene. "It was unfair of Jerry to blame Mac. It's unfair to blame anyone. No one's addiction is the fault of another person. That's just passing the responsibility. Jerry knows better."

Back then I didn't. Maybe I was feeling guilty myself, and blaming someone else made things simpler. Anyway, for too long I did resent Mac.

In my mind's eye, I prefer to go back to a happier moment that included both Anita and Mac. It happened in the small apartment Anita

Above: Dancing with Anita, the sixties. Below: Anita, early eighties

and Jimmy Douglass had shared on 60th Street, right across from the Atlantic offices. One night they invited me over for an impromptu jam between Dr. John and Leon Russell. In some circles the word was out that Leon was copping off Mac's music and even Mac's costumes. "Some of the witches back in New Orleans are burning candles on Leon," Mac told me. But that night Mac and Leon were switching off instruments, going back and forth between guitar and piano, piano and guitar, with Jimmy on bass, until Mac sat down at the keyboard and rang out a thunderous rendition of "Tipitina." At that point Leon got up and removed the large and elaborate crucifix he wore on a gold chain, then carefully placed the cross around Mac's neck.

Recalling this night at Anita's, as I often do, has laid my bad feelings to rest. Mac's career is in high gear as I write this, and I wish him all the best.

THE
SECOND
TIME
AROUND

*B*y *1972,* Shirley had enough. For years our relationship had been going down slow. Instead of attending her needs, I'd been out there making music, fulminating against the corporation, looking for hits, indulging my penchant for certain artists and styles.

"The word was that Jerry had started to bury his head in the sand," says Mark Myerson. "His signings weren't paying off. He brought in the Electric Flag and Canned Heat after their time. He recorded roots artists like Dr. John and Doug Sahm *before* their time; they were friends and wonderful musicians, but back then they were too esoteric for the market. Jerry had the knack of being too early."

Things had drastically changed since the days when I was both a producer and a promotion man. I had comfortably worn both those hats in the fifties and sixties. Also, in those early days Shirley had been one of my main business advisors. But by the time the seventies rolled around, no more. I was focused on production while promotion was in the hands of people I hardly knew. New distributors, different disc jockeys . . . it was a strange world.

The old Atlantic headquarters—on 56th Street, on 57th Street, on Broadway—were part and parcel of the music: our offices were down the hall from our studios, our control room, our mixing facilities. It was all there and all beautifully organic. I could operate with celerity and efficiency. I could rip and run with anyone—sign the artist, make the record, get it played, hype the press, fire up the sales staff, tout key retailers. I was in the middle of it all. In the summer of 1973, however, Atlantic moved into the Rock, 75 Rockefeller Center, the elegant symbol of corporate power. We were on a low floor, and the bosses—Steve Ross and his support group—far above us.

I was starting to see that by removing myself to Miami, I'd taken myself out of the loop. I had hoped for relaxation, a less stressful life. But in fact I was still working like crazy, and cut off from the action in New York.

Confusing matters more, I'd fallen in love with another woman. The affair began before my marriage had officially ended, but long after it was emotionally spent. This marked the beginning of a long period that would see me moving back to New York—not to nearby Long Island but right into Manhattan, which, after all, was where I'd started out. It was also the beginning of a new love, and I was excited, stirred by feelings I hadn't known in years. I'd had brief affairs, but never with anyone for whom I'd consider changing my life.

I met Renee Pappas in 1971 when I was working on Dr. John's *Gumbo* album and she was working for the Beach Boys, directing their personal appearances. She came to my bungalow at the Beverly Hills Hotel with a tape of the live Beach Boys concert that closed the Fillmore East, which I was considering releasing as an album. Renee was twenty-four; I was fifty-four. One era was ending, another beginning—for the Beach Boys, for music, for me.

Renee was young and fresh and pretty, filled with an irresistible optimism and innocence. I pursued her for a long while. She had a boyfriend, so I invited them both to an Aretha Franklin concert at the Cocoanut Grove. Several months later I invited Renee, who was then working for David Geffen, to join me in Tyler, Texas, where I was producing Freda and the Firedogs, a group led by singer Marcia Ball, to this day a tremendous talent marking time in Austin.

Doug Sahm had introduced me to Marcia. What Mac is to New Orleans, Doug is to Texas. From Western swing to Lightnin' Hopkins's Houston blues, from Tex-Mex ditties to polkas, Doug integrated it all and came out with something singular: his own sound on guitar, his own voice, his own songs. I also loved the irony of his calling his great sixties group the Sir Douglas Quintet, the Texan passing as a Brit to entice American ears. I was proud to produce his album, documenting Sahm's soul, embracing everything from T-Bone Walker to Bob Wills. We recruited an eclectic bunch of sidemen—Dr. John, Bob Dylan, Arif on electric piano, *conjunto* accordionist Flaco Jiminez, and Fort Worth tenor man Fathead Newman, formerly with Ray Charles and long a star in his own right. The album, *Doug Sahm and Band*, didn't sell. Due to contract disputes, the Freda and the Firedogs record wasn't even released. But I was defiant, proud of them both, and determined to follow my bliss.

Renee was part of that bliss, part of a new hope. She had survived a tough childhood: a father who died when she was eight and her sister, Connie, only six; a mother who went through the father's money and burdened her daughters with heavy emotional and financial insecurities. I was impressed that both girls had triumphed over a cataclysmic beginning, showing character and real mettle. (Connie is Elton John's manager in America; her husband, Chris Hillman, formerly of the Byrds and a superb bluegrass musician, is presently in the Desert Rose Band.)

My son, Paul, claims it was Anita who first told Shirley about Renee. "Anita told my mother," he says. "Anita precipitated the end of my parents' marriage, though God knows it was doomed anyway."

My own memory is that I told Shirley.

"I really don't remember who said what," says Shirley. "But there's no doubt Anita wanted to drive a wedge between me and Jerry. That was hardly necessary, since the wedge was already there. I remember the incident that brought it all down. Tommy Aprea, who had become part of our family and closer to the kids than Jerry himself, wanted to put a tuna tower on our skiff in Miami Beach. I gave him the money and Jerry gave me holy hell. Jerry was so incensed he took away my checkbook. I knew there was more to this than the stupid tuna tower."

There was. The tower didn't make sense—it was like putting a penthouse on a Toyota truck—but I had a hidden agenda. I wanted out, and I knew Shirley would never tolerate my taking her checkbook away. She didn't.

By then I had come to think of Shirley, Tommy, and the kids as a unit that no longer included me. On the dozens of trips I made to Muscle Shoals and California, Shirley never accompanied me. We had compartmentalized ourselves; we had lost each other and the childhood love we thought would last a lifetime.

I proposed to Renee, and she accepted. Divorce negotiations went quickly and easily: Shirley would get both houses—Miami Beach and East Marion, Long Island—and a load of municipal bonds. My plan was

Renee

to return to Manhattan in style, buy a co-op, jump back into the swing of things. It happened in a flash. No one—not even my best friends—had a clue.

"My wife, Corky, and I had visited Shirley and Jerry in Miami during Thanksgiving," recalls Mike Stoller. "In December Jerry called to invite me to his wedding. I assumed he and Shirley were renewing their vows. 'No,' said Jerry, 'I'm marrying Renee.'"

A big wedding had been planned, but I canceled it. At my age, with three grown children, I felt a high-profile ceremony would look inane. In 1973, days after the divorce came through, Renee and I were married in judge's chambers with only a few family members present. Of course my mother was there. Cy Ampole was best man.

"Jerry's mother was always there," says Renee. "Once, after we were married, we took Elsa out to eat with some friends. She looked around the restaurant and said to Jerry, 'Oh, Gerald, I bet everyone here thinks you and I are married and these are our children.' In truth, Elsa didn't look much older than Jerry."

Perhaps, in marrying me, Renee hoped to regain the father she had lost so early. I don't know, but that's the opinion of her sister—and Renee herself, reflecting on the marriage years later, seems to agree.

"Jerry was a wonderful teacher," she says. "He was nothing like the music-business creeps I'd known. He knew about art, literature, food, travel, everything that fascinated me. Looking back, I can now see I fell into the role of a child rather than wife. While Anita became more of a problem—dropping out of college, unable to hold jobs—I went to college under Jerry's tutelage; I was the good daughter. And for a short while, the relationship worked."

For the first few months, I was in a sickening vertigo, feeling I'd lost the one woman who understood and loved me. I started calling Shirley, writing long letters, urging her to try one more time, arguing that we still needed each other. Shirley wrote back that it was too late, that we'd drifted too far apart. And besides, she'd found someone else: Tommy Aprea, who'd been with her through the bad times; who was tight with the kids; who, like Renee, was decades younger than either of us. I had no arguments. Tommy was a sweet, good-hearted man. He figured to treat Shirley right and I wished her well. Before long she and Tommy wed, and they are still married today.

Renee and I moved to Park Avenue, where we geared up in style: Rosenthal china, Baccarat crystal, a driver, a cook, fine wine, haute cuisine, Magrittes in the hallway, and gold records in the den. I enjoyed the perks—for use, consumption, or mere contemplation. But soon a series of dubious types began to appear at dinner: assorted rockoids, epicene second-growth record-biz types and their actor companions, a run of hyphenated Brits slumming on Park, marginal interior decorators. Occasionally there were good parties, when friends like Earl McGrath or John Hammond or Carol Friedman graced our board; but Renee was trolling for other fish. I guess she was disappointed. Hard times were in store.

Renee got pregnant, and I urged her to have an abortion. This was a mistake. We had firmly agreed in advance not to have children, but I should've seen that enforcing that agreement was foolish and might be damaging.

"I had the abortion," says Renee, "but afterwards I built an emotional wall around myself. I went about my business of being Jerry's respectable and dutiful wife. I went to Finch, Marymount, I earned my degree; I became president of the board of our apartment building, took cooking courses, classes in furniture design, went into business as an interior decorator—all with Jerry's help and support. As I grew out of the role of his child, though, he became more threatened. Would I still need him? Would I still love him? Would I still be obedient?"

For my part, I took my work frustrations out at home. Same old same old.

CHANGING
SOUNDS

Miami was over. I was back in New York, but things had truly changed. The company didn't need me. Jerry Greenberg had replaced me as daily op man; Ahmet was scoring big with rock acts; the venues I was familiar with—nightclubs, festivals, and concert halls—no longer dominated the scene. Arena rock was king, rock with a hundred thousand spectators, Yes and Zep and Emerson, Lake, and Palmer.

"When Jerry got back to New York, it was a little too late," remembers Mark Myerson. "He didn't know how and where to fit in. Even worse, he was costing the company money—a prime example being the country division he began."

I can't agree with Mark about that. The country division lost money and didn't last more than a couple of years, but I consider it a proud accomplishment if only for one reason: I signed Willie Nelson. According to Willie, that signing helped turn his career around.

I had hired Russ Sanjek's son, Rick, who'd gone to Yale and was working the Nashville music scene, to open an office there for us, but it didn't work. Other than Willie, we never broke any artists. Given time, I'm sure we would have pulled it off, but as Atlantic's chief financial officer, Ahmet made the call: it's in the red, so close it down.

For me at least, Willie Nelson was more than enough. Willie's one of my heroes. Strange as it sounds, with his scraggly beard and calm wonderful eyes, he reminded me of my father when Harry was at peace with himself. Willie exudes love. He also shares with Sinatra a gift for incredible vocal rubato—prolonging one note, cutting short another, swinging with an elastic sense of time that only the finest jazz singers understand.

With Willie and Arif in the studio

Willie's understanding is vast, and before meeting him I prepared scores of Western swing dubs, not simply Bob Wills but also obscure regional bands: Adolph Hofner from the German villages of East Texas; the Light Crust Doughboys; the Pipeliners; Harry Choates, the Cajun fiddler and creator of the country standard "Draggin' the Bow." This was music I had first discovered at college in Kansas in the mid-thirties, music that had always held me enraptured—music to which Willie was the legitimate heir.

We met through Doug Sahm—both Willie and Bob Dylan are Sahm fans—and I was immediately touched by his genuineness. We hung out for days going over tapes and songs. It turned out that we both dug Western swing and melodic jazz. It was 1973, when Willie was looked down on by Nashville's assembly-line producers as eccentric. But his eccentricity was exactly what attracted me. I suggested he use his own band, something he'd always been denied, since I wanted him to be comfortable. Most of his first record for Atlantic was cut in New York, with Arif providing the perfect production ambience. Fuck the notion— sheer idiocy—that Willie was a renegade; just let Willie be Willie.

"I wasn't entirely comfortable at first," he says. "Things weren't happening as quickly as I wanted. Recording in New York was strange. So I went back to my hotel and started pacing. Listening to the radio. Search-

Trading hats with Willie

ing for an idea. Finally sat on the toilet and spotted this sanitary napkin envelope I could write on. I wrote, 'Shotgun Willie sits around in his underwear, biting on a bullet, pulling out his hair.'"

Shotgun Willie, his first album for us, included the title cut, Johnny Bush's "Whiskey River," and "Sad Songs and Waltzes," all of which have become Nelson classics. When I suggested that we do his second album in Muscle Shoals, everyone in Nashville thought I was out of my mind. They said Muscle Shoals was too R&B for Willie; I said Willie was too R&B for Nashville. Willie was willing. He'd learned the hard way that when it came to country music, Nashville could wear blinders—as they did with Elvis. He also knew I heard the blues in him and that his blues were strong.

This time his blues were brilliantly conceptualized in something he had never tried before: a cohesive suite of songs. He called it *Phases and Stages,* and—set against the rhythm section of Barry Beckett, David Hood, Roger Hawkins, and Pete Carr—the album flowed from start to finish. We cut it in two days, the first side taking a woman's point of view on the highs and hurts of romance, the second seen through the eyes of a man. ("I Still Can't Believe You're Gone," written for his drummer Paul English's late wife, is as poignant as any love song in the history of heartache.) "Nearly everything about the album represents a departure," wrote country music critic John Morthland. "It's rife with contradictions; it's got more jazz inflections than anything Nelson has done, yet it's also true to his Texas country roots."

I still see Willie sitting there with his old beat-up, Scotch-taped acoustic guitar. When he hits the strings the tape resonates, buzzing in the mike; when he sings there's always that Spanish, Texas-border tinge to his voice that sets my heart pounding.

Phases and Stages and its single—"Bloody Mary Morning"—sold respectably, not spectacularly. Yet the album is a milestone, at least in my mind, of solid American music. Unfortunately, no one at Atlantic shared my interest in country music, which in the long range probably served Willie's interests. When the Nashville division was eliminated, the resources necessary to nurture a country artist were gone. Not wanting to leave Willie dangling, I got him an unconditional release. It hurt to turn him loose, but *Phases and Stages* had earned so much praise that his freedom was worth a lot of money. Suddenly Willie was hot. Mo Ostin wanted him for Warner; I tried to help Mo, but CBS prevailed. And it was on CBS that Willie broke through with a long string of multi-platinum albums, beginning with *Red Headed Stranger,* the logical successor to *Phases and Stages.*

*A*lthough I could see that the longest phase of my working career, my association with Atlantic, was deteriorating, there was at least one respite during this otherwise sobering period—a party to end all parties, Atlantic's twenty-fifth anniversary in 1972.

"Ahmet went all out," Mark Myerson recalls. "He chartered an Air India 747 and flew everyone to Paris. The polite little Indian stewardesses were shocked when, as soon the jet took off, the gang started lighting joints, snorting coke, and partying seriously. We had a blast. We stayed in a luxury hotel, and there was nothing but good vibes—except for one encounter. It happened during a ten-course gourmet meal at a five-star Parisian restaurant. In this ambience of extreme elegance, Nesuhi and Jerry got into a hot debate over who was the greatest jazz violinist. Nesuhi, in his Napoleonic manner, championed Stéphane Grappelli. Wexler would have none of it. His man was Joe Venuti. The two of them went on far beyond the bounds of reason. Nesuhi beat his fist on the table; Jerry roared back at him. Of course nothing was resolved, and, after a while, the rest of us were too high to care."

Within a year or so, the music I cared most about didn't seem to be selling. My last big hits with Aretha, for example, dated back to 1971, with "Rock Steady" and "Day Dreaming," and I realized she could use another producer. When she told me that Quincy was interested in co-producing a jazz album with me, I jumped at the idea. I'd admired Quincy's work since his priceless small group arrangements for Dinah Washington on Mercury. After much procrastination, though, I learned through Quincy's man, bassist Ray Brown, that Quincy preferred to produce solo.

The problem was that Quincy took forever and a day to cut the sides, well over a year, a critical period when Aretha could ill afford to be out of the spotlight. Moreover, the album somehow changed format from jazz to watered-down pop. *Hey Now Hey (The Other Side of the Sky)* lacked direction, and the artwork—a flying hypodermic needle—was appalling. Only one song took off, the beautiful "Angel," written by Aretha's sister Carolyn. The album sold poorly, yet no worse than the final three I'd produced for Aretha: *Let Me Into Your Life, With Everything I Feel in Me,* and *You.*

If I was in a slump, the label was not. In a historic twist, an act that had died on Motown came to life on Atlantic. Stimulated by the spirited inventions of Thom Bell, the Spinners were red hot—"I'll Be Around," "Could It Be I'm Falling In Love"—forerunners of disco, a genre that I found somewhat tedious. No matter; the Spinners were keeping the Atlantic R&B best-selling tradition alive, and I wasn't.

I was accused of favoring friends like Donnie Fritts, one of my favorite people, with homespun Muscle Shoals albums that somehow missed the mass market. I also recorded singers like Gary Farr and Maggie Bell, artists I admired but couldn't sell. Music was changing, and no one understood it better than Anita, who had cleaned up and was working in A&R for Mercury, where she produced and mixed cutting-edge sides for Michael Henderson, a student of Marcus Belgrave (a member of the original Ray Charles septet) and former bassist for Miles Davis. "You're a purist and I'm a purist," she said, "but that doesn't mean you can't make the new funk music."

I heard her and I didn't. I listened to Funkadelic and Parliament, I appreciated George Clinton, but my mind kept drifting elsewhere. Maybe because the people in Muscle Shoals were both friends and admirers. Maybe because Muscle Shoals made me feel the way I'd felt when I first arrived there back in the sixties—like a participant in the music, a member of the rhythm section. Maybe because Muscle Shoals was an escape from the madness of Manhattan. Whatever the reasons, I found myself going back again and again, getting the special feelings only Muscle Shoals offered—driving from the studio across the moonlit Wilson Dam as Merle Haggard or George Jones or Patsy Cline sang their heartbreak songs on the radio. I fell into a groove of comfort, familiarity, nostalgia. I lived on the salty ham at Carl's Cafe, the homemade biscuits, the soft scrambled eggs, the buttery grits. Renee didn't accompany me. I was alone, a Jew in deep country retreat, far from hearth and family, immersed in a celibate cocoon, hooked on bittersweet music, the ideal soundtrack for an extended wallow in self-pity.

"Don't come back from Muscle Shoals with the same old stuff," my children would tell me, and I'd laugh. But sure enough, I'd come back once more with a sound I dug—and another flop album.

GOODBYE
AND
GOOD
LUCK

I was going through a period of rising discomfort at Atlantic. The people I'd hired had all been co-opted. Meetings were going on and I wasn't invited; if I walked in, silence fell. It didn't help to realize I'd brought this on myself, that when I went to Miami, I'd created a vacuum that had to be filled.

As these frustrations grew, so did my temper. Once, during a posh luncheon for the heads of the Warner labels at the Beverly Hills home of Joe Smith, president of Elektra Records, I lost it. Once again my adversary was David Geffen. To me he was still the original Sammy Glick.

Geffen and I had been vying for Dylan. Geffen won out and signed him to the Asylum label, where he wound up recording one album, *Planet Waves.* Naturally I wasn't thrilled about seeing him. As the potlatch began, I said, "Okay, David, you've got Dylan—now let's just forget the whole thing."

David couldn't resist baiting me, and I blew up. Right there in front of Steve Ross and the rest of the honchos—Ahmet, Nesuhi, Mo Ostin— I pitched a hissie.

"I couldn't believe it," remembers David. "No one could. Jerry's face turned red. The veins on his neck looked like they were going to pop. I thought he was either going to have a heart attack or put a knife through my heart. He yelled at the top of his lungs with such violence and vitriol everyone stopped what they were doing and just held their breath."

"You *agent!*" I recall screaming. "You'd jump into a pool of pus to come up with a nickel between your teeth."

Joe calmed me down, but the damage had been done. Steve Ross had the privilege of an in-your-face view of one of his execs losing it. And Donnie Smith's cold salmon buffet was ruined.

Later on, David piled it on when he conned Ahmet into merging Atlantic and Asylum. Ahmet and Geffen were to be joint chairmen. I couldn't believe it. And when the formal announcement appeared in *Billboard* and *Variety,* I went into orbit. Financial head Sheldon Vogel and my replacement, Jerry Greenberg, were in instant agreement about the potential for disaster. We would lose the advantages of two separate labels, and middle-level executives were panicked about losing their jobs. Almost no one thought the idea made sense. I finally got through to Ahmet: One day, I told him, you'll cry tears of blood from this wonder boy of yours. (And indeed, later on, the two men became bitterly estranged.)

"The only reason Ahmet reversed himself," says Geffen, "was because the co-chairmanship was being seen as a demotion for him. I don't think Jerry changed Ahmet's mind." In the final analysis it's not important. What matters is that the deal was undone. Merging the two companies would have caused an unholy mess, and despite my personal circumstances I still felt protective and deeply involved. Atlantic was my child, and I wanted its well-being with all my heart. I was proud of it. I still am.

Even in the midst of my troubles, I took pleasure in knowing that my favorites, Tom Dowd and Arif Mardin, were thriving. Since his landmark work on *Layla,* Tom Dowd had become one of the industry's outstanding producers; his work with Rod Stewart was bringing him universal recognition and respect. Arif was also taking off. Bette Midler had recently signed with Atlantic, and the records he produced—"Do You Want to Dance?" and "Boogie Woogie Bugle Boy"—were going through the roof and winning Grammys. He also hit big with the Average White Band and Chaka Khan.

I had turned the Average White Band over to Arif after I heard them for the first time at my friend Alan Pariser's Laurel Canyon enclave of hi-fi equipment and high-octane fun. I walked in and couldn't believe what I was seeing and hearing. This band of Caledonians was so tweedy and Scottish I expected to flush a covey of grouse. Their funk hit me where I lived, their tape was great, and I wanted to sign them on the spot. But they were already under contract to Uni, and Uni wasn't letting go. I cued them to hit on Uni exec Artie Mogul for heavy bucks, something on the order of $25,000. "If that doesn't get it,"

I told them, "jump on Artie's desk and pitch ashtrays through the windows."

The upshot: Good old tricky Artie, whom I had dubbed "the lovable felon" years before, went along and turned them loose, and for $10,000 he threw in the tape I'd heard at Alan's. I thought it needed work; the drummer had to be reintroduced to the bass. But when we tried the Band-Aid job at Criteria, it didn't work. Arif recut the entire record. When the album came out, Uni was sure it was the original tape and demanded their override, but we had no trouble proving it was a re-make. The results were smokers like "Pick Up the Pieces," "Cut the Cake," and "If I Ever Lose This Heaven," all produced by Arif with a little kibitzing on my part. Essentially, though, Arif no longer required any kibitzing.

Toward the end of April 1975, I couldn't tolerate the situation at Atlantic anymore, and I confronted Ahmet with my beefs—chiefly my exclusion from decision making. I reminded him that he was on record as agreeing that he, Jerry Greenberg, and I would sit as a troika. His response was that he worked too extemporaneously to adhere to such an arrangement.

I said I was eminently available.

He said people had grown out of the habit of reporting to me. He reminded me that I had brought it on myself.

There was the matter of my personality. Ahmet informed me that I was viewed as abrasive, derisive, and cynical, a maverick at meetings, a flaunter of my quick sales of option stock, an undiplomatic critic.

Okay, I thought. Could be. But what was Ahmet's own opinion?

His objections had a different spin. He felt I had no interest in the overall company, that my concerns were selfish and parochial, that I cared only for my artists. He reminded me of the Nashville office and my penchant for hiring the sons of old friends. He pointed out that he himself was in constant contact with heavy rock artists, managers, and lawyers. I agreed that he was indeed, and that I admired him for the physical stamina and psychic muscle it took to be always on with these types.

But I had not been exactly idle. What about the Jackson Five, with whom I'd concluded a contract in recent months? What of my negotiations with Elton John and the Band? And have we forgotten the profitable sale of Delaney and Bonnie? (The Jackson contract was awaiting signature, a done deal for a million dollars; but Atlantic nixed it as "too expensive," so the kiddies—including Michael—were trundled over to CBS. Elton and the Band never came through.)

It was embarrassing to have to list my credits, but I needed to make the point that not all my productions were Smithsonian pieces. What about the current roster? I asked him. Wasn't I producing the sound-track to *The Wiz*? Hadn't I brought in Willie Nelson, Led Zeppelin, John Prine, the Average White Band, Donny Hathaway, J. Geils—all current signings?

Then I got to the real question: After decades of fifty-fifty partner-ship, had Ahmet now become my *boss*?

Ahmet tried to be gentle. "Not exactly," he said. "But since I am accountable to Corporate, they want me to have final word." Again he brought up the changes that resulted from my defection to the subtrop-ics. God knows it was all true. And I acknowledged that Corporate nat-urally would look to him. But this new arrangement—given my history and personality—could never work. For me it was parity or nothing. No parity, no Wexler.

For a time we left it up in the air. But on May 3 I wrote him a letter, reviewing our talks and concluding, "Under no circumstances, Ahmet, can I be your employee. That's the bottom line."

Ahmet seemed genuinely upset by my decision. "Man, you can't quit," he said. "It's unthinkable."

I had lived and breathed Atlantic Records for a good part of my adult life, but it was the end of the road. After twenty-two years, Ahmet helped me terminate. I don't believe that Ahmet or anyone else, even finding my prelapsarian presence inconvenient, deliberately set about to make me uncomfortable. And despite the abrasions, Ahmet was my champion in the termination process. He went to bat with Corporate to help me get a decent settlement, and ever since has always been gra-cious and generous. In response to the liner notes I'd written for a Charles Brown album on the Rounder label in 1990, Ahmet wrote, "How moved I was by your incisive recollection of times that we will never live through again."

In an odd way, I was glad to be leaving. The industry was going big-time, entering an era in which middle executives ran companies with

perfunctory approval from above, and top executives had become too involved with mega-million-dollar deals to spend much time thinking about . . . what, music? I'm a man who lives by and for his enthusiasms. I listen to music all day every day (except on the golf course). Music plays all night in my bedroom. I thrive in the studio. I belong there. Hands on is what I want.

Ironically enough, two years later, in 1977, I took a job inside the Warner group. Mo Ostin gave me a vice-president's title and an office and staff in midtown Manhattan. I would be Warner Records' bird dog in the East, heading up the New York A&R department. Without the right to sign new acts and recruit my own staff, I wouldn't have taken the job. I hired two talented staffers away from Epic—Karin Berg and Steve Baker. Dire Straits, the B-52's, the Gang of Four, and the Roches were among the groups Karin in particular helped me sign. I was back in business.

SIXTY

CANDLES

It was a new life, and in some ways I was more comfortable than ever. We had a Park Avenue apartment and, in East Hampton, an English Tudor built in 1928 on nine and a half acres. Renee loved the elaborate grounds and manicured gardens.

"The house was magnificent," she says. "And Jerry restored it in wonderful taste. The problem was that he couldn't enjoy it. He worried what it was costing him. He worried all the time."

So, maybe I wasn't completely comfortable. But I hit right away with Ed Sanford and John Townsend's "Smoke from a Distant Fire," which went top-ten pop in 1977. The song had a beautiful Doobie Brothers feeling—hard-driving, yet seamless and smooth.

"It was the first thing Jerry and I co-produced," remembers Barry Beckett, who by now had outgrown the Muscle Shoals rhythm section and had become a producer. "It was a hell of a send-off for the Wexler/ Beckett team. Jerry worked the vocals so hard I thought he was going to tear out Ed Townsend's throat."

If there was any constant in my life, it was Muscle Shoals. I dreamed of getting Ray Charles down there, convinced my boys would put him back in the pocket he'd slipped out of years ago. We had a long discussion about the prospect, but Brother Ray was unmoved and unwilling. "Pardner," he said, "you got your ideas and I got mine."

My next trip south was a little different. I was so intrigued with Ronee Blakley's singing in the movie *Nashville* that I called Joe Smith at Elektra, made a deal, and took her to Muscle Shoals. But there were conflicts; the magic never happened. In fact, during this session—for the first and only time—I lost it in the studio. When Ronee called one of my lyric suggestions "stupid," a dead silence fell upon the session. The musicians looked down at the floor. A red rage started in my shoes and crawled all the way up my spine. I started to walk—but Ronee capitulated and persuaded me to stay. The Sturm und Drang was wasted; the record bombed.

There were no personality conflicts between me and Kim Carnes when Barry and I produced *Sailin'* at the Shoals. Kim's album yielded no hits but was tremendously satisfying nonetheless. I don't think I've ever enjoyed greater rapport with a singer. With Kim in the studio and me in the booth, the good feelings flowed back and forth almost mystically. A nod of my head and she understood what I was saying, where I was pointing her. She's a fine musician, her sultry voice a marvelous instrument.

The experience was especially happy because of the presence of my son, Paul. "Kim's album was a reconciliation point between me and my father," he says. "We had been alienated for a while. Just before I was about to graduate from Cal Arts, Anita had come to California. She was working—she'd developed into a terrific music producer—but she'd gone back on heroin. On the way back from the airport she nodded out in my car, her cigarette falling from her mouth and burning the seat. I saw fresh tracks on her arms.

"I was alarmed, so I phoned my father and said, 'Look, Jerry, I know you think Anita's clean, but she's not. If you're supporting her you should stop, because the money's only feeding her habit.' Next thing I knew, Anita had convinced Jerry that she hadn't really nodded out. She told him sleeping pills had made her drowsy; the tracks on her arms were old. She said she was clean. Jerry believed her. Loving eyes never see.

"There'd always been a loving bond between the members of our family, but the bond between me and Jerry had been severed for years. And the Anita problem made it worse. That's why helping him on the Kim Carnes project was such a joy. He picked up on my suggestion to use Dave Grisman, this killer mandolin player, who turned out to be one of the bright spots on the album. Jerry respected my input and treated me as a peer."

I was especially proud later on when Paul helped produce Van Morrison's *Wavelength* album, doing a superb job in organizing the band and selecting tracks. He also produced the Go-Go's first hit, "We Got the Beat."

Anita and Paul in the seventies

At home things were slipping. Perhaps it was Anita's problems, perhaps the strain of a May/December marriage that never quite got on track. In 1977, the two merged when I rashly permitted Anita to move in with us on Park Avenue after Renee, out of concern and affection, suggested it.

"Anita had a way of throwing Jerry's liberality in his face," she explains. "She not only shocked him with her drug habit, but also her promiscuity. At a certain point, she surrounded herself with lowlifes. We had drug dealers coming around the apartment, serious criminals."

It was hard for me to understand. There were two sides of Anita: one was brilliant and talented, my partner and soulmate in things musical; another was cunning, self-destructive, and dangerous. She got involved in prescription forgeries, for example, and I spent enormous time and money in bailing her out of real trouble with the law. Her life had turned into a bad dream. Finally I could take no more. She promised to enter a rehab center, Su Casa, if I helped her get one last fix. We argued back and forth, but finally I agreed. I drove her up to Harlem, where she made what she swore would be her last score.

"Giving up," sang Donny Hathaway, "is so hard to do."

Shortly before Anita went to Su Casa, Renee had planned an extravagant sixtieth birthday party for me at the Carlyle Hotel. It was a gala

At my sixtieth birthday party, 1977. Seated: Lisa, Elsa, Wex. Standing: Anita, sister-in-law Connie Pappas, Renee, Paul

event, and everyone turned out—Paul Simon, Ringo Starr, Clive Davis, Mitch Miller, my children, a bunch from Atlantic, my mom. Even so, I was miserable. Maybe because I felt unworthy, or maybe because of too much partying. One after another, my Los Angeles buddies took me into the john for some birthday blow. But I was down and just couldn't get into the celebration.

The thing that brought me up was music. I was excited to learn that someone I had eyes to produce for twenty years had requested my services: the great Etta James.

I ran out to L.A., where we cut the sides at Cherokee. It was a stomp from start to finish. For my money, Etta's one of the pioneers, up there with her label mates at Chess: Muddy Waters, Howlin' Wolf, Bo Diddley, and Chuck Berry. And Chess is where, after being discovered by Johnny Otis, she claimed her fame and recorded her enduring hits— "Trust in Me," "Something's Got a Hold of Me," "At Last." With Rick

Etta James

Hall's help, she stormed into the Soul Era with "Tell Mama." Like Aretha, Etta is a church in herself, her voice a mighty instrument, her musical personality able to express an extraordinary range of moods.

Larry Carlton laid down the rhythm tracks and led the section, which included Jeff Porcaro, Chuck Rainey, Cornell Dupree, and Richard Tee—all the right guys. I picked the tunes, varying from the Eagles' "Take It to the Limit," Alice Cooper's "Only Women Bleed," Kiki Dee's "Sugar on the Floor," and Hank Williams's "Lovesick Blues" to Dorothy Love Coates's (of the Original Gospel Harmonettes) "Strange Man," a story-in-song in which Jesus matter-of-factly turns up in Alabama on a Tuesday evening. An eclectic mix, perhaps, and probably overly ambitious. But I wanted to capture the essential Etta—a woman used but not spent, abused but never defeated, vulnerable but, through sheer strength of will, victorious.

"It didn't sell like we had wanted," Etta admits. "But I still consider it my best album." That's good enough for me. I was also touched when Etta, out of the goodness of her heart, took her whole band and played a free concert at Su Casa, where Anita was rehabilitating.

During the sessions in L.A., another good thing happened. Bob Dylan happened to drop by.

"GOTTA
SERVE
SOMEBODY"

I've always argued that a producer must serve the artist and the artist's project, so when Bob Dylan said he wanted me to produce his new album I wasn't troubled that he was primarily folk rock whereas I was R&B. He'd gone through his acoustic trip, his electric trip, his Nashville Skyline trip, and now was interested in keyboards, background vocals, horns, and big textures—the polished R&B sound. He had the songs ready, and needed only the right musical context.

When Dylan walked into the control room at Cherokee, everyone backed off, forming a *cordon sanitaire* around him. No one spoke until he did, so powerful was his aura.

If I was relaxed around Bob, it was probably because we'd met through our mutual pal Doug Sahm five years before, when we'd spent a weekend at my place on the Bridgehampton dunes. They played their acoustic guitars while I beat the conga, waves crashing on the Atlantic, the three of us bonded by music, memories, and the good herb. Bob volunteered as a sideman on the first album of Doug's I'd produced, and it was an up for all of us. During a break, Bob and I were kicking back in my office when he said, "Man, I've done the word trip—now I want to do the music trip." I knew what he was getting at.

Not long after, Dylan asked me to help him co-produce Barry Goldberg, Michael Bloomfield's gifted soulmate from the Electric Flag. We went to Muscle Shoals. Bob showed up a week late and spent most of the time meditating in his van with his wife Sara. He contributed only marginally to Barry's effort, but there was good feeling between us. I was a quarter-century older and had been there when one of my dearest friends, John Hammond, discovered him. Back then, after his early records on Columbia didn't sell, Dylan was called "Hammond's Folly." But John had the last laugh.

That afternoon in Cherokee, Bob told me he'd been writing on the piano. Since Dylan famously composed on guitar, I was intrigued. He walked over to the piano and played a series of chord progressions with the enthusiasm of a child. I thought it was great. Then, back in New York a few weeks later, Bob asked me to produce his next album. I alerted my man, co-producer Barry Beckett. Naturally I wanted to do the album in Muscle Shoals—as Bob did—but we decided to prep it in L.A., where Bob lived. That's when I learned what the songs were about: born-again Christians in the old corral.

I was surprised, but I'd produce Bob Dylan singing the yellow pages if that's what he wanted. Besides, I liked the irony of Bob coming to me, the Wandering Jew, to get the Jesus feel. Once he saw his sermonizing had no effect on this dyed-in-the-wool atheist, everything was cool.

After Ray and Aretha, Dylan was the third real genius I'd worked with. From the first day, I was impressed by his command over the material. His music was a direct expression of his rough-hewn and quixotic individuality.

Beckett and I had just come off a successful production for Dire Straits, whose *Communiqué* album was getting rave reviews. We were brimming with confidence. We'd had a great time cutting the sides in Compass Point, Nassau, where I solved our only problem—lousy local meat—by importing squab, roast, and loins of pork from Lobel's, a fancy Manhattan butcher. The music was wonderful. Mark Knopfler is a remarkably versatile guitarist and luminous musical mind. Each night we'd sip fine wine and dine by candlelight in a grandiose mansion by the sea, and the sessions were just as smooth. Barry and I were able to help the rockers get a bluesy edge, the Bahamas providing a cool and calm setting. Dire Straits was an example of how funky Englishmen can be when they pay attention. (It was also the most commercial of my post-Atlantic ventures; the band has an enormous worldwide market, and the royalty checks are still coming in.)

Knopfler was still very much on my mind when I started rehearsing Dylan. I thought Mark and his drummer, Pick Withers, would be perfect supplements to Bob's sound, new elements both to stimulate and to complement. Mark's vocal phrasing is deeply influenced by Dylan, and his subtle guitar mastery, I was certain, would inspire and push Bob in a

Barry Beckett and Dylan

couple of different directions. Bob dug the idea. "Mark does me better than anybody," he said.

Still, doing Dylan was tricky. He came to me because he wanted the sonority he'd heard in Aretha and Otis as opposed to those hard-scrambling Woody Guthrie guitar-on-your-back out-of-tune see-you-down-the-line 13½-measure out-of-time phrases. I have always believed that Dylan's "mistakes," his imperfections, were part of his peculiar gift, his naturalness of expression. Slick, seamless Dylan wouldn't have been any good, satisfying neither him nor the demands of his singular voice.

Bob began by playing and singing along with the musicians. We were in the first stages of building rhythm arrangements; it was too soon for him to sing, but he sang on every take anyway. I finally convinced him to hold off on the vocals until later, when the arrangements were in shape and the players could place their licks around—not against—him. To me, having the singer present when the charts are crystallizing is mandatory. When other singers—Sinatra, for example—waltz in after the arrangements are frozen in place, it bothers me. I want the singer there for the whole process, molding the music around his vocal phrasing.

In Muscle Shoals, Bob was uncomfortable wearing headphones, and I could see that the thing still hadn't come together. "Everyone get together on the floor," I suggested, moving the musicians out of their isolation booths. "Pull up chairs and face each other."

With all of them gathered around, there were tons of leakage—a killer detriment to decent recording—but I knew I needed them to be clustered to find the groove. I had Steve Melton, the engineer, roll the quarter-inch tape, and when he bitched about the leakage I had no time to explain, because now the boys were jamming. I'd asked Mark Knopfler to play like Albert King, not Mark Knopfler, and the pickers were cooking. Now I had them hurry back to their booths, put on phones, and play along to the rough tape. Soon they locked into the groove, and we turned off the quarter-inch. I had them stop for four or five silent beats, then Barry counted off and kinetic memory kicked in. Now we had the groove—with the right separation and definitions. From then on, we burned. In a week's time, using this method, we finished the rhythm tracks and Bob completed his vocals.

Bob called the record *Slow Train Coming*. It was a hit, the single "Gotta Serve Somebody" going top ten. It also got Bob his first Grammy. When he wondered what to wear to the awards, I said, "Why don't you all get the latest tuxedos and look fine?" When the curtain went up on Bob Dylan and his ragamuffins in their formal wear, the Dorothy Chandler Pavilion erupted. (My own Grammy history is short. In the Aretha years, for example, they still discriminated: no Grammys for R&B producers. My only two came for "Respect"—as Record of the Year—and the cast album of *The Wiz*.)

Jann Wenner called *Slow Train Coming* "the best album Dylan has made since *The Basement Tapes*. In time, it may be considered his greatest. Like Dylan, Wexler has his finest LP since those fabulous Sixties, one that ranks with his greatest achievements." I was, for once, in total agreement with *Rolling Stone*.

"The strength of *Slow Train Coming*," says Paul, who did the mastering, "is the passion. Dylan's Jewish fans may have cringed, his freethinking anarchistic followers may have retched, but there was passion in Dylan's Christian convictions, passion in his view of the Crucifixion, passion in his born-again beliefs."

Above: Jamming. Below: Augie Meyers, Jack Barber, George Raines, Wex, Doug Sahm, Dylan, Atwood Allen, Roadie

The follow-up, *Saved,* didn't match the intensity of the first. This time Dylan used pretty much his own band, which included Tim Drummond on bass and Jim Keltner on drums, plus Spooner Oldham and Beckett on keyboards. One Jesus album from Bob was fine; two was stretching it. But the phenomenon of Dylan–in–Muscle Shoals left some indelible memories.

"When he arrived for the *Saved* album," recalls local historian Dick Cooper, "I picked up his entourage in Nashville. Dylan was with Tim Drummond and three black singers—Regina Havis, Mona Lisa Young, and Clydie King. We stopped for burgers in Pulaski, Tennessee, birthplace of the Klan. So there we were, three white boys and three gorgeous black chicks in spandex and sequins. The white waitresses out front were outraged; the black cooks in the back were delighted. It was a hell of a scene."

A scene that sticks in my mind is Dylan on the back porch of the Muscle Shoals studio, trading licks on acoustic guitar with Eddie Hinton. They buddied up and for a while were inseparable. To me, Eddie is one of the great enigmas of Southern music. I always saw him as the Anointed One, the white Otis Redding (the man, in fact, hired by Otis's wife, Zelma, to teach her son and her nephew how to sing). Eddie wasn't a master technician, but dear God, the boy could play some funk. A poet, a part of the Alabama landscape, a disturbed soul who never quite got it together—it was always "next year" for Eddie. "Eddie needs just a little more seasoning," I'd tell myself. While I was producing Mavis Staples and the Staple Singers in Muscle Shoals—two albums I consider subpar efforts on my part—Eddie had something of a nervous breakdown, screaming and yelling in the middle of a session. His anguish was directed at no one in particular. It was simply that his demons couldn't be silenced. I was delighted years later, though, when Hinton's *Letters from Mississippi* album came out on Capricorn, a strong document of the singer's deep-bottomed soul.

How strange and wonderful, then, to remember Bob Dylan and Eddie Hinton as soul brothers—two poets, one world-renowned, the other known only to a few friends, neighbors, and fans, both riveting artists, both brilliant.

SONGBIRD

RIDDLE

*T*he *segue* goes from Bob Dylan to Linda Ronstadt, with the soundtrack for a movie in between.

Louis Malle, the superb French filmmaker, was a committed jazz fan. He came to America in the sixties to do a film on Jelly Roll Morton and homed in on Leiber and Stoller. The timing was wrong, and the movie never happened. Ten years later he tried again, this time using Jelly Roll's music in the background. I'd read the reports in *Variety* and thought to myself—here's the project of my life, the one I'd been preparing for now for fifty years. I didn't know Louis, but, unbidden, our mutual friend Shep Gordon asked him to call me. Just like that, Louis hired me to do the soundtrack for *Pretty Baby,* a sensuous period piece that unfolds in a New Orleans bordello. It was Brooke Shields's first important film and also starred Keith Carradine and Susan Sarandon.

Three key elements came into play. The first was pianist Bob Greene playing Jelly Roll Morton. The initial choice had been my longtime pal Dick Hyman, jazz great, Woody Allen's music man, and encyclopedist of piano styles; but lawyers' obfuscation got in the way, so Bob Greene stepped in, and astounded me. Bob had studied Jelly Roll so devotedly that he could demonstrate in any given chord which fingers Jelly Roll had pressed the hardest! His reproductions were absolute.

Then, to replicate the Louis Armstrong Hot Seven sound, I put together a pickup band led by Kid Thomas. Kid's trumpet opens the movie a capella. A broad dolly shot sweeps over early-morning New Orleans, and Kid's quivering vibrato blues, like the sunrise, eerie and evocative, rises over the city.

The third element was the New Orleans Ragtime Orchestra, led by

violinist William Russell, keeper of the flame and the saintly musicologist responsible for Preservation Hall and the whole New Orleans trad
revival.

Making the track turned out to be both simple and serendipitous.
Movie music involves two kinds—source cues (for example, when a
character walks into a bar and hears the jukebox) and underscoring
(mood music under the scenes, for which a composer is usually hired).
Louis gave me a free hand. I cut a bunch of New Orleans–feeling
themes that worked in with the scenes; my favorite is James Booker singing Jelly Roll's ribald "Winin' Boy Blues." I never used a composer, and
brought in the total recording costs for under five thousand dollars—an
unheard-of amount in Hollywood.

The sensuousness of the music matched the film's, which of course
is what I was after. In one scene, Keith Carradine, as the photographer
Bellocq, is shooting Susan Sarandon, who plays a prostitute, in a French
Quarter courtyard. Susan's nude, and Keith, gently powdering her
breasts for the right photographic effect, looks into her eyes and sweetly
says, "My, you have fine skin." The line tingles, and so does the movie;
so, I think, does the music. Anyway, whenever I've seen Susan since
then, my opening has been "My, you have fine skin."

Pretty Baby did well, and the music was nominated for an Academy
Award. Renee got herself a Mary McFadden gown and we headed to
the Coast for the ceremonies. Quincy Jones had also been nominated
and was seated next to me. In spite of our Aretha misfire, I like Quincy.
(He calls me "Miss Quick" because of my expeditious approach to record making. It comes from a line by golfing great Gene Sarazen: "Step
up to the ball and miss it quick.") We were sweating it out to see who
won; the tension was unbearable. "Fuck it," said Q. "Let's get a drink."
We did, and returned just in time to learn that we'd both missed it quick:
Joe Renzetti had won for *The Buddy Holly Story*.

*W*ith *Dire Straits* and Dylan under my belt, I felt I'd weather the move
from Atlantic. The seventies were coming to an end, and I was growing
into the role of Superannuated Hipster. But Renee and I were barely
holding on to our marriage.

"It got to a point," says Renee, "where Jerry got crazed behind the
minutiae of household matters—eating schedules, food preparations.

His need for control got out of control. His temper would flare; he'd rant and rave over nothing."

Renee's interior decorating contacts had dried up. And my business was certainly not as spectacular as it could have been. At Atlantic, for example, Ahmet was nailing acts like Chic, Sister Sledge, AC/DC, Foreigner, Genesis, and Laura Branigan. "I know Jerry's career wasn't going as well as he wanted," adds Renee, "and I'd urge him to option books and try his hand at producing movies. For someone with Jerry's intellect, I saw that as a logical move."

I did, in fact, with my friends Roger Berlind and Tim Horan, option a nonfiction piece from *The New Yorker* about Addison and Wilson Mizner, two charismatic characters—gamblers, playwrights, art collectors, prizefight managers, real estate tycoons—from the early part of the century. But nothing came of it, and music was my life in a way that neither movies nor anything else ever could be.

*B*oth *Renee and I* were friendly with Linda Ronstadt. (Before we married, Renee had worked for David Geffen, who was then Linda's manager.) At one of our dinner parties in 1980, Linda and Glenn Frey were among the guests to whom I enthused over a singer I'd heard in Austin, Lou Ann Barton. I played some rough demos and heard in Lou Ann a combination of Kay Starr and Dinah Washington—one hell of a mix. Linda and Glenn felt the same way and persuaded Joe Smith to give Lou Ann a deal at Elektra with Glenn and me producing. We went to Muscle Shoals and assembled the regulars, the forever funky rhythm section of Beckett, Hood, Johnson, and Hawkins. But the album, *Old Enough,* just wasn't good enough.

I love Lou Ann, but—at least back then—she was less than masterful at engineering her own life. Her raw musical energy had convinced me that she was the next Janis Joplin, and I'm sorry I wasn't able to make it happen for her. Since then, though, she's made some excellent records for Clifford Antone out of Austin.

I had high hopes of producing a Linda Ronstadt small-band date— at least that's what was in the back of my mind when she and Jerry Brown, then governor of California, came to spend the weekend with us in East Hampton. I was not reluctant to lecture on the subject of jazz history, and Linda was an eager student. I played her some of the great

Glenn Frey, Lou Ann Barton, Wex

thirties and forties singers, with special emphasis on Mildred Bailey and
Lee Wiley. She was captivated by their combination of vulnerability and
sophistication, the juxtaposition of little-girl innocence with big-woman
sensuality. "These are some songs," Linda said, "I have to sing."

I suggested she do a sneak gig at some small club in Jersey City to
test out the material, but she thought we ought to go right into the studio
and cut demos. So much the better. I nabbed Tommy Flanagan, world-
class piano accompanist (dig his work for Ella), and George Mraz, the
world's most in-tune bassist. We laid down three or four sides—"I've
Got a Crush on You," "Someone to Watch Over Me," "What'll I Do"—
which Linda promptly played for John Rockwell of the *New York Times*.
He told Linda it would make a great album; Linda asked me to produce it.

In my mind's eye, the metaphor was a necklace of perfect pearls to
place around Linda's neck. Each pearl was a master musician, the necklace a symbol of my dream band. My models were those elegant, timeless combos that had backed Billie Holiday in her vintage Columbia
period. Tommy Flanagan would be my Teddy Wilson. And who could
play the Lester Young role better than one of Prez's favorite sons, Al
Cohn? I had Al write the sparse, swinging arrangements and blow his

lush Lesterian tenor into Linda's ear. Ira Sullivan played mellow trumpet, and Tal Farlow added quiet fire on his light bop guitar. What a sextet! Linda and I flew out to the L.A. studio Fleetwood Mac had built, Village Recorders, and she laid in the vocals.

It wasn't easy, and Linda was unexpectedly uncomfortable. I'm not certain why. Maybe it was the strange new chord progressions of songs like "Lover Man," "Ghost of a Chance," "Falling in Love Again," "Crazy He Calls Me," "Keeping Out of Mischief," "Never Will I Marry." It took Linda, a superb musician herself, an extremely long time to get the melodies straight. She was tentative about interpretation—too shy here, too aggressive there. But at the end of an excruciating process, we got the goods—a forties jazz album, refined and relaxed, reinterpreted for a new generation. Even though I knew Linda wasn't entirely convinced, I heard it as an intriguing sleeper.

By then I had sold our house in East Hampton and had decided to accommodate Renee by renting a house in Greece for the month. "Jerry was never comfortable outside America," says Renee, "especially in non-English-speaking countries. But for me Greece represented comfort. It's my ancestral home. Greece allowed me to relax. But by the time Jerry showed up he was anything but relaxed. The Linda Ronstadt sessions had run overtime, and it was already the third week of our month before Jerry arrived. All he did was stay on the phone to New York and L.A. Then word came that Linda had decided to shelve the sessions, and he was devastated."

I took Linda's decision hard. I thought then—and still believe—she was wrong to can the record. Her manager/producer Peter Asher wasn't happy with the results, but I never heard any specific criticism. Joe Smith was neutral. It was a lot of work down the drain, not to mention the dream band, the classic songs and Linda's sensitive vocals. Not long afterwards she worked with Nelson Riddle on a series of smash albums in which she utilized pretty much the same material.

The difference, of course, was that Nelson surrounded her with a symphony of violins and violas, French horns and flutes. When she came to the end of a line on my record, there was nothing between her and the next downbeat but space and rhythm—scary business. Nelson's full-blown orchestrations cushioned Linda, I believe, because her voice no longer hung out there alone. It was the antithesis of the small-combo dates in which I tried to accentuate the drama of a lone, lorn woman singing in bittersweet solitude. Linda wanted her gowns and hats and

Working with Linda

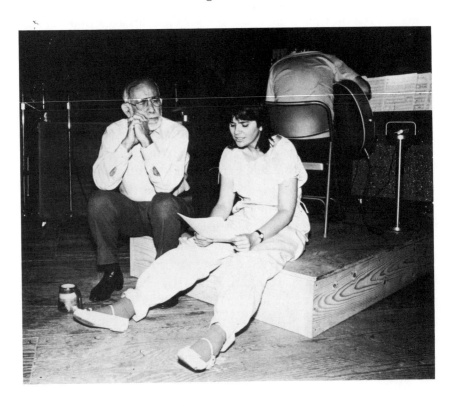

stoles. I still hold out hope, however, that one day Linda will listen to those simple, subtle charts of Al Cohn (may he rest in peace) in which she captured the sensibility of an earlier era.

The collapse of the Ronstadt project coincided with the collapse of my marriage. When I got to Greece, I saw it was all over. When friends asked what happened, I joked, "It was generational—she liked Jackson Browne and I liked Ray Charles." Of course it was far deeper than that. The marriage had not been marked by fidelity, so I should not have been surprised to learn what had happened: she'd fallen in love with another man.

"The turning point came," Renee remembers, "when Jerry and I saw a French film called *La Dentellière* (*The Lacemaker*). Isabelle Huppert plays the part of a working-class girl who falls in love with a man far more sophisticated and intellectual than she is. She never feels adequate or competent to converse with his friends. In the end, she goes mad and winds up in an asylum. So strong was my identification with that character that days after viewing the film, I swore that wasn't going to happen to me. I'd given my ego over to Jerry's, put my life in his hands, played the part of the subservient wife/child for far too long. I had to get out. I had to rescue myself. And I did."

We tried to save the marriage, went to a shrink, went through a series of tortuous turns, all in vain. Both of us lacked the heart. The thing was dead.

Inside I felt dead. A ten-year relationship had turned to ashes. I'm from a generation of men who really never learned to talk intimately with other men. For all my friends and soulmates in the music business, there were none in whom I could confide. A new young friend, the jazz photographer Carol Friedman, became my best buddy. She understood what I was going through and comforted me through some desperate times. We shared a lot of meals and soul baring—everything but bed.

At the start of a new decade, the eighties, I was a sixty-three-year-old man about to go off the rails, ready to become a certifiable voluptuary.

SEXUAL
HEALING

I don't want to name them. But I do want to say that they filled a need. They were the ladies I encountered during the lonely years after my divorce. I sought companionship without commitment—lubricity without complicity.

I was especially taken with an attractive singer. We hung out for the best part of two years. Maybe I looked foolish showing up at my friend Elia Kazan's house for dinner with a gorgeous blonde thirty-five years younger than me wearing thigh-high boots on a body that wouldn't quit. When my darling mother, well into her late eighties and not at her sharpest, met this voluptuous lady, she exclaimed, "And when are we going to hear wedding bells chime?" I wanted to escape through a trapdoor.

The release, of course, came from music. This time it was Carlos Santana to the rescue. Barry Beckett and I went out to San Francisco to do Carlos's *Havana Moon* album, which the *Village Voice* called "the most masterful '80s Santana LP, a *roots* move, with blues galore, a calypso Chuck Berry cover, a kindly Willie Nelson lament." It was a romp. First of all, Carlos is a monster musician—Jimi Hendrix and T-Bone Walker and Jimmy Page and John McLaughlin and flamenco all rolled up in a guitarist of rugged individuality and tremendous integrity. Integrity is Santana's middle name. He reveres his Latin roots; he has shrines with votive candles in his home to John Coltrane, Miles Davis (who was actually influenced by Carlos himself), and Wayne Shorter. He's at once New Age and old-time Tijuana ballroom blues.

For the session, we recruited Booker T., the Tower of Power horns, the great accordionist Flaco Jiminez, bassist David Hood, and the Fabulous Thunderbirds, a group of black-blues Texas rednecks who'd been killing me for years. I tightened up right away with Kim Wilson, their singer, and Jimmy Vaughan, their lead guitarist.

Some time earlier, I'd heard Jimmy's brother Stevie Ray at the Continental, a bucket of blood in Austin. Next morning I placed a call to Switzerland to my good friend Claude Nobs, the blues maestro, who runs the Montreux Jazz Festival. "Claude," I said, "I have no tape, no video, nothing to send you. Just book this guy." Sure enough, Stevie Ray was a smash. Subsequently, David Bowie hired him as lead guitarist and Jackson Browne gave him unlimited studio time to record at his place in California; John Hammond heard the tape and signed him to his subsidiary at CBS.

Anyway, in the middle of Carlos's session we ran off to Texas in Bill Graham's private plane, bouncing down the coast in a wild sky of thunderstorms, racing over to Austin, where Willie Nelson had said sure, he'd sing a song for me, sight unseen. We got to his Spicewood Ranch and dubbed his voice over the tape of Carlos, Booker T., Flaco, and a slew of Latin percussionists (including Armando Peraza) doing "They All Went to Mexico."

Back in California, Carlos and Jimmie did a beautiful thing on "Lightnin'," a heartfelt homage to Hopkins. We burned up Bo Diddley's "Who Do You Love" and celebrated John Lee Hooker in "Mudbone"; and "Havana Moon," in Carlos's words, is "a classic piece written by Chuck Berry, the man who represents the heart and soul of American music." When the sessions were over, we all went out and got drunk. Kim Wilson threatened to kidnap me and take me on the road with the Thunderbirds, but I finally convinced him I had other fish to fry.

I co-produced a musical, *One Mo' Time: An Evening of 1920's Black Vaudeville*, with Village Gate owners Art and Burt D'Lugoff. Another labor of New Orleans love, the show featured legendary trumpeter Jabbo Smith and replicated a typical 1923 bill at the famed Lyric Theater in the French Quarter, with echoes of Jelly Roll and Bessie Smith. The show enjoyed a four-year run at the Gate, and road companies took it all over the U.S. and Europe.

Later, another project of mine at the same off-Broadway venue, a gospel revue called *Shout Hallelujah*, never caught on. And in the early eighties there were more flops. When Beckett and I produced

McGuinn-Hillman, Renee's sister said, "I'm afraid Jerry's trying to turn Roger and Chris into Sam and Dave." I was taking what I could get, trying to stay busy, doing everyone from José Feliciano to Donovan to Tony Orlando. (Barry Beckett, I should note, through his work with Alabama, Hank Williams, Jr., and other C&W artists, has earned a reputation as one of the hottest producers in the country—a fact that makes me exceedingly proud and happy.)

With the help of guitarist Jimmy Johnson I produced what I consider a hell of an album for Billy Vera, one of the great singers and scholars of soul. I'd first signed Billy in the sixties, teamed him with Dionne Warwick's cousin Judy Clay, and formed the first salt-and-pepper male-female duo—not exactly a conservative move for those days. Billy and Judy had two hits, "Storybook Children" and "Country Girl—City Man," so this was an especially joyful reunion. There were beautiful tunes on the record, especially Billy's "Hopeless Romantic," but it all became hopeless when the small Japanese-financed label went belly up.

There were hot moments—a Montreux Festival blues evening I produced, bringing the boys from Muscle Shoals over to play behind Luther Allison, Johnny Copeland, Johnny Mars, and B.B. King. Like Ray Charles, B.B. had grown a little complacent with his routine band, and I figured my Alabamans would kick some ass. I was right. B.B. loved them; that night Switzerland sizzled.

My deal with Warner was winding down. Meanwhile, ABC/Paramount Records had closed its doors, leaving my old pal Seymour Stein without a corporate home. I brought his indy label, Sire, into the Warner fold, and before long Seymour signed Madonna—not bad. Without much hope, I hit on chairman Mo Ostin for a finder's fee; Mo said no go. I'd also asked Warners to sign Eddie Murphy for comedy records, but the brain board dragged its feet. By the time they okayed the signing, Eddie had gone with Epic. Such peccadillos aside, I have always viewed Mo as a sagacious and classy guy.

With the passage of time, I have come to respect and admire David Geffen (who now has had three separate careers). And my hat is off to Clive Davis. Teaming Aretha with Arif Mardin, Luther Vandross ("Jump to It"), and Narada Michael Walden ("Freeway of Love"), Clive brought Lady Soul back to the charts; her pairing with George Michael ("I Knew You Were Waiting") was a smash. Not to mention the job he has done with Cissy Houston's daughter Whitney.

I myself produced a song for George Michael when he was still with

Wham!, "Careless Whispers." We did the strings in Nashville and the vocals in Muscle Shoals. Jimmy Johnson and my son, Paul, assisted, and we were thrilled with the finished product. I was impressed by George's vocal and production chops. He was a highly evolved young man, and a reader; I whipped my copy of the complete short stories of V. S. Pritchett on him for the flight back to England. But unfortunately, when the single was released, his management decided to go with an earlier production of the same tune recorded in England. Our version came out only in Japan, though some think, because of the live fiddles, the American rendition has the edge.

Paul was also my main man in helping me put together the soundtrack for Richard Pryor's *Jo Jo Dancer, Your Life Is Calling*, his deeply moving autobiographical film. When I flew out to California to audition for the gig, Pryor was in a sweat. This was his directorial debut, and given the extremely personal nature of the material, he was really putting his ass out there. We had dinner at Spago; I worked my show and he hired me on the spot. Pryor's affection for Motown—especially Marvin Gaye—complemented my own sense of soul sounds, old and recent. I also had the good fortune to be able to hire Herbie Hancock for the underscoring.

My favorite moment in the movie is when the grandmother, played by Carmen McRae, is dying and says to Jo Jo, then a little boy, "I'll always be with you." Next thing we hear is Mahalia Jackson singing "In the Upper Room," a spiritual of extraordinary poignancy, which has haunted me ever since my *Billboard* days, when I reviewed her version on Apollo Records. Mahalia's supernal voice tells us that the grandmother has passed even before we see the casket. Then we cut away from the funeral parlor to Richard, back home, scrabbling on the floor for scraps of cocaine as Mahalia continues to moan. The effect is chilling.

The reviews were even more chilling. The critics ravaged Richard, and, in my biased opinion, unjustifiably. I found the writing and acting superb, the story an act of dramatic courage. The film's failure, though, had such a hurtful effect on Richard that I'm not certain he's recovered yet.

By the mid-eighties, then, I was more or less back on track—and so was my daughter Anita, whose life seemed to have finally taken a happy turn.

SITTIN'
ON THE
DOCK
OF THE
BAY

*A*nita *married* a man fourteen years younger than her. The marriage seemed happy, healthy, and productive. Gary was an air-conditioning engineer who adored her. She got a job at ABC Television and went from answering the phone to heading a department, with a secretary and her name on the door, all within a year. That's how bright she was. When Capital Cities bought out the network, she survived the purge and was given still another promotion, to head of finance. Anita was on a roll. She'd been going to Twelve-Step meetings, taking it a day at a time, doing everything necessary to maintain her recovery. For a couple of years, things were beautiful. She was beautiful.

Then, terrifyingly, her past reached out and seized her. She tested HIV positive. So did Gary.

Anita was domiciled in an apartment near Lincoln Center where Elsa had once lived. My mother had died in 1987, aged ninety-two, after a long period of deterioration. We moved her to the Hebrew Home for the Aged, and towards the end it was agonizing to look at this woman who once had been so gorgeous, animated, and filled with enthusiasm for life.

Anita was determined she was going to get well. The onslaught of AIDS brought out the quality of her character. She was eager to make amends to people she had hurt in the past. "I was astonished," says Renee. "Anita called to apologize. She was completely genuine, filled with remorse for upsetting my life. She was expressing appreciation to everyone who had tried to help her. She had reached down into her soul and found a reservoir of goodness and compassion. I can't remember being more moved by any single act."

"The miracle about Anita," explains Shirley, "was that in the midst of her suffering she found strength. She was brave. She reexamined herself and discovered so much love. Her manipulation melted away. Her disease brought our family together in a way I never thought possible."

As the illness evolved from Epstein-Barr to pneumonia and full-blown AIDS, Anita became a leader, an inspiration to others. She appeared on "The Oprah Winfrey Show," openly discussing her former addiction, her present condition, her hopes and fears. Anita also produced a full-length documentary, *Aids Alive: A Portrait of Hope,* which, in realistic fashion, offered further hope. As an AIDS patient caught between holistic and traditional medicine, she described her struggle and, looking into the camera, said, "It's about facing fear." She faced her fear, and in doing so helped others. (I was especially moved when Shirley and old friends like Ahmet, Willie Nelson, Paul Simon, and even the Warner Corporation helped finance the film.) Anita's demonstration of courage and spirit remains her great legacy.

She died in 1989. She was thirty-eight. In the final months, my daughter Lisa devoted her life to her sister. Paul was a strong and steady companion. Shirley was there as a tremendous source of comfort. Anita's husband, Gary, who was to die shortly thereafter, did everything he could to assuage Anita's pain and offer support; he showed heartfelt generosity. We all did what we could.

It is an unnatural and unspeakable act for a parent to bury a child. Shirley and I buried our baby, our beautiful daughter, in a cemetery on Long Island that sweeps down to the bay. On her tombstone is a musical staff and the first six notes of the song I'll forever associate with the warmth, intelligence, and radiance of her being: "(Sittin' on) The Dock of the Bay."

FALLING
IN LOVE
AGAIN

I got lucky back in 1985. I met the right woman. In Sarasota, Florida, my dear friends Annie and Syd Solomon (he's the abstract expressionist painter) introduced me to Jean Arnold, a playwright and novelist. Love at first sight. I fell head over heels, putting an end to my ripping and running. I had never been happy single. Jean lifted my loneliness and brought me the gift of love. We were married less than two months after we met.

There was a period of adjustment—I damn near messed up the marriage thing for a third time—but finally, after a lifetime of temper tantrums, I learned to chill. I recognized Jean's need for her own space and time, and have great respect for her writing. The *New York Times* called *The Scissor Man,* her most recent novel, "a fully accomplished mature work, combining technical mastery with an engrossing story," and I'm proud and supportive of her efforts. My present situation is fabulous. We're about to celebrate our eighth wedding anniversary.

"Retirement" has been a blessing, too, since the projects keep coming. I've even enjoyed my Hollywood adventures. Producer Bob Evans hired me to do the music for the film *The Cotton Club.* When he wildly overspent and Francis Ford Coppola was called in to salvage the effort, Francis wanted Ralph Burns for the score. I've known, loved, and utilized Ralph's work for thirty years, but in my book no one could replicate the music of the Cotton Club better than Bob Wilber. Francis insisted on Ralph and fired me.

Meanwhile, I had made friends with Richard Sylbert, the brilliant set designer who rebuilt the Cotton Club for the movie. During a big night at Elaine's, Dick and I learned we shared a common passion for

With my wife, Jean Arnold

the novels of William Kennedy, and together we optioned Kennedy's *Billy Phelan's Greatest Game*. Furthermore, Dick recommended Kennedy to Coppola, and Kennedy became Coppola's main collaborator on the script to *The Cotton Club*. Postscript: Kennedy, a rabid jazz fan, is best buddies with Bob Wilber—and Wilber wound up, through Kennedy's influence, writing the score. Now ain't that some shit!

The current music scene: heavy metal, rap, hip-hop, house . . .

Rather than end on a sour note, I'd prefer to turn it over to my children.

Lisa has developed into a superb drummer, a flawless timekeeper who anchors Big Sister, an all-girl blues band—and I do mean blues. "I'm playing the blues music I turned a deaf ear to as a kid," she says. "When Dad brought his work home, I sometimes tuned out. Now there's nothing I love more than pure blues."

Paul has talent as a record producer; his views on the present state

Above: My daughter Lisa. Below: My son Paul

of funk are far more on the money than mine, and he's out there earning his grits doing publicity and PR for Atlantic.

Paul can make his own music tracks with his own hands, something I could never do. "The effect of the new technology," he argues, "is positive. It's stimulating creativity. The invention of the drum machine paved the way to rap. The old R&B drum patterns were beautiful but growing predictable. The drum machine lifted that predictability without discarding the essence of dance. Obviously James Brown is still the man. But there are new syncopations, and the syncopations are complex. If these souped-up syncopations have led to hip-hop, then hip-hop has saved R&B and brought it back as a syncopation-propelled art form. If R&B was slicked up in the seventies, it's become raw in the nineties. And that's what I like. I'm attracted to reggae, rap, hip-hop and dance hall, just because those forms are not calculated, not predictable. Black music has always led the way, and, as far as I can see, that remains as true now as it was in Jerry's day."

My day isn't entirely over. I did have a minor heart attack a couple of years back, but I'm 100 percent now. I work out, swim, play golf. I've also reached that age when funerals of friends are all too common. Cy Ampole passed in 1991. Saying goodbye to him and to my lifelong pal John Hammond and to my marvelous partner Nesuhi Ertegun was especially painful. I miss them so much.

I'm mildly insomniac. I have tapes by the side of my bed, tapes that get me through the night. It's music that's close to my heart . . . Lester Young's record of "You Can Depend on Me" with Roy Eldridge's incandescent sound. To recognize that Roy's trumpet line is the brass section's out-chorus of Fletcher Henderson's version thrills me. Smack has been one of my deepest loves, especially his bands from 1934 on, one with Red Allen and Coleman Hawkins and the other with Chu Berry and Roy. I don't play as much Louis Armstrong as I used to, because he started sounding too familiar. But I do play Johnny Hodges, Ben Webster, and Gypsy-guitar genius Django Reinhardt. I love the lyrical trumpet players—Bobby Hackett, Warren Vache, Bix Beiderbecke—and I'm blessed to have many recordings by haunting saxist Frank Teschemacher. I love Red Allen—like Bix, way ahead of his time. And I love Hank Crawford, especially the early Atlantic sides. They are a magic distillation of Ray Charles's sound that in some mysterious way even transcends Ray. These sounds are the ones that still sustain me.

When sleep still doesn't come, certain lines come to mind: T-Bone singing, "I drink to keep from worrying and I smile to keep from crying to keep the world from knowing exactly what's on my mind." The blues: feeling good about feeling bad. Certain feelings have stayed with me for forty years: Elmore James's guitar lick, for example, which shines before me like a fine filament, a hammered silver wire that starts at the Mississippi Delta, where Robert Johnson played it and passed it on to Elmore, whom Ahmet and I had the good fortune to record with Joe Turner—the same lick we gave to the Clovers, who sang it on "Down in the Alley" in vocalise, and then, in turn, was covered by Elvis Presley, who took it worldwide. To have tracked this phenomenon, to have somehow participated in the universalization of black music from its country origins to its place in world culture—this was the privilege of a lifetime.

These are the midnight thoughts that get me through the night. Lately I've been involved with two New Orleans musicals on Broadway, furnishing the tunes. *Jelly's Last Jam*, based on the life of Jelly Roll Morton, stars Gregory Hines and is a huge hit that's likely to run for a while. The other was *The High Rollers Social & Pleasure Club*, a rhythm-and-blues revue featuring Allen Toussaint, which flamed out after a week. This one cost me a few kopecks.

I'm still producing. My most recent record is with Etta James, and making this was a special satisfaction. Not only was I working again with one of my favorite singers, but I was also back at the scene of many previous crimes, Muscle Shoals. All the way back home. Both Etta and I were determined to make a quintessential rhythm-and-blues album—no compromises, no nonsense, just righteous and raw.

Clayton Ivey, a keyboard wizard, was my point man in the studio, while Lucky Peterson—Etta called him "the cat who's burning down the cornfield"—tore up the guitar and Hammond B3. Steve Ferrone of the Average White Band was on drums, Willie Weeks on bass, and Steve Cropper on rhythm guitar.

I asked Steve Winwood if he'd sing with Etta, and he flew over from England, along with his Traffic mate Jim Capaldi, just for the session. The result was "Give It Up." Stevie's a true gentleman—a fabulous musician, a genuine soul singer—and on his duet with Etta he was thrilled to be reunited with bassist David Hood, drummer Roger Hawkins, and guitarist Jimmy Johnson, the red-clay rhythm section that toured with Traffic in the early seventies.

The icing on the cake was provided by the arranger, my man Hank Crawford. His charts were lovely, and he came down to Alabama to play his alto. Imagine having Hank step out of a horn section with Nashville session men and deliver an ungodly solo in one take. It was like having Bird or the Rabbit blowing on my set.

Etta and I had did our share of pushing and pulling over vocals—she's as strong-minded as I am—but musically we wound up in each other's arms. I especially loved the way she read the ballads "Evening of Love" and "You've Got Me," and her rendition of "Nighttime Is the Right Time" rivals the Right Reverend Ray himself.

For the title of the record, three words seemed to reflect both Etta's revitalized career and my own status quo. We called it *The Right Time*.

SELECTED DISCOG-RAPHY

Music produced
or co-produced
by Jerry Wexler

The following list is neither complete
nor inclusive of singles. All titles are on
Atlantic except where noted; all are cur-
rently available on compact disc except
those followed by an asterisk, which are
out of print.

THE FIFTIES

LaVern Baker, *Soul on Fire: The Best of LaVern Baker*
Ruth Brown, *Miss Rhythm: Greatest Hits and More*
Ruth Brown, *Ruth Brown* °
The Clovers, *Down in the Alley: The Best of the Clovers*
The Drifters, *Let the Boogie-Woogie Roll, 1953–1958*
Champion Jack Dupree, *Blues from the Gutter*
Chris Connor, *Sings the George Gershwin Almanac of Songs*
Chris Connor, *Chris Connor* °
Chuck Willis, *King of the Stroll* °
Chuck Willis, *Chuck Willis* °
Ivory Joe Hunter, *His Greatest Hits* °
Ray Charles, *The Birth of Soul: The Complete Atlantic Rhythm and Blues
    Recordings, 1952–1959* (three CDs)
Ray Charles and Milt Jackson, *Soul Brothers*
Ray Charles, *The Genius of Ray Charles*
Joe Turner, *His Greatest Hits*
Joe Turner, *The Boss of the Blues*
Atlantic Rhythm and Blues, 1947–1974 (eight CDs)

THE SIXTIES

The Drifters, *1959–1965: All-Time Greatest Hits and More*
Solomon Burke, *Home in Your Heart: The Best of Solomon Burke*
Wilson Pickett, *A Man and a Half: The Best of Wilson Pickett*
Betty Carter, *'Round Midnight*
Lurlean Hunter, *Blue and Sentimental*°
Patti LaBelle and the Bluebelles, *Dreamer*°
King Curtis, *Plays the Memphis Greatest Hits*°
Sweet Inspirations, *Sweet Inspirations*°
Esther Phillips, *Set Me Free*°
Aretha Franklin, *I Never Loved a Man (The Way I Love You)*
Aretha Franklin, *Aretha Arrives*°
Aretha Franklin, *Lady Soul*
Aretha Franklin, *Aretha Now*°
Dusty Springfield, *Dusty in Memphis*
Cher, *3614 Jackson Highway*°
Shel Silverstein, *Inside Silverstein*°
Aretha Franklin, *Queen of Soul: The Atlantic Recordings* (four CDs)
Atlantic Rhythm and Blues, 1947–1974 (eight CDs)

THE SEVENTIES

Aretha Franklin, *Spirit in the Dark*°
Aretha Franklin, *Live at the Fillmore West*°
Aretha Franklin, *Amazing Grace*
Aretha Franklin, *Young, Gifted and Black*°
Barry Goldberg, *Barry Goldberg*°
Sam and Dave, *Can't Stand Up*°
Lulu, *Melody Fair*°
Delaney and Bonnie and Friends, *To Bonnie from Delaney*°
Donny Hathaway, *A Donny Hathaway Collection*
Ronnie Hawkins, *Ronnie Hawkins*°
Dr. John, *Gumbo*
Doug Sahm, *Doug Sahm and Band*°
Doug Sahm, *Doug Sahm and Friends: The Best of Doug Sahm's Atlantic Sessions*
Donnie Fritts, *Prone to Lean*°
The Wiz, Original Cast Recording
Willie Nelson, *Shotgun Willie*
Willie Nelson, *Phases and Stages*

Maggie Bell, *Queen of the Night*°
Aretha Franklin, *Queen of Soul: The Atlantic Recordings* (four CDs)
Atlantic Rhythm and Blues, 1947–1974 (eight CDs)
Allen Toussaint, *Motion* (Warner)°
Tony Joe White, *The Train I'm On* (Warner)°
Bob Crewe, *Motivation* (Elektra)°
Ronee Blakley, *Welcome* (Elektra)°
Kim Carnes, *Sailin'* (A&M)°
Sanford/Townsend, *Smoke from a Distant Fire* (Warner)°
The Staples, *Unlock Your Heart* (Warner)°
Etta James, *Deep in the Night* (Warner)°
Pretty Baby, Motion Picture Soundtrack (ABC)°
Dire Straits, *Communiqué* (Warner)
José Feliciano, *Sweet Soul Music* (Private Stock)°
Bob Dylan, *Slow Train Coming* (Columbia)

THE EIGHTIES

McGuinn-Hillman, *McGuinn-Hillman* (EMI)°
Bob Dylan, *Saved* (Columbia)
Billy Vera, *Billy Vera* (Alfa)°
One Mo' Time, Original Cast Recording (Warner)°
Lou Ann Barton, *Old Enough* (Asylum; since reissued by Antone Records)
Carlos Santana, *Havana Moon* (Columbia)
Jo Jo Dancer, Your Life Is Calling, Motion Picture Soundtrack (Warner)°

THE NINETIES

Kenny Drew, Jr., *Kenny Drew, Jr.* (Antilles)
Etta James, *The Right Time* (Elektra)

INDEX

PERMISSIONS

ACKNOWLEDGMENTS

Grateful acknowledgment is made to the following for permission to reprint previously published material:

Famous Music Corporation: Excerpt from "The Day You Came Along" by Sam Coslow and Arthur Johnston; copyright © 1933 by Famous Music Corporation, copyright renewed 1960 by Famous Music Corporation. Used by permission.

Goldsen Music: Excerpt from "Mean Old World" by Aaron T-Bone Walker and M. H. Goldsen; copyright © 1945 by Michael H. Goldsen, Inc., copyright renewed 1973 by Michael H. Goldsen, Inc. Used by permission.

Leiber & Stoller Music Publishing: Excerpt from "Poison Ivy" by Jerry Leiber and Mike Stoller; copyright © 1959 by Jerry Leiber Music & Mike Stoller Music (Renewed). All rights reserved. Used by permission.

MCA Music Publishing: Excerpt from "How Deep Is the Well," words and music by Percy Mayfield, copyright © 1953 by MCA Music Publishing, a division of MCA Inc., New York, NY 10019; copyright renewed. Used by permission. All rights reserved.

MCA Music Publishing and EMI Music Publishing: Excerpt from "Swing! Brother, Swing," words and music by Walter Bishop, Lewis Raymond, and Clarence Williams, copyright © 1936 by MCA Music Publishing, a division of MCA Inc., New York, NY 10019; copyright renewed. Used by permission. All rights reserved. Rights in the UK reprinted by permission of B. Feldman and Co. Ltd., London WC2H 0EA.

The Estate of Titus Turner, Sr.: Excerpt from "Grits Ain't Groceries" by Titus Turner (Titus Turner Songs). Reprinted by permission of Titus Jr., Bonnie, and Tiberious on behalf of The Estate of Titus Turner, Sr.

Warner/Chappell Music, Inc.: Excerpt from "Bad Blood" by Jack Dupree, copyright © 1959 by Unichappell Music Inc. (Renewed); excerpt from "The House That Jack Built" by Fran Robbins and Bobby Lance, copyright © 1968 by Cotillion Music, Inc., all rights administered by Warner-Tamerlane Publishing Corp.; excerpt from "Oke She Moke She Pop" by Lou Willie Turner, copyright © 1954 by Unichappell Music Inc. (Renewed); excerpt from "Shake Rattle and Roll" by Charles Calhoun, copyright © 1954 by Unichappell Music Inc. (Renewed); excerpt from "TV Mama" by Lou Willie Turner, copyright © 1954 by Unichappell

PHOTOGRAPHIC
CREDITS

Jeff Albertson: p. 257
Dick Cooper: pp. 275, 289
Carol Friedman: pp. 300, 302 (both), 313 (bottom)
David Gahr: pp. 190, 205, 209 (both), 274, 295 (top)
Bob Gruen / Star File: pp. 248, 254, 288
Michael Kimble: p. 312
Elizabeth Marshall: p. 270
Stephen Paley: pp. 179, 212
William "Popsie" Randolph: pp. 68, 79, 118, 128, 146, 191, 234, 239, 283
Rod-Tex Pictures: p. 238
Paul Wexler: pp. xii, 313 (top)

All other photographs are from the collection of Jerry Wexler.

A Note on the Type

This book was set in a digitized
version of Caledonia, a Linotype face
designed by W. A. Dwiggins (1880–
1956). It belongs to the family of
printing types called "modern face"
by printers—a term used to mark the
change in style of type letters that
occurred about 1800. Caledonia
borders on the general design of
Scotch Roman, but is more freely
drawn than that letter.

Composed by Graphic Composition,
Athens, Georgia
Printed and bound by Courier Book
Companies, Westford, Massachusetts
Designed by Iris Weinstein